DATE DUE

Opposition Planning in Wales and Appalachia

Opposition Planning in Wales and Appalachia

Pierre Clavel

Temple University Press Philadelphia

Temple University Press, Philadelphia 19122

Published in 1983
Printed in the United States of America

Library of Congress Cataloging in Publication Data

Clavel, Pierre.
Opposition planning in Wales and Appalachia.

Includes bibliographical references and index.
1. Regional planning—Wales. 2. Regional planning—Appalachian Region. 3. Opposition (Political science) I. Title.

HT395.G72W254 1982 361.6′09429 82-10322
ISBN 0-87722-276-2

Contents

Preface vii

Chapter 1. Introduction 3

Territory 4
Opposition 19
Planning 25

Chapter 2. Theory 39

Liberal and Marxist Conceptions of Regional Development 39
A Theory of Territorial Politics 51
Additional Relationships of the Model to the Literature 60

Chapter 3. Planning in the Context of Welsh Separatism 73

Welsh Institutions and the British State 73
Centrally Initiated Regionalism: 1964–75 88
Local Response to Government Policy 97
Opposition under a Separatist Program: Plaid Cymru 104
Conclusion: The Role of Planning 112

Chapter 4. Appalachia 116

Federal Policy toward Appalachia 118
Regional Planning under the Appalachian Regional Commission 124
Opposition to ARC 132
Local Government as Opposition? 146

Chapter 5. Territorial Opposition 153

Evidence of Territorial Opposition 154
Underlying Conditions 158
Explanation 166
Choice of Strategy 175

Chapter 6. Planning 177

Dualism: Official Planning and Opposition 178
Planning and Hegemony 189
Differences in Planning: Hegemony vs. Hierarchy and Polyarchy 193
Planning in the Transition to Separatism 195
Wider Applications 205

Notes 213
Index 242

Preface

When in 1975 I decided to study regional planning in Wales and Appalachia, I did so thinking that it might be useful to explore the country–city polarities inherent in these places, as a perspective on the class, race, and sex divisions that seemed to be the main topics of urban planning in the United States. The regional perspective had a history among planners, particularly the perspective that stems from the work of Patrick Geddes, and this had been perhaps unwisely driven out of fashion. It seemed to me that, if I interviewed some of the important actors in significant regional struggles in two important industrial countries, I could get a feel for the way city–country polarities influence, confuse, or reinforce other polarities. I would then try to reformulate what I thought about the role of planning. If I could do this for regional planning in these peripheral places, I thought I could at least have a jumping-off point for thinking about urban planning and perhaps other issues facing modern societies.

Conceptually, what follows has two foci. On the one hand, I look for the *basis* on which majorities and minorities organize themselves. This is my perspective for studying the politics of peripheral regions: how effectively have groups and institutions been able to use such bases as territory or class or economic interest to stabilize their support around issues? There was a point in my writing when I concluded this was the prior question. It was a question of politics and economics, of how the system works. Only after getting a conclusion on it could I move on to other issues. The first part of the book is mostly taken up with this question. In Chapter 1 I derive a typology of regions, and in Chapter 2 I review the literature that forms the basis for a theory of the causes that make regions shift from one type to another. Chapters 3 and 4, case histories of planning in Wales and Appalachia, are themselves taken up in part with politics and economics. Chapter 5 reviews the cases in order to elaborate further the perspectives developed in Chapter 2.

The second focus of the book is an organizational question. Given a perspective on types of regions and their transitions, how is it best to organize planning? The premise is that the organization of planning appropriate for one area may not be appropriate in other types of areas. This alone might not mean much, except that in fact Wales and Appalachia are different kinds of places from the metropolitan contexts in which we have most recently tended to see planning. Wales and Appalachia are obvious cases of externally dominated "hegemony" and provide a kind of planning that is a distortion of what we are used to. Official planning is distorted, and in both places a kind of opposition planning developed. Much of what I present, therefore, is a simple report of planning practice and its organization. This is the main subject of Chapters 3 and 4. In addition, the last part of Chapter 1 introduces the organizational problem for planning, and the final chapter of the book reviews the evidence from Wales and Appalachia and provides an alternative way to plan.

In the course of research and writing I became indebted to many people and institutions. I was initially encouraged and supported by Cornell University's Western Societies Program and the scholars that directed it: Sidney Tarrow, Douglas Ashford, and Steven Kaplan. They provided travel funds and also helped organize the study groups and conferences where I developed my ideas. I am further indebted to Dean Kermit C. Parsons of the College of Architecture, Art, and Planning and to Chairman Sidney Saltzman and my colleagues in the Department of City and Regional Planning for providing additional travel support and allowing me to take time off for writing. Other institutional support at Cornell came from Barclay G. Jones, director of the Program in Urban and Regional Studies, and William Goldsmith, director of the Program on International Studies in Planning.

In doing field interviews, I received help from many generous people. Professors Anthony Goss and, later, Michael Bruton of the University of Wales Institute of Science and Technology in Cardiff, provided office space and services that made the whole enterprise much easier, and that put me in touch with head technician Winston Gough and the faculty of the Department of Town Planning there. Jeremy and Brenda Alden and Gareth and Teresa Rees entertained me at different times and helped arrange travel and contacts, then entered into long conversations, some of which led to main points in what follows. Ken Corey let me use his house for a week. In Appalachia, I benefited from the hospitality of Jerry Starr, Harley Johansen, and John Williams of the University of West Virginia in Morgantown, and had an office provided by the Regional Research Institute. Others who helped me particularly with logistics and ideas included Annette Anderson, Robb Burlage, Jon Hunter, and Rick Simon.

Many persons commented on all or parts of the manuscript: Carolyn Adams, Jeremy Alden, Douglas Ashford, Joseph Braunhut, Robb Burlage, Harold Carter, Anne Clavel, John Davis, John Forester, Bill Goldsmith, Fran Helmstadter, Charles Levine, Ann Markusen, Gareth Rees, Tom Reiner, Alan Scott, Donald Spencer, Lauren Stefanelli, Bert Swift, David Walls, Robert Warren, David Whisnant, Donald Whitehead, Phil Williams, Chris Yewlett, Darrell Williams and Frank Young.

The whole effort benefited enormously from my excellent office coworkers. Helena Wood typed, retyped and corrected the manuscript. There was varied and intelligent support from Verlaine Boyd, Lynn Coffey, and Donna Wiernicki. I thank them also.

Opposition Planning in Wales and Appalachia

Chapter 1

Introduction

This book is about territorial movements and planning. The cases and events described below, in Wales and Appalachia, include territorial activism by opposition groups. They are cases where, in addition to advocacy on specific issues, oppositions engaged in long-range planning that allowed them to challenge central authority in fundamental rather than superficial ways and to raise issues central to the future of the modern state. The agitation in Wales helped motivate schemes to reorganize central government. In Appalachia, the opposition got a new awareness of the choices between dependence on corporate development and local control. In both places, new relationships between workplace and community organizing developed.

What follows is addressed to persons engaged in these kinds of issues. The argument has three connected parts. First, it describes the partial but definite territorial political mobilization of these two places, the partial transition from external domination toward separatism. That this occurred at all is worth reporting, and I present a theory of territorial mobilization. Second, I draw conclusions about oppositions, about their contemporary roots, and about how workers and other popular factions can participate in territorial oppositions: I argue that, under the conditions prevalent in places like Wales and Appalachia, workers can apply more pressure on the system—central governments and centers of economic and social control—through a move toward separatism than through more traditional industrial strategies. Third, I advocate a role for planning in supplementing and reinforcing such a territorial strategy and opposition.

Territory

Why Wales and Appalachia? First, they are the most culturally distinctive parts of their respective countries, which results in a distinctive territorial politics. This profoundly affects my analysis. Appalachia, particularly its central portion, maintains a mountain yeomanry that has been culturally resistant to the introduction of coal mining and industry since 1900. Wales remains the major area of linguistic distinctiveness with Great Britain. It is more compact and more accessible than Appalachia, yet nearly one-fifth of its population of 2.7 million spoke Welsh in 1971, and numerous local festivals and organizations attest to a flourishing—if threatened—culture. Second, extractive industry, coal, has dominated the economies of both places for a long time, accompanied by largely externally induced development. Coal and iron manufacture in Wales was one of the earliest events of the industrial revolution, and Appalachian coal became the major energy source in the United States by the late nineteenth century. But the legacy of this early development is that Wales and Appalachia are poor regions within rich countries. These regions remain significantly below the national standard as measured by indicators such as family income, unemployment, and net out-migration, though the differences are decreasing.[1]

The result has been political conflict. It is not the classical "sectionalism" of a homogeneous region opposing a differently developed central economy, though this was the case in both places a century ago. Trends in income, migration, and industry suggest integration of Wales and Appalachia in their larger economies. Their homogeneity has been reduced by penetration of centrally headquartered firms and government agencies. Yet they remain "peripheral" in important ways. This has caused a new political conflict that has hindered any transition toward fusion with the larger country. The new polarization is between the indigenous populations and institutions, and the newer, metropolitan-oriented groups and agencies.[2] Cultural antagonisms between insiders and outsiders, economic differences and educational inequalities, and class differences between rich and poor all cause schisms within these areas. These kinds of antagonisms overlap and unite as territorial issues. Thus, the promotion of Welsh language or of Appalachian folk history are controversial issues between the territory and the larger country, as is the relative poverty of many citizens of Wales and Appalachia, as are the frustrations of local people trying to deal with agencies of the central government, and the interests of local workers versus the national firms that employ them.

This can be a different kind of political conflict from the muted, regulated conflicts characteristic of the "pluralism" advocated by the national political parties and agencies of the central government in both countries. Pluralism reflects the interests of well-organized economic and class organizations: the Confederation of British Industries, the Ford Motor Company, the National Farmers' Union, the Trades Union Congress, the National Manufacturers' Association, the United Mine Workers, and various industrial-sector interests, consumer groups, and voluntary associations. Pluralist politics operates at the national scale. It adapts to territorial interest groups by absorbing them. A preeminent mechanism is the establishment of "regional" offices, for example, in the cases I describe here, the Welsh Office and the Appalachian Regional Commission. The functions of regional offices are to mediate, represent, interpret, and program territorial interests. They defuse and channel protest, but never offer a fundamental challenge to central policies.

Territorial politics in Wales and Appalachia are something different: locally rooted, mass-based opposition politics challenge the agendas and projects of the central government and propose alternatives. In Wales this is most clearly indicated in Plaid Cymru, the nationalist political party that received as much as 11 percent of the total Welsh vote during the 1960s and 1970s, and it is reflected in a number of other organizations. In Appalachia the territorial movement of the same period was a kind of regionalism rooted in community organizing, with minimal electoral activity, but that left an extensive network of contacts and developed a policy and rationale similar to that in Wales.

This evidence, of territorial political mobilization and the apparent conditions that cause it, is all the more striking because it occurs in two nations whose formal structures of government and planning differ widely. Great Britain's unitary state provides for a great degree of formal centralization of policy, in contrast to the federalism that characterizes the United States. In Britain, even the details of local policy are made in parliament and central ministries and then administered locally. In consequence Wales, along with other regions, has been subject to an official coordinated regional policy toward factory location and population distribution. In these and other ways that I indicate below, Britain is centralized. In contrast, the U.S. federal system disperses formal authority and fragments policy making, despite tendencies toward centralization in the economy and federal administration. But no regional policy toward population distribution has ever evolved. Consequently the regional planning machinery that was set up in Appalachia was quite different from that in Wales. Wales had a formal planning apparatus in the Welsh Office that was mandated to do a plan that would coordinate the policies of the central government. The Appalachian Regional Commission, in contrast, was dominated by the governors of its thirteen states, and its staff avoided formal planning.

But these differences, though important, did not preclude significant similarities in the two cases. Often what appeared relatively elaborated in one place was present but rudimentary in the other. There were similarities, and they tended to rivet my attention. This led to an approach that is comparative, but not in the usual sense. A more common method would entail paying attention to government structure and trying to explain differences in behavior from the differences in structure. What evolved here, however, was a comparison of periphery with the metropolitan center, across national states. I pay attention to formal structure, but focus on territorial movements and how they use planning to further their programs.

Liberal and Socialist Doctrine. Although territorial politics exists, the dominant political and economic ideologies view regional political mobilization as both ineffective and ideologically undesirable. Liberal and socialist ideology hold that territorial bases are ineffective foundations for political clienteles, that functional or class groupings are more effective as well as more exact descriptions of the direction in which most political alignments move, especially as nations modernize.[3] Furthermore, regional politics is ideologically controversial. Functional groupings are the rationale of liberal politics, class mobilization the rationale of socialist politics, justified in each instance by their purported effect of reducing inequality.[4] Liberals' hopes for equality rest with the idea of competition among national interest groups and firms, mediated by national parties, legislatures, and administration. Socialists argue that equality is best furthered by working-class participation in government as a class, through their own institutions, notably trade unions. Each doctrine sees regional political mobilization as a diversion at best, a force for reaction at worst.

These powerful ideas dominate Western politics and represent actual economic forces. Yet regional politics can be based on equally potent ideas and forces. First, there is the *fact* of regional politics. Despite some present confusion about the meaning of "regionalism," regionally based political movements are evident. On the one hand there is a proliferation in Western countries of what might best be termed regional nationalisms, which often represent true political mobilization: Wales, Scotland, Brittany, Catalonia, the Basque provinces, Quebec, and Puerto Rico are examples. On the other hand, administrators and politicians try to take territorial interests into account as they oversee increasingly centralized state machinery, which has resulted in a proliferation of regional councils, regional administrative districts, and regional authorities of various sorts. The second kind of "regionalism" is very different from the first, which directly and dramatically represents a political movement toward autonomy from central government. But it is important to acknowledge that the second kind of regionalism is often a response to a political feeling, perhaps an attempt to defuse it or keep it within bounds.

Neither liberal nor socialist ideology provides any theory to incorporate the evidence of regional political mobilization. This is a serious problem: it implies that neither government officials nor critics have any way to recognize regional mobilization. They will, for example, provide centrally initiated services and subsidies to regions where there is a demand—which they will not recognize—for participation and autonomy. But the absence of regional theory also reflects more important, more fundamental, more general flaws in liberal and socialist ideology.

Socialist theory does not address the effect of territorial mobilization on working-class mobilization. For socialists, the basic thesis is that their goals—most prominently, the reduction of inequality—will result from working-class political mobilization against exploitation in the workplace, regardless of other affiliations, even national boundaries. But other goals, in the meantime, also mobilize workers—causes involving race, sex, and territory. The most important territorial goal has been nationalism, raising the "national question" in the Marxist literature.[5] Should socialists, for example, support a war? Their consensus position on this question is based on pragmatism; there is no theory.

Similarly, their theory does not answer the question of whether, or under what conditions, socialists ought to support regional or community political mobilizations. If the goals of socialists are political mobilization of workers, or increased equality, this may turn out to be as serious an issue as the "national question." If socialists uniformly respond by espousing centralism, they run the risk of alienating, not mobilizing, workers in some regions. If they uniformly support community and regional political movements and interests, they might in some instances oppose the mobilization of workers. There is evidence for both sides on this question. What is needed is a theory that states the conditions under which regional political mobilization fuels or derails working-class mobilization, and that accounts for the impact of regional mobilization on inequality generally.

Liberal regional policy does not provide any theory either. It fails to take into account the possibility of regional politics.

Instead, the main doctrine is a regional adaptation to the needs of the increasingly dominant national firm.[6] In Western countries, market development is the predominant liberal policy, with the main variation being the extent to which governments use intervention to make markets work. Although classical liberalism calls for very little government intervention, and although this has intermittently influenced the liberal democracies in their regional policies—during the Eisenhower administration in the United States, and under Conservative governments in Britain, for example[7]—the dominant trend has been toward an interventionist, market-oriented regional policy. This policy—generally bipartisan—has been accompanied by the following features: (1) attempts to establish employment generators in regions identified by national criteria—low income, high unemployment, out-migration—as problems, through subsidies based on location combined, in Britain, with restrictions on new factories in the South East; (2) provision of public works concentrated in growth centers within the peripheral regions; (3) encouragement and subsidy of agencies for regional planning.[8] Liberal policy is as noteworthy for what it fails to do as for what it does. By being generally undiscriminating about what kinds of employment to attract, or where to locate growth centers, or what regional planning should do, it ends up accommodating the interests of metropolitan-dominated business. In a general sense, liberals justify this metropolitan bias by emphasizing the role of new branch plants, growth-center development, and planners as providing market institutions conducive to entrepreneurship: better communication, better access to capital and government grants, better job mobility, and, ultimately, pressure for a more competitive politics.[9]

Socialists have differed from liberals by placing less emphasis on markets and by attempting to use the state to serve the interests of the working class.[10] But, in Western countries, policy toward regions and planning has differed only in degree.[11] Socialists have acquiesced to a situation where most of the wealth and productive apparatus is privately controlled. What results is the mixed economy, where the state regulates the private sector and the nationalized industries, but does not subject them to thoroughgoing popular control. Even in state-owned enterprises, a managerial class dominates, not too much different from the private-sector counterpart.[12] There are those, both in Britain and in the United States, who have attacked these basic premises of socialists and liberals, arguing that the main cause of inequality is the concentration of wealth and power in private corporations and central bureaucracies. But these critics are not dominant in any major national party, nor have they connected this premise to issues of *regional* politics.[13]

Regionalism. A conceptual basis for regional politics began to develop among planners and reformers in the early part of this century, but was later rejected by modern regional scholars. This early regionalism was a response to industrialization and national development, which many observers thought was destructive of regional cultures and institutions. Patrick Geddes in Europe and India, Lewis Mumford and the Regional Planning Association of America (RPAA), Howard Odum and the southern regionalists, and the Tennessee Valley Authority (TVA) of Arthur Morgan presented a notion of regional consciousness—generated by the interaction of people and natural environment—that they expected to produce regional institutions independent of established business interests and political units based in the metropolis.[14] If liberals saw the basis of economics and politics in entrepreneurs and business firms, while socialists saw it in working-class mobilization, the regionalists countered with the notion of community. Geddes, Mumford, and others stressed the values of moderately sized city and community life, and they constructed proposals for city plans on the premise that the collective motivation to produce good communities would win out over the alternative motivations provided by the business firm or by class.

What was also distinctive about these writers was their approach to politics. It was a curiously ambivalent political doctrine. On the one hand, they believed that a particular kind of political consciousness would develop out of the interaction of citizen and environment. This would be a consciousness of the requirements for balance between man and nature, of continuity between environment and institutions. Thus, Geddes advocated conservation not only of the natural environment, but of those buildings and institutions that adapted to it: village reservoirs in India, for example, and slum tenements in Edinburgh. Since most of the economic and political trends in the early twentieth century were devoted to tearing down and replacing these things, this kind of consciousness was potentially revolutionary. Geddes believed that planners and other reformers would help generate a groundswell, a mass movement that would sweep politicians and businessmen before it. But on the other hand, politics, as practiced within its existing forms, was irrelevant. He thought that he had identified, in regional consciousness, an inevitable transformation, that all that was necessary was to help clarify what was happening.

Those who came later with similar programs were perhaps less optimistic, but their politics were in some ways similar. Mumford and the RPAA operated as an informal intellectual conclave, its members mostly writers or planners and architects, but not engaged in electoral politics. Odum was a nationally known intellectual who served on New Deal committees, but none of the southern regionalists got involved in political organizing.[15] The New Deal programs influenced by these regionalists, and in which they participated, were made possible by a unique set of circumstances marked by an *absence* of local-level political organizing. The radical elements within TVA were able to survive only because of central support, as they found the locally entrenched people from the land-grant colleges hostile to them.[16] Arthur Morgan's influence in TVA, the separate programs of the Resettlement Administration, together with other elements not traceable to the regionalists, were products of the *early* New Deal, which found major business interests temporarily disorganized and quiescent, and Roosevelt particularly responsive to his "brains trust" and other intellectuals. But the political coalition that elected Roosevelt did not ultimately support the regionalists' doctrine.[17]

Refutation of the regionalists' ideas has been supplied by events, not theory: in assuming that community would prove a more potent force than the functional and class mobilizations of this century, the regionalists were simply wrong, or at best ahead of their time. What is probably true, however, is that neither the liberal, nor the socialist, nor the regionalist doctrines are adequate to account for the current emergence of community and regional politics. We need a theory that views class, functional, and regional politics together. Under what conditions does one kind dominate, reinforce or contradict the others, and with what results?

Toward a Theory of Territorial Politics. What I found in Wales and Appalachia were community and territorial movements in varying stages of formation, reinforced by opposition planning. What is needed is a theory that explains this.[18] The explanation here consists of a set of independent and dependent variables. I think of them as "variables," though initially I simply describe phenomena. I describe "territorial politics" as a construct, a dependent variable. Next, I propose a typology of situations that capture the independent variables: explanations for the occurrence of territorial politics. Finally, I describe planning and opposition planning. A more elaborate theory is presented in Chapter Two.

"Territorial Politics" means territorially based interest groups, coalitions, and parties that have a mass base. Such groups include nationalist and regionalist parties and movements, but also individual communities and groups within communities whose aims are limited to such modest goals as the preservation of a neighborhood against the encroachments of highways or factories. They may be highly ideological or reflect pure economic self-interests that happen to coincide with a territorial policy (e.g., farm subsidies, sales of federal land, the creation of recreation and wilderness areas). The following characteristics seem to be common, however:

1. At least some tendency toward separatism. For example, in Western Europe and North America there are numerous nationalist movements of one sort or another. A recent survey listed about fifty in Western Europe, each of them a sizable territory within an existing nation.[19] Among the prominent

examples are Brittany and the Basque provinces, Wales and Scotland. In North America most recently there is the example of Quebec, but Puerto Rico might also qualify. Nevertheless, it is important to distinguish nationalism from a demand for separation of institutions and for economic independence. Some nationalisms are not separatist, others have no interest in economic autonomy. Rather, nationalism is used to further demands for access to a central government. The idea of independence, on the other hand, is more ambitious. It is also more general, for a measure of independence can be demanded without demanding nationhood. Thus in Appalachia now there is a demand for local control of major energy-producing corporations. Similar political movements exist in many areas without a demand for nationhood. Other groups that demand nationhood invest at least as much energy in the pursuit of a measure of economic independence: Indian tribes in the United States are an example of this.

2. The defense of community. Many community and neighborhood groups have formed for the purpose of defending territory against such potential disruptions as factories, highways, nuclear plants, or airports.[20] These organizations have provided much of the basis for advocacy planning, where professional planners oppose establishment planning agencies and other bureaucracies. Territorial defense has also been a main issue in the aggregation of smaller groups in regional organization. In Wales, as will be indicated later, it was a main theme in the development of Plaid Cymru, the nationalist political party. Its chairman said:

> The Government want to maximize the mobility of labour to solve economic problems which they see from the point of view of Britain as a whole. We, on the other hand, want stable communities in Wales, and so we are against labor mobility and in favour of the direction of industry. We want to limit the migration of Welshmen out of Wales to the natural level which would match the number of Welshmen returning to Wales or indeed other young people coming to Wales to find employment.[21]

In this the goal of stable communities was raised to a regional issue, and the main elements of government regional policy, migration and industrial incentives, were tied to it.

Similarly, experiences of individual communities have aggregated in more general positions by regional groups in other places. Appalachia is one of these, but there are other cases: Vermont's Liberty Union, a political party that ran local and statewide candidate slates, largely around the issue of absentee property ownership; Puerto Rico's nationalist movement.[22] Certainly Quebec's separatism has been based partially on a desire to preserve the culture in the community.[23]

3. An appeal for working-class support as an element in the strategy for building a mass party. Many territorial groups, acutely aware of the possibility that community and nationalist goals might become "fringe" appeals, or elitist strategies, have consciously and sometimes painfully recruited working-class support. The Basques in Spain have, for example, received support from the producer cooperatives in Mondragon.[24] In both Wales and Appalachia a strategy for involving the working class is evident.

The Differences among Regions. Why should territorial politics occur? When one encounters it, as in the case of Plaid Cymru in Wales, and in some of the opposition groups in Appalachia, one also encounters a set of ad hoc explanations. The most prevalent explanation, that of common culture and national background, as in the case of the Welsh, seems partly correct and explains the relative weakness of territorial coalitions in Appalachia. But as I noted earlier, the evidence from Wales and Appalachia and from other peripheral regions suggests other, underlying factors: the relatively highly developed and intrusive extensions of metropolitan institutions into these areas and, compared to this, their relatively undeveloped community and territorial politics and economies. These factors are capable of abstraction and measurement as theoretical constructs, although I need only define them relatively crudely here.[25]

The first refers to the relative centrality of the area. The concept is one of access, representation and recognition of the area within the larger society. Most obviously, centrality is a matter of position, as if the society were displayed as a sociometric diagram, with "centrality" conferring many communications links between the region and central institutions business centers or central government. These links can be either physical or organizational, and they provide access and representation for a region at the center. Thus a plant of British Steel or the Welsh Office in Wales provides high centrality, as would comparable institutions in Appalachia. But centrality also is more than access. It is representation and recognition in the center. It implies some alteration or change at the center. The term *relative* centrality suggests a rank ordering of regions at the center. A change in relative centrality would thus imply a change in the rank ordering used in thinking about policy and making policy at the center.

Local development means local private or public capacity to act in a complex economic and administrative environment. I will refer to it below as "local capacity." It entails both administrative structure and the necessary popular support to administer effectively. In the private sector this means the development of decision-making and managerial capacity within the firm, use of support services such as consulting engineers and marketing experts, and a wide array of local product recognitions; in the public sector it means similar decision capacity interacting with local political support and services.

These two explanatory factors produce the following theoretical possibilities, which I elaborate in Chapter 2:

1. They separate analytically factors that typically are confused and lumped together as "modernization" or "development" or "urbanization." Thus, they help avoid a simplistic, unilinear approach.

2. They explain the *interaction* of national with local phenomena.

3. Both factors can be thought of as material underpinnings for cultural factors and for the ebb and flow of central control over regions, thus obviating explanations in which "ideas" are the ultimate cause.

The interaction of local development and centrality can be

demonstrated in a simplified four-case typology:

Centrality: Relative penetration of central institutions	Local capacity	
	Low	*High*
High	1. Hegemony	3. Polyarchy
Low	2. Hierarchy	4. Separatism

The cases can be described as follows:

1. Hegemony. This is found in the modern peripheral region, as I observed in Wales and Appalachia. On the one hand, externally based enterprises and government offices are well entrenched. In Wales the most prominent examples are the nationalized coal and steel industries, utilities, the port-related facilities and private industry along the south coast, and various offices of the central government. In Appalachia the examples are coal, along with a variety of manufacturing, all undergoing a transition of ownership from local elites to national and multinational firms. Government is perhaps less of a factor in Appalachia than in Wales; government certainly is more fragmented in Appalachia—the states play a role not matched in Great Britain. But in both places the growing influence of the central government and externally based industry have increased the ties of local economies and politics to the larger nation. Thus centrality is high.

Local capacity, on the other hand, remains undeveloped. Local economics and politics have changed, but not as much as centrality has changed. The locally controlled economy does not produce great wealth. Entrepreneurship and leadership are often lacking, particularly in the economy; and the external presence, due to its resources, is able to coopt such local leadership when it does develop. Local businessmen are absorbed into subordinate roles. The work force is engaged in minimum-wage or relatively low-wage occupations, or is absorbed and supported by welfare-state subsidies. Polarization between insiders and outsiders is prominent, impeding political development, while sustaining a small vanguard of territorial and class opposition.

2. Hierarchy. This is the classic rural case. I refer to it as "hierarchy" despite possible exceptions to the contrary. The key characteristic is the combination of low local capacity and low centrality: remoteness, resulting in a lack of the underlying (though perhaps suppressed) cultural conflicts of the hegemony case. Hierarchy is the *Gemeinschaft* of community studies and generally does not exist anymore in modern countries. But, some area approach it more than others. Parts of Appalachia that are relatively unaffected by central institutions qualify in this sense; and parts of Wales.

A review of the conditions necessary for any area within a modern country to remain in a state even approaching "hierarchy" is revealing. First, the economy must support people in activities that are integrated in the larger system only through loosely connected trade channels, for example, subsistence farming, some kinds of fishing, locally owned mines, craft manufacturing, tourist homes, and independent retailers and wholesalers. The presence of large-scale commercially profitable farming, deep-sea fishing, corporate mining, most manufacturing, nationally franchised motels or chain retailers would violate the low centrality condition by providing access to centralized capital and, in many cases, to standard business practices. Second, this type of area would have to insulate itself from the influence of a central government. This is perhaps possible, particularly in the United States, if the political representatives of the area are powerful and able to contain or distort central administration in line with local practice.

All of this refers only to the centrality dimension, perhaps the most obvious and intrusive means by which "hierarchy" is transformed. But local capacity could also remain low. Conceivably local capacity could remain low through decades of selective out-migration of the brighter people, a demographic factor that could cripple development of any political or economic organization and capacity. A second way for an area to maintain low capacity would be through isolation and antagonism among local units and failure to develop an areawide (regional) network of support services, communications, and political cooperation. In the extreme case, there could be no compensating factor, such as in-migration of persons who settle and become part of the local community.

3. Polyarchy. Polyarchy is the case of high economic organization and political pluralism, usually associated with metropolitan regions.[26] These places are characterized by high levels of entrepreneurship and innovation, and well-developed services and communication networks. Politics is characterized by bargaining among many interests. Conflict is organized, and participants understand the rules. Public agencies and local governments interact in a marketlike fashion, buying and selling services.

In the terms used above, centrality is high in these areas. In general, access to markets and political representation in the most important national centers of power are not an issue for the territory as a whole. The kind of collective action around centrality issues—for example, demands for highways or other transportation subsidies—that can develop in other places is absent here.

Local capacity is also high. The result is that political demands tend to be organized around economic sector and class rather than territory, which takes on a secondary significance. Class and sectoral development are reinforced by the generally high local capacity under polyarchy; and the general concentration and communication accompanying high levels of local capacity and economic development means that workplaces and specialized businesses will be less isolated *within* the polyarchical region.

4. Separatism. Lacking high levels of centrality, a relatively organized area with high capacity is apt to cut those ties that it cannot use to its own advantage. The muted insider-outsider conflict of hegemony is transformed to a highly mobilized campaign around an external target. The extreme is nationalism, but within this general type of area would fall any case where the reduction of centrality is a significant political objective.

The transition to separatism is described in Chapter 2, but it may clarify the definition to note that under separatism local capacity substitutes for centrality. Centrality, which primarily is a characteristic of the relationship of an area to the larger world, also seems to confer a kind of organization locally. Local interests organize their plans and expectations around the existence of a branch factory or government office, as indicated in the description of hegemony above. But what happens when these externally based institutions are withdrawn? This could happen in places like Wales or Appalachia, when centrally based corporations or government agencies can no longer supply the resources necessary to coopt significant leadership groups. Small oppositions then grow into larger ones. Central authority is challenged, resulting in a fluid situation not governed by the normal rules and fraught with conflict between the local units and representatives of external authority, whether within the area or outside. But this conflict can be creative, helping to build further the local capacity that precipitated it, as participants develop a consciousness of their own position and the myths of hegemony are unmasked, as victories are won, and as new ways of working together develop.

Opposition

Inherent in territorial politics is the opposition of center and periphery. It is not a picture of official functions of government that encompass various interests through bargaining, negotiation and compromise. Instead it features oppositions who differ profoundly in culture and economic status from the dominant elites and central government, and who intend to force their way to more advantageous positions. And then it says that their success in doing this will depend both on their own efforts and on the structure of forces at the center.

At this point I will introduce two additional issues: (1) why should opposition be more important now than it has been previously? and (2) granting its viability, how can opposition maximize popular representation?

Contemporary Roots of Opposition Movements. The oppositions in Wales and Appalachia are occasioned by and indicative of more general issues, for which no major policy or theory can present a settled explanation. A preliminary assessment, however, would note the following features:

1. Western nations have entered a difficult period marked by inflation, unemployment, and a marked slowing of growth rates. There is debate over the causes, but general agreement that the problem is both widespread among Western countries and relatively long-term rather than cyclical.

2. The most fundamental political effect of the reduced rate of economic growth has been the fragmentation of coalitions that, through the 1950s and 1960s, had been built around growth. These coalitions had emerged around such programs as economic management and—in varying degrees—planning, together with innovative social programs whose premise was a wider distribution of shares of growth. These programs, in one way or another, characterized each of the major political parties in the United States and Britain. In Britain, the Labour Party resolved internal conflicts in favor of a "modernization" program in the late 1950s, while it was the Conservatives who introduced a measure of national planning in the early 1960s. There was a similar convergence in the United States, where various social comentators were proclaiming the "end of ideology." But after about 1970, this set of programs went into eclipse. On the surface, it was a matter of changes in party: from Johnson to Nixon in the United States, from Wilson to Heath in Britain. More fundamentally, the reduced rate of economic growth was exerting pressure to which these programs could not respond. A major outgrowth was the defection of business from the coalitions that had fostered social programs and planning in the 1960s. The 1970s were marked, in contrast, by a heightened degree of overt class conflict in both countries. Most dramatic, perhaps, were the coal strikes in Britain and the United States, in 1974 and 1978, respectively. By the end of the

1970s commentators on both sides of the Atlantic were remarking on the corporate effort to "roll back" the workers' gains of the previous period.

3. The slowdown in economic growth had similar—and sometimes sharper—political effects at the local level. In many places, coalitions favoring urban growth had formed around urban improvement schemes, but with the decline in national economic growth, a combination of factors made these coalitions less viable. One factor was demographic. Many cities were affected by an in-migration of blacks and other ethnic minorities, while their middle classes went to the suburbs, thus making programs of urban renewal of facilities for a middle-class clientele (downtown shopping malls, middle- and high-priced housing) less viable politically. What took the place of these projects was a services-oriented politics aimed at increasingly dependent populations, but in most cases hampered by two additional factors. On the one hand, the central cities had lost tax resources that, combined with overall national economic decline, put city administrations in a fiscal crisis where expenditure demands outpaced revenues. Second, urban service bureaucracies were difficult to reorient to the needs of their new clients, at least partly due to race and income differences between bureaucrats and clients.

4. The logic of the corporate response to both national and urban economic crises was a more or less coherent program that emphasized efficiency of some services delivery, combined with relatively capital-intensive, high-technology solutions to particular problems. These developed on several fronts throughout the 1970s. Within industry, there was a major thrust toward mechanization, with more capital-intensive processes replacing labor, while corporations put pressure on labor to accept limits on their shares of increasing productivity, in part by forcing plant closings and migration of production to areas with cheaper and less well-organized labor. In municipal services, there was a move toward curtailment of labor-intensive operations. There were school closings—and consolidation in large schools, hospital closings—and the privatization of hospitals with resulting increases in costs, and general service cuts

forced by such initiatives as Proposition 13 in California and Proposition 2½ in Massachusetts.

5. Local and regional responses to these trends abounded during the 1970s, so that the overall picture was one of contradiction rather than the dominance of any one approach. Each move toward more capital-intensive, high-technology approaches to production or services seemed to generate a countermove somewhere. Plant closings, to take a fundamental part of the corporate strategy, were met with increasing resistance, including community and worker repurchase. Perhaps the most celebrated example is British: that of Lucas Aerospace, where a combined shop steward's committee gained worldwide attention with its proposals for new products and its negotiations with management on issues of enterprise management and planning. In the United States there were a number of schemes that approached the Lucas example in one way or another: The Vermont Asbestos Group, Mohawk Industries in New York, the Rath Meatpacking Company in Iowa, and a number of community-initiated innovations in Jamestown, New York, are prominent cases. There were also cases where public enterprise and state and local offices intervened to influence the quality and performance of local economies and firms. Massachusetts established a Community Economic Development Assistance Corporation to help finance locally controlled firms, and a National Consumer Cooperative Bank was established in Washington in 1979 to offer financing and technical assistance to producer as well as consumer cooperatives. In Britain, the Industrial Cooperatives Association was formed by Parliament to aid worker cooperatives. In both cases, funding was limited, but large amounts of local enterprise were encouraged by these central actions. Local governments in the United States, in a few cases, took initiatives to make job retention and job creation a public function, rather than leave it in the hands of businesses. The cities of Berkeley, Hartford, and Cleveland introduced innovative schemes when "progressive" leadership came to power. These ideas were reported and promoted by the establishment of public-interest organizations like Conference on Alternative State and Local Policies in the mid-1970s. There

was also the impressive development of non-official neighborhood and community organizing during the decade. Cleveland, to cite one example, had perhaps one viable neighborhood organization at the beginning of the decade, and ten by 1980. ACORN and other organizing coalitions grew to national stature, and neighborhood and community organizing had developed its own infrastructure of national organizations, training institutes, and, within the federal Department of Housing and Urban Development, an Office of Neighborhoods.

6. These counter-moves against what I will call—in an oversimplification—corporate hegemony, had their reflection in urban- and regional-planning circles. This was in some ways weak and scattered, yet also of crucial importance in that it offered a possibility of organizing separate local responses into a coherent overall response. The most dramatic examples of a planning response were regional in scale. Other local examples suggest an even wider base for "opposition planning." In the area of health-care, there was widespread organizing to counter privatization moves, using the opportunities afforded by federal legislation requiring and inviting (despite frequent local official opposition) citizen participation. Housing issues have occasioned a good deal of organizing around rent control and other topics. There had been a kind of "radical" organizing element within the planning profession since at least the 1960s in both the United States and Britain. In some cities in the United States "official" planners had taken at least some positions counter to the prevailing corporate strategy and in one—Cleveland—planners had produced an official "Policies Plan" whose announced goal was to serve "those who have least" with specific strategies on topics like mass transit, public power, housing, and downtown development. These policies anticipated by several years the "progressive" initiatives of the Kucinich administration.

Popular Participation. Opposition often is mobilized to increase popular participation, and that is the case for the territorial politics defined above. But opposition also faces its own problem of elitism. Faced with a hostile central government, spies, and the whole panoply of cooptation possibilities, how can an opposition maintain its own internal democracy? This is an organizational question that has two facets. The first is the strategic issue of how to compose the organization: what coalitions to form, whom to invite as allies. For if one can invite the right interests as allies in the first place, the conflicts and pressures that would limit participation may be postponed. The typology of territorial politics presented above is a basis for understanding what sorts of coalitions will most likely maintain popular participation. It suggests that under conditions of hegemony, the interests of working-class and regional political mobilization will coincide, and opposition planning can reinforce this. Business interests will tend to be isolated from the mass of people due to their ties to outside capital and power, increasingly perceived as exploitative.

Furthermore, for reasons that I suggest later, hegemony is unstable, and under some circumstances a transition to separatism can occur. If this begins to happen, various local consumer and even business groups will be motivated to seek closer ties to labor. The insider culture will encourage this, as external domination and exploitation becomes more apparent. The interests of labor and some local business and their affiliated middle class will coincide. Opposition planning, by pointing out such links and unities of interest, will help this along.

This mutual reinforcement of territorial and class interests is not likely except as hegemony is transformed to separatism. Under hierarchy, local elites are dominant, and the basis for opposition is lacking. Under polyarchy, neither of the factors forcing working-class and bourgeoisie together operate. In all these cases, a socialist strategy might best proceed to focus on working-class organization, and view regionalism as a diversion from this, though perhaps one to support opportunistically. But there would be no theoretical reason for support of regional political mobilizations.

Opposition planning, under these conditions, might still be appropriate, but its economic and political support would be different. It would look to working-class support in these cases, rather than a regional or territorial base.

Another facet of opposition organization is less strategic, and more a matter of structure. My main conclusions on this score concern the incorporation of planning into the opposition organization, and influencing official planners to adopt forms of planning hospitable to opposition programs.

Planning

Planning, as used here, means undertaking to put together courses of future action for some community, territory, or nation. It is a generic concept, unconnected to who plans what is planned, method, or success of implementation. Such a definition, though widely used, contrasts with more restrictive conceptions that are coordinated exercise of executive will imposed from above; it *can* be a relatively uncoordinated, incremental endeavor by participants who may disagree on goals, but agree on the need to define a course of future action.[27] It is not necessarily an activity of the established authorities (official planning), but can be undertaken by others, including the opposition (opposition planning). According to this definition, planning is always an activity for, on behalf of, some community, territory, or nation. That is, it considers more than the needs of special interests.

Planning is important not only for initiating future actions, but because it can become doctrine. Doctrine is an accepted set of principles and explanations shared by many persons: it can pervade organizations, become established in specialized school curricula, and indirectly influence actions. An example of doctrine in regional development was the Tennesee Valley Authority's early emphasis on local grass-roots organizations, later altered and "refined" to mean reliance on the land-grant colleges and the cooperative extension service. An elaborate rationale became TVA doctrine on this topic. Another example of doctrine, which is central to the case histories of Wales and Appalachia, is the growth-points doctrine: the idea that economic development proceeds best when capital investment is concentrated in a few places, rather than thinly spread over smaller communities.

In its classic form, planning can reinforce doctrine in dramatic ways. An example would be a plan for a new town that portrays in detail the concentration of investments in a growth point and even specifies the regional growth points that are to take priority. But even planning that does not meet this classic definition, planning that is an incremental, uncoordinated mapping of future actions, can reinforce doctrine. If the planners, despite the lack of a formal plan, still talk informally of growth points and their rationale, and if an uncoordinated set of individual projects nevertheless concentrates investments, the effect can be similar, if not as well debated.

Both official and opposition planning can either inhibit or reinforce the transition to separatism. In Wales and Appalachia, planning of some kind played an important role in territorial politics. Official planning provided a focus around which territorial oppositions formed; in addition, a kind of opposition planning also developed, providing thematic coherence to individual opposition positions. Thus while there was a history, related below, of political conflict between centrally oriented and territorially oriented interests (e.g. the Labour and Conservative governments, themselves in conflict, versus Plaid Cymru); there was also a parallel development of official and opposition planning. A less focused but similar set of events occurred in Appalachia.

Official planning began differently in each place, in the mid-1960s. In Wales, it began with a flourish and in the classic form appropriate to Britain's unitary form of government, while in Appalachia it began modestly, subordinated to the fragmented structure and informal style of the separate states involved. But there were many convergences, and in both places there were difficulties from the start. In Wales, planning had been the responsibility of a separate ministry, the Welsh Office, since 1964, but the only formal plan, a 1967 report discredited by all factions outside the Welsh Office, had never been revised, and apart from that no official planning position existed for Wales, though there had been numerous special studies and a good deal of informal monitoring of the economy. In Appalachia the official regional planning body since 1965 had been the Appalachian Regional Commission. Appalachia did not have the official status Wales did, because it consisted of only parts of thirteen states, and because the commission's power base was the governors of those states, hence the commission took a rather passive role as a planning agency. Its own planning was largely in response to that of the states. It had been able to prod the states to plan, but had little control over the result. In both places, official planners described their work as largely "indicative" in style, that is as largely a statistical operation designed to facilitate the policy of others, rather than an instrument of official command.

Official planning has its counterpart in planning that resists metropolitan penetration and class domination, that is locally rooted and unique. I call such planning, opposition planning. Generally, opposition should include all conflicts between centralized authority and opposition groups: examples would include rank-and-file labor and class groups, like the Miners for Democracy or the Welfare Rights Organization in the United States, and industrial-sector oppositions, like the Trades Unions Congress in Wales. In Wales and Appalachia territorially based opposition coalitions fused class, sector, and territorial consciousness, providing a context for opposition planning. These parties and movements posed a fundamental challenge to regional policy and planning by altering agendas proposed by central agencies and in official plans. In Wales Plaid Cymru prepared a well-researched plan that challenged the idea of growth centers, the migration policy, and the emphasis on public works in official plans, and proposed conservation of Welsh communities as an alternative.[28] This document, written in 1969, gave the party a strategic advantage over the government and contributed to an atmosphere that allowed debate on government projects. In Appalachia a diffuse opposition existed. Each state was different. But a network of activities and a critical policy and planning literature developed, contributing to the belief that an alternative to official planning by regional agencies was possible.

In this context attacks occurred, sometimes successful, against specific project proposals. In Wales there were a series of successful oppositions to new towns and other government development projects. A frequent argument was that the new plans would disturb the social structure by introducing English-speaking migrants or by fostering too-rapid growth, and so cause social pathologies, such as delinquency, and the destruction of local institutions, such as Welsh schools; another argument was that the plans would depopulate existing communities. In Appalachia similar opposition was grounded in similar arguments, such as resistance to the federal government's clumsy plan for flood-recovery and to its unpopular scheme for housing and urban development.

Planning Doctrine. Efforts to apply planning in Wales and Appalachia reveal that the official doctrine is inadequate in these situations faced. None of the approaches mentioned above provide an adequate conceptual framework for those who wish to practice planning or understand its failures in these places. Not only was the growth-point doctrine inadequate, most of those who opposed it had no adequate alternative concept. There is little in planning doctrine to support the notion of opposition planning. Planning has, instead, been preoccupied with the problem of opposition *to* planning, a major theme in liberal politics and in countries like Great Britain, where strong support for socialist programs is matched by strong market-oriented forces. There has also been little place in planning doctrine for planning as agenda setting, or for other than market-oriented methods.

The history of planning in Western countries has been marked by a retreat from its earlier, synthetic conception. Communities have been ambivalent, wanting at times the order of plans, and at other times the creative workings of markets and pluralist politics. In this framework, professionals and academic commentators steadily moved toward accommodation to market and pluralist values. Doctrine changed. It is an instructive history. Until the postwar period, market models did not dominate thinking in the social sciences and professions the way they did later. City and regional planning was an offshoot of disciplines that can be characterized as synthetic rather analytic: architecture, landscape architecture, and engineering; and planning's most important "theorists" were people like Le Corbusier and Frank Lloyd Wright, while important subordinate themes came from synthetic thinkers in the social sciences, such as Patrick Geddes. In the 1930s, when market values were called into doubt by world depression, a kind of synthetic, classic planning was widely, if vaguely, regarded as the necessary remedy. National planning was adopted on a large scale in the Soviet Union, and there was a good deal of agitation for planning in the United States and Great Britain, from both the left and the right. There were experiments with local, regional and national planning. In all cases this was classic planning—the relatively authoritative elaboration of controls that would implement the goals of leadership, much as in business.

This sort of planning was debated sharply during and after World War II. Planning was under ideological attack in the United States, part of the anticommunism of the period. In academe, the classic model was attacked on conceptual grounds: a central planner could not know enough to allocate resources as well as the market; and if governments tried partial planning, there would be continual and great political temptation to broaden the plan.[29]

Much of what has been written about planning since that time has echoed these criticisms in one way or another. Planning is defined as a function of either a central staff or a semiautonomous agency, interest group, or lobby.[30] The vast majority of studies have reached the same conclusion: in a complex, polyarchical system it is difficult to know enough or have enough authority to plan or implement according to the classic model (agreed goals, laying out steps to achieve them, coordinating the relevant actors to take these steps). A famous case study described planners as frustrated in moving from goals to detailed steps for implementation. The main theme was the inappropriateness of such planning in a political system marked by conflicting interests and general reluctance to plan at the expense of free competition among these interests. A host of case studies have made this criticism of planning in the Western democracies, whether at the national or local levels.[31]

Planning's viability as a discipline was saved from this criticism by inventing the idea of "indicative" or "incrementalist" planning to describe how some public bodies were influencing economies in a broad and comprehensive way despite official reluctance or refusal to adopt outright the classic model of planning. Thus the debate over "planning" versus "the market" was said to be a sterile activity: in fact both could coexist, though command and hierarchy would be found to have limited uses.[32] In the late 1950s much attention was given to the French method of national planning, which was described as "indicative": less a plan than a prediction around which a consensus of private-sector decision-makers would develop.[33] This notion of planning caught on, and by the mid-1960s many nations were emulating the French. Planning came to be seen as a way to reduce the uncertainties that faced private business and thereby encourage investment in the right sectors at the right time, rather than as an instrument of heavy-handed government control.[34] Planning seemed, in fact, a major factor in the postwar economic growth common to many countries, and thus a benefit to all. Similar arguments were made for regional and urban planning.[35] Martin Meyerson, in an article that was influential in local planning circles in the United States, described planning as mainly concerned with predictions that would aid the market, not replace it.[36]

This more modern planning doctrine, whatever its popularity and promise in national capitals, made less progress in places like Wales and Appalachia. It did percolate to enclaves of technocrats in government and among the more modern business men, but there were obstacles to more general diffusion. First, indicative planning required that government be in a position to negotiate with business. In Wales and Appalachia, many of the most important businesses had their headquarters elsewhere, and local managers either could not negotiate or, when they did, did so on orders from above. Second, indicative planning depended on its perceived role in assuring a stable, growing economy. But the economy of peripheral regions was notorious for growing more slowly than the larger national economy, and for feeling downturns more quickly. Finally, indicative planning required a consensus on the importance of modernization. In Wales and Appalachia, polarization between insiders and outsiders was more the rule. As I will show, indicative planning applied in such a context tended to exacerbate, rather than to reduce, polarization.

Meanwhile, both kinds of planning doctrine came under attack not only in peripheral regions, but generally in Western countries after the end of the 1960s. The promise of indicative planning had reached a peak in the mid-1960s and then began to go into eclipse. Economic crises caused a collapse of national planning, and financial constraints in urban areas engulfed urban planning.[37] None of the procedural or technical innovations that had seemed so promising to planners and their supporters in the previous two decades were nearly a match for the political and economic pressures of that period. Planners, who had earlier begun to take a modest share of credit for national economic advance and some isolated urban developments, were forced to hastily adopt defensive positions and to endure ideological backlash and budget cutbacks. In Great Britain, national planning was abandoned during a crisis over balance of payments in the late 1960s, and urban planning faced retrenchment in subsequent reductions in general support for local government. In the United States the Vietnam War diverted funds from the domestic economy, and economic crisis slowly developed through the 1970s, with the financial squeeze on state and local governments a threat to planners throughout the decade.

Much of the difficulty encountered by planning agencies in Wales and Appalachia can be explained by the typology of regional politics I outlined earlier. The characteristics of hegemony, a concept typified by these places, make it difficult for official agencies to find clients in the region, or to be entirely clear in their policies when they do find them. Hegemony explains the polarization, the need to focus on agenda setting and the inappropriateness of methods that were designed for other kinds of systems. I deal with this problem in detail in Chapter 6.

Most of what has been written about planning takes account of neither centrality nor local capacity. In effect, the literature assumes the polyarchy case: centrally linked institutions are balanced by strong local politics and administration, and competing interest groups agree on the rules. The only variation is toward a less differentiated system with less competition, more hierarchy.

The planning I observed in Wales and Appalachia is inconsistent with both of these conceptions, a fact that, for two reasons, can be attributed to the hegemonic politics and economics in these regions. First, the real effect of planning in both places was visible on political agendas: what projects would be brought up and debated, what topics would be avoided.[38] I noted earlier that this effect of planning tends to be obscured. Technical planning within a hierarchical framework is supposed to be a means of programming the detailed steps toward a goal, and people measure the effectiveness of this kind of planning by the speed with which the proposed actions take place. Indicative planning is thought of as more passive, at most suggestive. Indicative planning is said to work well when it helps other (technical) planners get their plans implemented more quickly. This may have been one effect of the plans of the Welsh Office and the Appalachian Regional Commission, but what is more apparent is their effect on the political agendas of their constituencies. Their plans occupied press attention and the attention of other public officials. By suggesting a project in any location, the planners could make it difficult for alternative proposals to obtain a thorough hearing. By suggesting projects like new towns and roads (in Wales) or highways and hospitals (in Appalachia) they ensured that these, and not other topics (like the ownership structure of natural resources or manufacturing) would dominate public and official attention. Second, in both Wales and Appalachia a wide-ranging opposition to official planning emerged. These opposition plans and statements can be viewed, like their official counterparts, as efforts to control the agenda of debate rather than as technical plans. As such, they had some success.

These characteristics of planning make more sense in the context of hegemony than in either hierarchy or polyarchy. Under hegemony, a potential opposition must be controlled; and official planning can help by setting the agenda for public attention, by performing indicative planning to service those interested in industrial development, and by keeping some deals quiet until it is too late for effective opposition to develop. Opposition groups, on the other hand, have a basis for organizing due to their insider cultural ties; and official plans (along with other activities of the outsider-controlled bureaucracies and economic structure) provide an issue around which opposition plans can develop.

New Directions for Planning? It is an important question whether planners can transcend these conceptual limits. The case studies that follow, and the analyses in Chapters 5 and 6, will suggest a possible and desirable role for planning. They will suggest a change in orientation and some developments in method. My argument is that the difficulties and disasters in which planners have become involved, in hegemonic regions like Wales and Appalachia, are not only avoidable but also indicate a more general set of mistakes that occur in other kinds of political and economic settings.

Planning has strayed from its constructive mission. This has been going on for a long time, but has been particularly true in the past decade or so, a time of marked turbulence and uncertainty in dealing with urban and economic problems. Since the early 1960s, planning has suffered attacks from both right and left.[39] It has been a period when, as a profession, the practice of planning has admitted large numbers of persons who, whatever their training, have had more access to authority and bureaucratic ties than they have had chance to reflect on and learn a distinctive professional role. It should not be surprising that a coherent, doctrinal response has been slow to develop. Planners at the outset of the 1960s had coherent doctrine and clear debates, limited and inadequate as these now seem.[40] At the local level they debated whether the appropriate institutional structure was the independent commission or the executive advisor, whether land-use analyses should result in plans or projections. Regional and national planners debated such issues as whether to do plans that pushed economies ahead all at once, or purposely stimulated unbalanced growth.[41] These were relatively simple debates, approaches from a common background by practitioners.

What happened to planners was that their clientele changed. The middle-class reformers who had supported planners through the 1950s in the United States fragmented into different groups, while new clientele groups, including ghetto minorities, corporate business interests, and civil service employees, became more important in big-city politics.[42] With all this, the federal government took an increasing role in local and regional planning, channeling funds that supported all or part of many planning agencies, and thus itself became an important new client.[43] The old doctrine and its concepts of planning were in no way appropriate or adequate as a professional response to these changes, though they could be used as a stopgap on occasion. That is, a planner could always identify himself with his land-use planning background if it would do him some good. In other cases he could simply make himself available as a helpful person with contacts, the one-eyed professional in the land of the blind, so to speak.

It is worth asking at this point, though, whether more coherent concepts and methods might ultimately develop among planners, concepts and methods that might be more useful for cases of hegemony and that might also be useful in other cases. I examine this question in more detail later, but at this point I want to review briefly where planning doctrine and technique was leading during the 1960s before it was overwhelmed by the events just described.

A major issue at the outset of the 1960s was whether planners ought to retain their traditional, somewhat artistic, approaches to land-use planning, or launch into much more complex analytical procedures that seemed to have unlimited potential for expanding their role in giving policy advice. A less significant issue at that time was whether either position responded to a broad enough set of clienteles, whether they both were not more elitist than planners wanted to be. On this second point, a minor shift in planning methodology and doctrine had the potential to broaden response, to increase, rather than decrease, the extent to which all interests (rather than a few) might be represented in policy making. This minor movement occurred largely in response to the rapid development of analytic techniques in transportation studies and land-use models, the introduction of the social sciences into planning curricula, and the entrance of highly trained professionals from engineering and other analytic disciplines into planning practice, all of which was part of what I earlier described as the shift to indicative planning, the shift from Geddes' regionalism to "liberal" regional policy. Britton Harris, an important academic and practitioner of the new analytical planning, had advocated that planners devote more time to the study and analysis of urban areas.[44] Only if they could predict such phenomena as the shifts in land use resulting from changes in transportation, he said, could they provide useful policy advice. Making statements about the goals of land use was not the business of planners, but of politicians. This suggestion was radical at the time, as most planners thought it was their business to suggest goals, to spend relatively large parts of their time elaborating ideal land-use patterns, and to spend relatively small parts of their time on scientific analysis of actual interrelationships among urban activities. Harris' suggestion, furthermore, implied rather large and complex models, long study of theory in urban sociology and economics, and extensive use of computer techniques and mathematics. These ideas gained increasing acceptance in the early 1960s and seemed to threaten more traditional ways of operating in most city and regional planning agencies.

Paul Davidoff and Tom Reiner, who had been colleagues and students of Harris, contended that Harris had made too crude a distinction, that the choice for planners was not between analysis and goal setting.[45] They suggested that between these two poles of activity there was room for another function for planning: the elaboration of sets of means and ends, sequences of activities that might be spelled out, compared and presented to potential clients for their edification and ultimate choice. Although it was, in part, simply reflection of ideas that were in the air among planners at the time, in retrospect the article by Davidoff and Reiner seems pivotal. It represented a crossroad in the progression of thinking about planning, an option not taken, an idea that had proved too fragile for its time. In making their point, the authors disputed Harris's contention that there could be no theory of planning apart from a theory about the city itself, and they asserted a connection between the goals of clients and the analyses and thoughts of professionals. They did not put goals and means in separate boxes, but rather described a procedure whereby the experts would have to make contact continually with their clients. They implied that out of this interaction might result the construction, not simply of goals, but of whole systems of thought. What they actually said was a little less than this: that planners would engage in thinking through and presenting the courses of action that might lead to alternative goals—writing scenarios, to use a phrase popular now. But still, this was an important departure both from the detached, positivist stance that Harris proposed, which allowed planners to spend a great deal of time building models and allowed little for client interaction; and from the somewhat more politically involved practitioners who, by not getting much into the scenarios of implementation, put up their own barriers to client interaction. Davidoff and Reiner implied both engagement in the structure of thought surrounding planners' proposals and sharing of ideas with those whom the proposals would affect. This was quite a radical idea, both politically and intellectually.

Another planning academician, John Dyckman, had come to somewhat similar conclusions at about the same time. Through the 1950s, planners had thought of themselves as providing an alternative to politics because of their special concern with goals. This view was challenged by academics on philosophical and technical grounds. Herbert Simon, taking his basis from an interpretation of the logical positivist philosophy of Wittgenstein, argued that social goals were meaningless concepts, and that planners and administrators should spend more time on surveying near-term alternatives and evaluating them.[46] Kenneth Arrow had shown the impossibility of creating statements of collective preferences from knowledge of individual preferences, thus undermining the assumptions of some planners that they might find a technical way to do what politicians claimed to do in a political way.[47] Dyckman, writing at about the same time as Davidoff and Reiner, then asked: "what might be left" for planners? The answer, he thought, was they would make "heroic" statements of courses of action communities might embark on. They would leave the development of generalizations about actual behavior, including the decision processes for implementing plans, to other fields, and attempt to project beyond this. He thought that the research of case studies of actual planning in its political context might produce a sociology of planning knowledge to guide them. Thus, if planners could build up a sense of what kinds of communities and groups produced what kinds of ideals and programs, they would have some basis for making plans of the "heroic" nature he sought.[48]

One other student of planning made suggestions that can be tied to this line of thinking. Alan Altshuler, a political scientist, carried out studies of planning in Minneapolis and St. Paul.[49] Like other political scientists who had observed planners, he was struck by the discrepancy between their ideal of comprehensive planning, and the political systems they worked in that withheld legitimacy from such activity. Politicians refrained from setting goals, allowed planners to go out on a limb with their proposals, and did not support them when they were attacked by special interests. Rather than question the whole notion of comprehensive planning, however, Altshuler tried to devise a means to institute comprehensive thinking separate from politics in a role like that of the judiciary, and he encouraged planners to think of themselves as contributers to the broadest debates in local affairs. He provided, in effect, a case study of the sort Dyckman proposed.

From these and other sources, one can identify a progression of ideas about planning. The key elements are: (1) an insistence that plans emerge from transactions between planner and client, rather than continue the separate development of research-oriented plans and popular consciousness; (2) the idea that this planning process involves not just statements about goals, but a structure of thought—means and ends—that can be agreed on and/or debated; and (3) the idea that somehow this planning—along with the development of consciousness—can go on alongside of the regular political process. That this set of conceptions of planning never came to dominate either the academics or the profession of planning is not the point here, though several writers extended this line of thought later.[50] The point is that a beginning of a new doctrine existed within the planning profession, and that doctrine might have allowed the profession to develop beyond the positions implied for it in any of the critiques it experienced subsequently.

For this doctrine to become dominant, at least two things have to occur. First, the economic, political, and clientele base have to develop. This is the subject of Chapters 2 and 5 below. Second, there has to develop a coherent doctrine and method of planning. How would planners actually involve themselves in the kind of planning described here? What procedures would they follow in doing plans that would allow for full transactions between planner and client? How might they develop whole structures of thought that might be debated and advanced? How would they proceed with this alongside of, rather than under fire from, a set of political institutions? I return to these questions in Chapter 6.

Chapter 2

Theory

Chapter 1 introduced the problem of territorial opposition and the possibilities this implied for the organization of planning—a theme that will be dealt with analytically in the concluding chapter. But so far there has been little discussion of a more fundamental issue: Why should there be a territorial (as opposed to some other) basis for opposition planning? The answer requires a set of hypotheses describing the conditions for transition from one type of area to another—particularly, from hegemony to separatism. This question precedes questions about the organization of planning. In this chapter, I first review the liberal and Marxist literature on this question. Then I elaborate the theory of territorial politics (first suggested in Chapter 1). I tie the theory to this literature, at least to certain themes in it. I note some theoretical antecedents and then return to the main body of liberal and Marxist literature on territorial politics, elaborating the model.

Liberal and Marxist Conceptions of Regional Development

If one theme dominates Western policy and theory toward regions, it is the inexorable disappearance of local territorial consciousness and organization and their replacement by a national and international system.[1] In this system, moreover, dominant organizations are instrumental, rather than ends in themselves. People join them not because of tradition, but in order to get something else: wages or political advantage, for example. This is true of business firms, labor unions, political parties, and most voluntary associations. The notion of community has thus undergone a drastic transformation, and, except for the nation-state, territorial community as a recognized institution has been replaced by other organizations. Consistent with this, Western political and economic theory and policy toward regions now emphasize: (1) a shift away from territorial bases of representation and identifications to a system of bargaining among classes and industrial-sector interests; (2) a sequence in which these shifts spread from central metropolitan areas to the periphery; and (3) a belief that the effect of these shifts is increased quality of economic and political participation. Based implicity on these views has been another: remaining territorial issues are matters of administration of centrally determined policies. This includes the problem of regional policy and planning.

The first of these points—the shift from territorial vertical interests—is fundamental to the literature on comparative politics. In the history of party systems in Western Europe and North America, social scientists have seen change as a dual shift in the locus of political conflict from that of local versus central elites (at one extreme) to conflicts among national elites, and from ideological issues to class or sectoral issues.[2]

Studies of political parties and alignments have repeated these themes often. V. O. Key noted the decline of sectionalism in his influential work, *Southern Politics*.[3] Lipset elaborated it in *Political Man*,[4] and James Sundquist repeated it, noting the penetration of modernist voters into traditional Democratic southern constituencies, which made the southern metropolitan suburbs, at least, more like other parts of the country in the issues they supported.[5] The working hypothesis of these analysts was the emerging and persistent class basis of political groupings, the decline of section and region along with other less persistent bases. At the same time issues were said to have become less ideological and polarizing, more a matter of stable coalitions in permanent bargaining arrangements.[6] One looks in vain for a suggestion that this shift to functional interests is reversible or anything but universal. Regional interests are seen as temporary or subordinate. There is an impression of inevitability about the general course of modernization. Nor is there, in most cases, any suggestion of a point of equilibrium beyond which evolution is not likely to proceed. There is, in addition, an implication (though I see no explicit statements) that the development is unilinear, at least in its most important outlines. Exceptions are certainly described (the South in the United States, the populists, nationalism in Western Europe), but as exceptions rather than as indications of basic alternative lines of development.

The second main theme is the proposition that the shift from territorial to functional interests and representation moves geographically by diffusion from metropolitan centers and capital cities to the periphery.[7] Political, economic, and administrative "modernization" leads to contact and demonstration effects. New attitudes are introduced into peripheral areas through extensions of metropolitan, so-called cosmopolitan, institutions: labor unions, savings banks, nursery schools, various kinds of business services, government agencies. One major phenomenon is the introducton of large-scale employers—branch plants or government agencies—that, because of their size or because they follow rules written in headquarters in the metropolitan areas, are said to recruit labor on performance rather than status criteria. All these examples can be thought of as mechanisms of diffusion. Diffusion is implied, if not explicitly stated, in the shifts from territorial to functional alignments described earlier. The establishment of national, class-based political parties imply diffusion. The literature on American federalism, urban politics and intergovernmental relations generally describes a process of diffusion in which private and public programs are transmitted and reshaped and information generally communicated in a multiplicity of channels from one government to another.[8]

Third, a more explicitly ideological dimension of the arguments for the shift to functional alignments and their diffusion throughout the territory of a nation portrays this shift as not only general and inevitable but also as leading to greater equality, both of material rewards and of political participation and power. Fundamental to this view is the proposition that the larger the political system, the less chance there is for any one faction to dominate. The classic statement, by Madison in the *Federalist Papers*, was later elaborated to justify national integration as an alternative to the sectionalism implied in the states' rights doctrines.[9]

Others link national integration with equality. There is debatable evidence that, in the course of development of nations (and states or regions within nations), there would be a progression, resulting initially in inequality, but subsequently in greater equality at a higher material level.[10] There were arguments for the role of national bureaucracies in advocating the rights of the poor.[11] Finally Selznick, in his study of the TVA, noted the conflict between such national goals and regional interests: an implicit case for the doctrine of national integration.[12]

Samuel Beer extended the images of modernization and diffusion in an analysis of the development of American federalism.[13] In this he conceived the shifts in federal-state-local administrative and political relationships as resulting largely from economic development. He typified the economy as moving from a segmented local structure to periods dominated in turn by the development of national corporations, and then a national labor movement, and most recently a large-scale economy based on science and advanced technology. The increasing centralization of the federal system was, he argued, a byproduct of new relationships between government and science. Starting with World War II, the development of science and technology required active participation by government and directly influenced public policy through public agencies, most prominently through defense, atomic energy, and health, but through all the other public agencies also. This created a new kind of demand for government action and centralization. Thus, government activities became so pervasive that they conflicted with each other or with the aims of private firms. Consequently, new government programs were established to coordinate these activities.

Another effect of the new prominence of science was the emergence of a "professional-bureaucratic complex" that represented and reinforced tendencies toward centralization: a research elite, professionals in the bureaucracy, private-sector interests who benefitted from the programs, and congressional elements specializing in specific technical aspects of policy making. Beer cited the instinctive tendency of professionals to seek national arenas of support and influence as one of the forces of centralization that accompany economic and political modernization.

The main alternative to pluralist and modernization theories is Marxist analysis. But Marxists (or those who may be grouped loosely in this category) have by-and-large dealt inadequately with territorial issues. The underlying differences between Marxist and liberal analysis are certainly profound. I would list the following as the most important differences: First, the norm toward which liberals see Western societies moving is that of permanent bargaining among interest groups, defined chiefly by class. There may be individual mobility, but classes will persist. Marxists, on the other hand, expect that the class basis of social organization will ultimately be transcended.[14] Second, Marxists view working-class consciousness and organization as the key to economic and political change. That is, the goal of working-class emancipation is to be achieved *by the efforts of the workers themselves.*[15] Liberals rely much more upon mediating agencies as crucial to the management of conflict among groups: regulatory agencies, police, markets.[16] Classes, for liberals, become less self-conscious, more inclined to bargain for incremental gains through those institutions.

Finally and fundamentally, for Marxists the economy is the origin of political change; material conditions provide the substructure and relationships upon which class relationships and politics rest. Liberals attribute causal importance to governments, techniques of leadership, and cultural traditions of interest-group adjustment. Thus, for them, government is the provider of remedies for problems. For example, the government's welfare policy in the New Deal was supposed to be the remedy for class inequalities. Marxists, in contrast, focus on class mobilization.

While Marxist ideas offer a telling critique of liberal thought, orthodox Marxism still leaves major gaps. One important problem is that Marxist thinking, by taking the principle of economic determinism too far, focuses exclusively on the economic substructure and resorts to dogmatic explanations of class and government organization. The truth of Marx's observation that exploitation on the shop floor might motivate working-class organization almost seems to have been too powerful. In concentrating on the immediate implications of this insight, Marxists have neglected some of its ramifications. They have studied the material conditions of labor exploitation as if such studies by themselves would lead to increased working-class consciousness, and as if class consciousness in turn would lead inevitably to political control and the eradication of class.

Recently, Marxist writers have addressed this bias.[17] The issue is how to supplement the process of mobilization that derives from consciousness of material exploitation, how to protect the process from crosscutting influences, how to reinforce it. Avoiding this issue—for whatever good reasons—has meant that at least two rather important practical problems have received little attention. One is the organizational question—the problem of government bureaucratization. Briefly, the problem of bureaucratization is that the ruling elite has usually found it more convenient to persuade the general population of the advantages of size, technical virtuosity, and mastery of procedure, in a party hierarchy or government agency, than to point out the costs of nonrepresentation, nonresponse, and oligarchical control. Michels presented the classic analysis: mastery of procedure always produces an oligarchy in organizations of any size, whatever the background of the rulers, whatever their committment to democratic goals, whatever the mechanism of parliamentary control.[18] For Marxists, committed in theory to working-class control, the question has been called "substitutism": the tendency for party to substitute for class in actual governing, and for party leadership to substitute for the whole party.[19] Despite recent attempts to open this issue to research and discussion, organization remains a problem. (The fact that organizational research in the Western liberal democracies has done no better is no help.)

A second question is that of the *basis* on which class consciousness and organization might develop. The central answer has been that the basis is material conditions of exploitation in the workplace. But in fact a number of other bases mobilize organization and consciousness: race, sex, religion, and territory are the most prominent contemporary examples.

My feeling is that these two problems should be confronted in this order: first, the bases of consciousness and organization; and second, the internal structure of bureaucracy. This leads to a reconsideration of territorial issues. I think more will be gained for the problem of organization by studying the relative roles of territorial versus workplace organization, than vice versa. Changes in bureaucracies tend to come from outside rather than from inside. I am not asserting an external determinism for organization. On the contrary, the internal momentum and persistence of organization seems to me to be much greater than most people realize. Even so, major changes, including organizational democratization, probably require that internal dynamics be coordinated with external pressures. Knowledge of the kinds of pressures possible from different kinds of organizational bases—e.g. workplace versus territory—would, I think, stimulate organizational innovation.

The two main sources for the analysis of territorial bases of organization in Marxist literature are studies of nationalism and studies of uneven regional development. Marxists, early on, had to confront the problem that, while in principle one might want to give priority to organization of the working class, in practice the dominant allegiance for all classes, including workers, was to the nation. In practice, therefore, the question was the extent to which Marxists ought to support nationalist movements. Marx himself had taken the position that workers had a right to free themselves of all oppression, including national oppression, and this was interpreted by many socialists as a justification for alliances with nationalist movements.[20] This was the case in Poland in the period before the First World

War; and in Germany the Social Democrats were torn by debate over how much support for working-class issues they should trade off for the political advantages of a powerful coalition. They ultimately supported the nationalist position of Germany in World War I. The chief intellectual opposition to these positions was mounted by Rosa Luxemburg, who attacked reform-oriented coalition practices, in general, and nationalism in particular. Her position was that nationalism was an issue peripheral at best to the interests of the working class, that the bourgeoisie would always dominate nationalist movements, that the best hope for working-class political movements was to focus on class movements internationally and at the national scale in the larger nations, seeking the support of the smaller peripheral national movements.[21]

Luxemburg's argument occasioned a famous series of debates with Lenin, conducted in the journals of the period preceding and during the war. Lenin supported nationalists on the grounds that self-determination would ultimately lead to working-class control. In practice, after 1917, he adopted a two-pronged policy: (1) allowing peripheral nationalities national self-determination, including separation as independent states, while (2) enouraging by all means available to him, including the use of the Red Army, the establishment of working-class dominated governments within these states.

But this was a pragmatic, not a theoretical solution. While Lenin more correctly perceived the strength of nationalist sentiment, and the military and economic advantages of large-scale national organization, Luxemburg's theory was never proven wrong.[22] Whether Marxists ought to support national movements in order to promote consciousness and organization among workers, is still an open question.

Nationalist theory has not provided a definitive answer to these issues and has not advanced the question much beyond Lenin's pragmatic solution.[23] Perhaps the most important recent work that deals with nationalism is Nairn's *The Break-up of Britain*, which links the recent emergence of separatist nationalism to uneven development, and which also attempts to move beyond a purely economic analysis to political outcomes.[24]

Most simply stated, Nairn's thesis is that while Lenin and other Marxists assumed an even spread of capitalism over the world, the main development that has produced nationalism is in fact uneven development. This means that we must give closer attention to the dynamics of the development of class consciousness from capitalism. If capitalism has spread unevenly, then obstacles to working-class organization and consciousness may also vary from place to place, necessitating new analyses specific to each situation and a comparative analytic framework that distinguishes the dynamics of different kinds of places. Nairn then identifies a particular discrepancy from the Marxist hypothesis for Britain's ruling class and develops a two-dimensional model for comparing the developments from this in different kinds of national contexts. For Britain, Nairn suggests that circumstances permitted the establishment of political control over its peripheral nations—Scotland, Wales, and Ireland—before the development of capitalism was complete, and this political hegemony allowed the formation of the British ruling class in a precapitalist, partly absolutist form. The result was that the development of the modern economy proceeded further in some peripheral areas, than at the center. Incorporation within such a precapitalist state, therefore, was a hindrance to economic development and also a brake on the development of class relations toward working-class participation. Therefore, in these circumstances, movements for national independence might lead to working-class control in the new state. Nairn extended this argument to suggest two main factors in the development of peripheral areas ("nations") that would enhance this probability: economic development and state history. By economic development he meant the existence of an independent and vigorous bourgeoisie. He found Scotland along with certain other European nationalist movements, including the Basques, very strong on this factor, while many former colonial states lacked this class. "State history" is the existence of a collective memory of governing, such as the memory in Scotland of the nation that existed until the eighteenth century. Nairn is not specific, however, about the connections between these factors and the class composition of the new state. His focus is on the regressive drag from the center, not the composition of forces at the periphery.

Nairn's reference to uneven development suggests a promising area of inquiry for the study of political organization. But so far, there has been little exploration of this aspect of regional inequality in the Marxist literature. The bulk of attention has gone to the causes of uneven development, rather than to its political consequences. The most fundamental question has been whether the cause of uneven development is to be found inside particular areas (e.g., in a regional history of class relations) or in external phenomena such as the development of international trade relations, the rise of the multinational firm, or internal colonialism. Marxist economists who have explored uneven regional development have acknowledged the lack of attention to the conditions of developing regional consciousness.[25] Even some of the best available work on regional politics, including Markusen's descriptions of western regionalism in the United States—as a contest for regional loyalty between corporate and working-class interests stimulated by the prospect of exploitation of energy resources—fall short of a theory that can account for the conditions under which class and regional interests might coincide.[26] Throughout this literature, there is plenty of concern lest regional (or national) loyalties might develop to the detriment of working-class interests, but little suggestion of the mechanisms under which this might or might not occur.

Other approaches touch on this problem but fail to come to grips with it in a fundamental way. A number of Marxists see general social tendencies toward inclusion of an enlarging group of occupations in the "working class" and thus an enlarging base for class organization—and this may support "regionalist" or "territorialist" strategies. Carrillo, for example, offered arguments like these for Eurocommunism, and Castells argued that "urban movements" might supplement class movements.[27] But neither of these suggestions answers the fundamental question of whether other groups will show solidarity with the industrial proletariat in the long run. An internal colonialism hypothesis has been formulated by several writers and applied to such places as Wales and Appalachia. This model, drawn from work on imperialism and Third World dependency, had the enormous practical importance of focusing the attention of activists on such issues as the control of property and the distribution of political power. It describes the mechanisms of external control through the use of local collaborators and cultural domination, and it suggests why local people might be expected at times to organize politically against external control. But it falls short of specifying very explicitly the conditions that might transform local populations into a working-class movement.[28] The most general criticism of the internal colonialism model is that it places too heavy reliance on external agents of domination. On the contrary, critics say, internal colonies have relatively permeable boundaries, making it hard to define any pure external force. Moreover, posing external sources of domination may only confuse the issue for local people if the real problem is capitalism and bourgeois domination, wherever it exists.[29] The general sense of this debate suggests a joint effect of internal and external phenomena, but researchers typically have avoided working through the implications for regional political organization.

The most important Marxist analysis of "regionalism" has been made by O'Connor, as the byproduct of his analysis of the causes and consequences of state fiscal crisis.[30] O'Connor's analysis delineates a "state" sector as developing because of the needs of "monopoly sector" and "competitive sector" private business and labor. With monopoly capital and labor taking an increasing share of private business, with typically high-technology, high-wage types of organization, there develops a set of problems that can be solved only (and only temporarily) by the expansion of government, that is, the state sector: the monopoly sector, highly productive, runs out of markets and requires the state as consumer; it runs out of capital and requires the state to participate in investment financing. Meanwhile, as an increasing part of productive needs are provided by the high-technology monopoly sector, there is created surplus labor that must be taken care of, and surplus entrepreneurs. For surplus labor and surplus entrepreneurs, the state is pressed to undertake programs such as welfare and reeducation; and to subsidize competitive sector business. The state sector thus takes on a dual role dealing with the problems created as the private sector shifts from competitive to monopoly form: it must use its taxing and borrowing capabilities to provide finance capital for monopoly business, and it must use its spending, persuasive, and coercive powers to care for the surplus workers and entrepreneurs and keep them from questioning the transformation that is occurring. Both of these problems, says O'Connor, lead to the creation of new government functions and a general expansion of state employment. One prominent form of this is the *regional* government agency. Regional functions replace local functions. Unencumbered with the kinds of electoral accountability characteristic of the local level, regional agencies are in a position to work more effectively with the monopoly sector. O'Connor sees regional agencies as the beginning of a possible "social-industrial complex," attacking both the finance and welfare problems of the modern state sector by using the technology- and capital-intensive methods developed by monopoly business.

Two things are worth noting about this analysis, in the context of the arguments I have been reviewing in this chapter. First, there is a certain convergence of O'Connor's Marxism and Beer's liberalism. Both note the development of a modern state sector in response to the elaboration of a large-scale, articulated private-sector economy, and they both note some of its key characteristics: growing professionalism, the contact between public- and private-sector professionals and technicians, the lessening relevance of legislative control. Where they differ is in emphasis. O'Connor pays relatively more attention to the force of the monopoly-sector profit drive and to possible popular movements to overcome and transform it. Beer pays relatively more attention to the way centralization has elaborated itself, taking the economic imperative more as a given. Certainly there are fundamental differences between the two analyses, but I am nevertheless struck by their convergence.

Second, particularly in O'Connor's argument, but also in Beer's, there is a suggestion of instability in the monopoly sector–state sector coalition, a suggestion of the possible development of popular forces that will challenge the particular combination of welfare and financing functions described as emerging. O'Connor sees the popular movement coming out of the fundamental discrepancy between a finance function that favors monopoly business and a welfare function that cares for the victims of the monopoly form of economy. He suggests that coalitions of government workers and professionals, and their clients, may force modifications in this program. This would, of course, change the form of regionalism in some indeterminate way. But O'Connor does not go much further. I find it useful to characterize O'Connor as making an important contribution in his assessment of the causes of state-sector behavior and internal conflict, but falling short in his description of the state as administrative and political configuration; while Beer does better on administration and politics, but takes too much for granted in economic causes.

A Theory of Territorial Politics

Neither liberal nor Marxist conceptions of regional development encompass the territorial movements described in Chapter 1, which include (1) indigenous control, (2) worker participation, and (3) defense of community—the transition to the separatism type of situation. Why not? I would specify the problem as a common belief in the unilinear nature of progress of society. It is not that these beliefs are the same in all respects. But each conception is in itself unilinear in its idea of progress. For the liberals, it is the doctrine of modernization. For Marxists, there is a unilinear development of capitalism suggested in *The Communist Manifesto*, and this theme is carried through the hypotheses about the development of the working class and its eventual rise to control, and the evolution of a classless society. Even the "national question" and the actual emergence of new nations failed to change this characteristic of Marxist theory. For both Marxists and liberals, the consequences of the unilinear overemphasis have been the development of national models at the expense of territorial (regional, local) ones and a failure to learn from local experience. Conceptually, local experience is relegated to the reports of case studies, incorporated through ad hoc theorizing only loosely connected with the main theory, and given inconsistent, pragmatic treatment in policy.

The basic theoretical problem in dealing with territorial movements is therefore to separate the themes that a unilinear development model lumps together. This is the purpose of the typology presented in Chapter 1. It separates the attributes of "centrality" and "local capacity" and asserts that places can develop on one of these dimensions without developing as much on the other. It separates dimensions from what would otherwise be one dimension, most recognizable as the classic concepts of sociological theories of development, "*Gemeinschaft-Gessellschaft*," the "rural-urban continuum." These classic concepts implied that there was only one path along which a place or region or nation could develop. The typology of Chapter 1 suggests a multiplicity of paths, summarized in the possible transitions among types of places displayed in the diagram.

By formulating development in this multilinear fashion, it is possible to hypothesize *interaction effects* of the variables defining the axes. Thus, centrality and local capacity are hypothesized to have effects together, through their interaction, that neither would have alone. Two such theories have been the basis for this model: that of Edith Penrose and, more explicitly, that of Frank W. Young. Penrose described what was in essence a theory of system-subsystem interaction for the growth of the business firm.[31] Overall growth of the firm, she said, depended on its ability to incorporate the operations of diverse branches into productive relationships with the larger firm. This was not simply a technical problem, but a long-term process of a central management team learning how to talk with production units and discovering ways to join productive capacities in the branch units with other parts of the firm and with marketing potentials. Her emphasis was on the management team and perhaps the main analogy is to my earlier discussion of the operation of central regimes. But there was also recognition of the unique characteristics of the production units, and here the analogy is to the region. Moreover, the focus of the Penrose model is on neither central management nor the production unit, but on their interaction. Both groups are seen to learn from one another over a period of time.

The kind of interaction between central management and branch unit that Penrose emphasized was largely one of the mesh, and the failure to mesh, of concepts. There was no mention of force or formal authority, or the availability and distribution of material resources, and very little exchange. These were assumed as the normal control relationships of the firm under capitalism, and what Penrose was doing was adding this dimension to them. But she saw it as a very important dimension, one that over a period of time became as important an organizational resource as any piece of fixed capital equipment. A branch plant producing farm machinery might then see itself as linked through particular expertise with an aircraft firm, with the joint product a crop-spraying airplane. The joint planning necessary to produce a competitive product might involve many years of work, but once accomplished, the ability to work jointly was a resource that might be applied to other projects, and the branch plant would attain prominence within the firm. Failures to achieve joint relationships would result in decline for the branch as well as the firm, resulting in divestitures and failed mergers.

By analogy, the Penrose model could be applied to peripheral regions within larger states. The farm machinery plant might literally be an economic component of the region, the larger firm an influential part of the central regime. The interactions between branch and center can be seen as repeated for other relations between units at the periphery and those at the center. The problem of the interaction could be seen as part of the public sector as well as the private sector, applied to branches of the agencies of the central government or to the relations of local to central governments.

Another interaction model was elaborated by Frank W. Young and applied to data for systems of villages.[32] The problematic variable, for Young, was the capacity of a village unit, or the capacity of a system of villages, to process information, to incorporate a diversity of types of information in its collective memory. Young's hypothesis was that, for any one village, changes in local capacity would occur as a result of the joint effects of its relative centrality and its existing level of local capacity. With centrality low in relation to capacity, there would be an intensification of solidarity within the village that would result in a move to a position of higher centrality and greater capacity. With centrality high in relation to capacity, the reverse would occur.

Thus, the interaction effect is the change in a third variable, which Young calls solidarity and which Penrose (less explicitly specifying interaction) describes as the integration of line and management components of the firm (at the point of production). This is a very intriguing concept that has stimulated much research.[33] My point now is that both Young and Penrose suggest a way of thinking about the effects of interactions between central regimes and peripheral capacity in the development of separatism. The parallels between Young's and Penrose's concepts are not hard to see. Capacity of the local unit is similar to Penrose's unit productivity, while the centrality of the locality is something like the incorporation of the production processes of the unit into the overall strategy of the firm. Young places a relatively greater emphasis on the local unit and achieves more precision; and his formulation of the dynamics of local-system interaction is more specific. His formulation of the role of local solidarity as a mediating process, forcing the transition between a particular configuration of local capacity and centrality, at one point in time, and a changed configuration at a later time, goes further than Penrose's. Penrose, whose formulation is not specific about these things, provides a more complete description of the processes of the central management team and the content of their communication with the local units.

Both Penrose and Young point out the phenomenon of unit solidarity as arising from the interaction of centrality and local capacity. Penrose makes the less explicit statement: over time, a fusion of central and local thinking may occur, resulting in the development of the local unit (i.e., an increase in capacity) as well as the larger system. Young is consistent with this, but more explicit. When a unit is of relatively low centrality and high capacity, it will experience a solidarity movement, moving it into a place of higher centrality and, as a result, higher capacity.

Two of the variables described here—centrality and local capacity—provided the basis for the typology of areas presented in Chapter 1. Penrose and Young also provide the basis for a set of hypotheses that explains the transitions possible from one type to another.[34] What follows is a summary of these hypotheses as applied to areas like Wales and Appalachia and a discussion of the possible role of planning in stabilizing or encouraging transitions. The hypotheses apply to the accompanying diagram.

1. First, unless external factors intervene, there is a tendency for centrality and local development to be in balance with one another. Thus, a place—B—with a high level of centrality will tend to have high capacity, and one with low centrality—C—

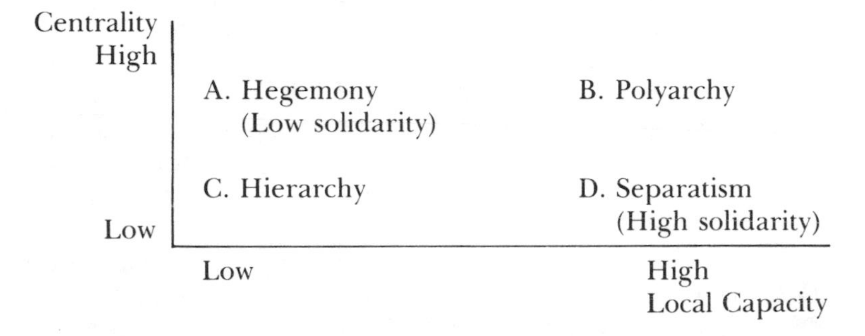

will have low capacity. This means that the hierarchy and polyarchy cases are relatively stable. Thus local capacity and centrality tend to reinforce one another. High capacity means a place has economic organization, jobs, and concentrated population, and this tends to sustain political recognition, representation, access to resources, and easy communications with other places. Once these latter attributes (centrality) are established, they in turn sustain capacity. The economic and class organization characteristic of polyarchy is sustained because of being tied into national networks. Entrepreneurs can develop specialized sectors more easily, having access to outside as well as inside capital and markets and political favors; labor unions can prosper with outside networks to support them.

At low levels of centrality and local capacity—Place C—the same tendencies toward stability would hold. Low capacity would not attract centrality, and low centrality would not attract higher capacity.

2. The hegemony and separatist cases—A and D—are unstable, because centrality and local capacity are out of balance. The basic idea is that high centrality fosters high local capacity that, if absent, sets in motion an adjustment. The reverse is also true: high local capacity also fosters high centrality, and if that is lacking another kind of adjustment occurs.

If hierarchy and polyarchy are stable, then why do transitions occur? Transitions occur because of the intrusion of external factors. Changes in technology or infusions of resources or even military power can upset the balance. Most directly, these external factors change centrality: they build transportation links, establish factories. Occasionally, they may directly and negatively affect local capacity, as when punitive measures are taken on political leaders or whole populations are removed. When these things happen, considerable exchanges of resources may occur, as when, under hegemony, wealth is extracted from an area while external resources are poured in to maintain order. This may appear to be a kind of "stable" dependency, though typically hegemonic areas are subject to great swings of economic fortune. But it is not the internal stability of hierarchy and polyarchy; it is costly to maintain and, generally short-lived.

Separatism is also unstable. The tendency toward balance would cause a shift toward either hierarchy or polyarchy. This would occur once any degree of transition toward separatism occurred. The case histories described below, and, as a result, my analysis, deal with the transition toward separatism (from hegemony) rather than any pure example. In what follows there is much on the transition, little on the practice of any region or nation after achieving separation, and little on any possible resolution toward hierarchy or polyarchy.

3. The causal variable in changes from one type of area to another is solidarity. Solidarity means the intensity of sentiments around a theme, which focuses the energy of the whole social system of the area. Solidarity is hard to measure in any objective way, though one gets a sense of it from descriptions by observers and participants. The defense of slavery, and the attack on it, occasioned the solidarity of the South and the North during the Civil War, revival or revitalization movements, regional and national mobilizations for economic development, like those in Manchester at the beginning of the nineteenth century or Sao Paulo in the late twentieth, are examples of cases where solidarity increased. Less well-reported are cases of decreasing, painfully lowered solidarity, but Wales and Appalachia have both afforded examples at times.

The causal mechanism is in the relationship of solidarity to the interaction of centrality and local capacity. There are two parts to this. First, changes in solidarity are caused by changes in the relation between centrality and local capacity. When centrality is high in relation to local capacity, solidarity decreases; when the reverse is true, when centrality becomes lower in relation to local capacity, solidarity increases. At first, this proposition may seem counter-intuitive. After all, ought not high centrality simply *increase* solidarity for any unit, even if capacity is constant? Not according to this theory. If you are already operating at capacity, the extra access and representation will tend to break up internal relationships; solidarity will drop in response to the added external contact. If on the other hand centrality *decreases* with no change in contact, there will be more time for solidarity, and it will increase.

The second part of the causal chain connecting solidarity to local capacity and centrality concerns the way changes in solidarity then result in changes in either centrality or local capacity. Part of this is that solidarity is by its nature a collective motivator. Quite possibly there is a comfortable level of solidarity for an area, but high or low solidarity, exhilarating and depressing respectively, are uncomfortable and therefore result in changes. Thus in areas experiencing either high or low solidarity, a search for resolution occurs. But resolution is possible through appropriate changes in centrality or local capacity, to bring them back into balance and thus bring solidarity back to a comfortable level. At this point there is no specific hypothesis about which kind of change will be sought. The possibilities are as follows:

a. Under conditions of high solidarity (case D—high local capacity, low centrality): Increase centrality by demanding new access and/or representation, or reduce local capacity by eliminating local institutions.

b. Under conditions of low solidarity (case A—high centrality, low local capacity): Increase local capacity by creating new local institutions, and/or reduce centrality by cutting representation and/or access.

4. Young provides a further element of this argument. When solidarity is low in the larger system, then the low centrality, high capacity cases will, after increasing solidarity, increase their own centrality, and then capacity. In my terms, separatism will move toward polyarchy. Young states the following for villages within a larger area, for the consequences of high solidarity:

> . . . It must be emphasized that solidarity is a communication strategy that is not always successful. Not all sects become churches, nor do all peasant uprisings force land reform. A key factor in the determination of whether a solidarity movement will survive is whether or not the new pattern of meaning subsumes or otherwise articulates with that of the larger system. And this in turn is a function of the degree of solidarity of other villages in the system. If there are a number of these, particularly if they already hold positions of high relative centrality, they will be likely to resist the upstart proposals. Having survived many such confrontations before, they are likely to be able to reject or subsume most movements from below. On the other hand, change must come if the intervillage system is to keep pace with other subregions, so villages offering reformulations are often able to force a compromise. Thus a sect or a political movement (assuming one that is based in a commu-

> nity) may settle for the status of denomination or third party, and a land reform effort such as organized "squatting" may be taken over by a government agency and legalized. It is true that movements often spread beyond community boundaries, but they can usually be analyzed in terms of these units.[35]

The Welsh and Appalachian oppositions were like Young's villages: groups which lacked centrality within a larger system, but which had developed over time a powerful set of ideas—local capacity, in my terms. Plaid Cymru, perhaps, dominated a few local areas and so in a sense were like Young's "villages," but even in Appalachia and throughout much of Wales, numerous localized groups of the opposition had minority strength which they could mobilize in futherance of a larger solidarity movement. A direct application of Young's formulation would have these oppositions contesting for centrality. Their success would depend on the extent to which the "new pattern of meaning" they project "subsumes or otherwise articulates with that of the larger system."

5. Planning can help stabilize or destabilize these situations, depending on how it is done and the type of area involved. Official planning can bring on opposition, and opposition, with or without planning, can cause basic changes.

Official planning, on behalf of a central authority, can be the focus around which opposition can form. It does opposition the favor of providing a position against which an attack can be launched. Governments tend not to do this sort of planning except under hierarchy or a surge of collective enthusiasm and optimism for planning.

Under polyarchy, indicative planning would be a stabilizing influence, as its main activity is one of servicing the institutions of government and the economy. Under hegemony, indicative planning would have problematic consequences. Powerful, externally controlled interests in the private sector might make any even-handed application impossible, forcing the planners into a handmaiden role. But even then, by helping maintain the appearance of polyarchy—the apparatus, that is, without the polyarchical constituency—indicative planners could be considered to be a force for the stability of hegemony.

On the other hand, even indicative planners may prove to be a source of embarrassment for a hegemonic regime. Even though they do not provide the lightning-rod effect that classic planning would provide for an opposition, the motions they go through and the doctrines they are obliged to advocate—even if they are playing only a fictional role, which most are not—can be attacked. Moreover, by drawing attention to development problems generally, they may help dramatize the obtrusive roles played by nongovernmental, externally controlled forces. In Appalachia, for example, even though the Appalachian Regional Commission took a low profile as a planning agency, it did promulgate a growth-centers modernization doctrine, and this in turn ultimately helped focus attention on the major energy companies' role in development. Despite ARC's initial disinclination to do any grand plan, when a degree of regional solidarity developed in the late 1970s, it was planning, ARC, and the energy companies jointly that formed the focus against which regional forces organized.

Finally, opposition planning can be the focus around which regional solidarity develops. It can be the vehicle for expressing, in Young's terms, "the new pattern of meaning [that possibly] subsumes or otherwise articulates with that of the larger system." It is to elaborate this idea that the chapters following are written.

Additional Relationships of the Model to the Literature

These concepts and relationships, posed here in relatively abstract form, can be tied more concretely to the literature I cited earlier. Centrality can be tied to uneven regional development and the associated structure of external control. Local capacity can be tied to other strands in the literature. The interaction model can then be elaborated, the cases noted in Chapter 1 described in more detail. It is then possible to relate the model to the possibility of popularly controlled separatism: to treat the effects of local-elite policy, central policy, and bureaucratic structure in a relatively concrete way.

Centrality and External Control. The model just outlined, with its relative changes of centrality, local capacity, and solidarity, should be looked at as a mechanism through which general shifts in Western economies operate in regions. The developments of technocratic federalism identified by Beer, of O'Connor's regional social-industrial complex, and of Nairn's uneven development express themselves through their effects on centrality. These then trigger other changes. I will try to lay out these relationships.

Centrality is particularly sensitive to these general changes, because it, unlike local capacity or solidarity, is a relational characteristic, a joint property of locality and larger system. Centrality has no meaning apart from the larger system, and so when the system changes, centrality is the property through which the locality is first affected.

More specifically, centrality is affected through the means by which the larger society exerts control over its parts. The changes that Nairn, Beer, and O'Connor refer to are, above all, changes in the way societies—their central governments and big enterprises—maintain control over regions. At present, the dominant characteristic of this control is the expansion of resources available to central regimes for inducing regional compliance, resources deriving from the enormous power of the economic units just noted: corporations, but also other national organizations. In feudal regimes, for example, central resources were limited to military force. Typically this control was sporadic and incomplete, and nations in their modern form did not exist. The modern nation-state emerged with capitalism, which made control possible through the manipulation of quantitative rewards first through the market, then through government bureaucracy. In the first form, called market capitalism, external control was largely in the private sector. Entrepreneurs and business firms influenced and ultimately dominated one another through the manipulation of the market. The role of government was to provide the legal framework for this economic expansion and exchange. In general, nineteenth-century governments exerted little *direct* control over peripheral regions, while businesses had major impacts. There was popular resistance to this, including, the United States, the Populist movement of the 1890s and, in part, the Civil War, but government action overcame it.

In the more recent form, called technocratic capitalism, government has taken on a much more active economic role and the market is supplemented very prominently by planning and bureaucratic bargaining on the part of big firms and government agencies.[36] The result was an enormous increase in rewards and favors available for distribution by central governments. It was possible to open up varied channels of communication, both physical and organizational, as ever-increasing proportions of the population became involved in market and political relationships. In this new institutional arrangement, the new role relationships of control operate as follows:[37]

First, the system is run by a technocratic elite, organized around certain values of capitalism, but lacking others. They are committed to the usefulness of profit as a central incentive, while they reject many dogmas of classical capitalism: they accept, for example large-scale government and the necessity of welfare programs. They are sustained in these attitudes by their membership in professional career networks. Recruitment, training, and a significant part of job motivation has become a function of national and even international networks that dictate the organization of work and affect the basic productive capacities of entire firms and agencies. Membership in these career paths confers competence in an array of techniques, symbols, and languages that cannot be matched by persons of purely local or organizational background. Most important, it confers qualification to exchange and bargain for rewards, personally and on behalf of the organization, outside of the more traditional market.

Market capitalism remains in many sectors. Nonprofessionals, persons in business for themselves or confined by the firm or organization career structure, are able to do business in the market. What is required is good knowledge of a moderate-scale production process or service (for example, family farming, some kinds of manufacturing, much retail and personal services) and the ability to put this output in contact with potential buyers. Detailed experiential knowledge of the process or the market is more important than the advantages of a national network and professional contacts.

Those involved in the large-scale career networks characteristic of technocratic capitalism play a different kind of game. They are typically involved in firms or agencies with others who play the market game, but have available the options and resources of the technocratic game. Its players deal in a different reward system with a different realm of competition. The rewards are as apt to be symbolic as quantitative; victory is as apt to mean organizational (and personal) status nationally as it is to mean profit (though financial rewards tend to be associated with status both for organizations and individuals). The typical organizations of technocratic capitalism include research universities, health-care establishments, the military, many high-technology businesses. What is characteristic of technocratic capitalism is that market capitalists and the organizations they control no longer dominate the economy or government.

Second, the type of control exerted by technocratic elites over a peripheral region is different from that exerted by market-capitalist elites. Market capitalists dominate the periphery by means of the market, while maintaining the ideological allegiance of the population to the market system. They make use of the principle that, in a situation where two partners have unequal resources initially, adherence to rules of "fair" exchange work to the advantage of the stronger partner. Thus external capital establishes itself in a peripheral region either directly, by establishing a subsidiary, or indirectly, by investing in a locally owned operation, and then by operating through market rules vis-à-vis smaller local businesses and a usually unorganized labor force. In doing this it can keep the prevailing local wage and the profits of most small business competitors at a low level.

Thus outside capital provides relatively low wages and other payments, in return for relatively high-quality wage labor and services. As this situation becomes pervasive, a variety of additional exchanges are possible for external capital to keep the system running: benefits to local police, government officials (e.g., part-time jobs and bribes), and to local clergy, newspaper editors, school superintendents (contributions, advertising revenue, political support), in return for general ideological support, all typically focusing on upholding the market system.

The kind of control exerted under technocratic capitalism maintains some of these features, conflicts with others, but above all adds an additional layer of unequal exchanges that primarily work outside of the private market. Negotiations between large corporations and local subsidiaries, between government agencies and local contractors, between federal and state agencies and local officials are often cases of exchange based on inequalities of training, contacts in national networks, and professional status. Like the market-capitalist domination, these inequalities are stabilized by supplementary arrangements with local institutions: welfare bureaucracies, law enforcement agencies, highway departments, school systems, newspapers and churches.

Third, technocratic capitalism's control system is relatively intrusive in localities. While market capitalism leaves large areas of the local social system intact, technocratic capitalism introduces professional and technical people who, with the support available to them because they circulate in national networks, demand changes in a range of local institutions. Because one of the main channels of technocratic development is government, there is additional force for change, leverage exerted through the public sector. What results is a kind of dualism, an uneasy but usually stable truce between two sets of people and organizations where, in spatial terms, there is rather close interpenetration. There is, as in market capitalism, exclusion of large parts of the local population from participation in the most important jobs. But the criteria of exclusion in the technocratic sector are different. Rather than ability to compete in the market, exclusion is based on lack of education, technical background, and facility with the symbolic attributes of technological modes of operating.

Fourth, the role of government, very important in technocratic capitalism for both its financial and legimitizing functions, becomes tied closely to the structure of control that has developed in the private sector. It is not the instrument of the private sector, but neither private nor public sector could survive without the other. The private economy needs welfare programs, partly to dampen class conflict. It needs subsidies for industry, both to reduce the risks of large-scale, capital-intensive enterprises and to ease the transition of small-scale entrepreneurs into new kinds of work. Most important, it needs government programs to justify the very structure of the economy, no longer consistent with prevailing values of independent work. It does this through schooling and welfare programs and the creation of a cadre of professionals and technicians oriented to dealing with urban and social problems.

Fifth, the result of its pervasive professional networks, its wider range of exchanges, and its dependence on government is that the control system under technocratic capitalism presents the *potential* for reciprocity. That is, there is the possibility that the subordinate parts of the system can exert control over the center, as the center does over the parts. Control may, therefore, relax or break. On the one hand, the professionalization of important sectors of the labor force and its spread into the public sector and to the local level, accompanied by the development of institutions of higher education, creates a demand pressure for participation in significant decisions, quite unlike anything that had existed under market capitalism, and far in excess of what the conventional rewards of market capitalism can satisfy.[38] Under technocratic capitalism, private and public authorities have gone to enormous lengths to provide participatory structures to absorb this demand without losing control, but it remains in doubt whether this will be possible.

The other fundamental pressure for reciprocity comes from the growing use of government to legitimize the basic structure of the economy through education-, welfare-, and economic-subsidy programs. This has provided jobs for professionals but also made possible alliances between government-employed professionals and their dependent clients, alliances that have forced participation and access to the basic governmental machinery in many areas: health, environmental control, and urban planning are salient examples.[39] So far, these alliances seem not to have breached the essential control points of the economy, but the trend is difficult to discern and its direction remains problematic.

These developments in external control systems affect centrality of regions. Most apparently, they affect local administration and planning through official agencies. The development of technocratic federalism would seem to give some places more central access, representation and recognition, some less. There would, possibly, be a general centralization in the pattern. But this hypothesis that centrality has been redistributed cannot be extended directly to the pattern of development more generally. It cannot be applied directly to the question of uneven regional development, because development is defined as having a second component, local capacity, whose shifts in pattern operate differently from centrality. A simple way to make the distinction would be to say that local capacity is much more sensitive to and overlaps with the cohesion and legitimacy of local politics. While one can think of centrality as nearly identical with administration, local capacity must include a broader range of phenomena, particularly a political consensus capable of activating administration, even capturing it. The relation of *this* to external control is less direct.

Local Capacity. While technocratic capitalism elaborates a system of control and affects centrality, it has less effect on local capacity. But local capacity—in this context, capacity to resist external control—affects regional mobilization. In feudal regimes, local capacity might have meant military force, natural defenses, loyalty and organization. Under capitalism it means the ability to avoid victimization through exchange and through the moral and administrative bullying of the public sector. What contributes to this capacity? Material resources would seem to be the first requisite. Other things equal, rich suburbs would have more capacity than poor ones, wealthy regions more than impoverished ones. But it is not only a matter of wealth. It is also a matter of economic organization in government, as is suggested by Nairn's emphasis on a native bourgeoisie and a state history. These resources, both in private economy and public administrative capacity, enhance a region's ability to negotiate with a central regime within a system of exchange. A modern bourgeoisie will fare better in resisting unequal exchange in the private sector, and modern administration will provide advantages in negotiating with the technocratic apparatus of modern federalism.

But resistance can occur in another way, by rejecting the very context of the exchange relationship. Several suggestions of this nature have been made. One is the distinction between growth and antigrowth coalitions of local elites. The first group corresponds, roughly, to other conceptions of a local bourgeoisie, but the antigrowth coalition is posed as immune, to some extent, from the need to join forces with external sources of capital and organization. Middle-class professionals, workers, government employees and businesses whose profits depend on sales elsewhere, rather than on local expansion, and who anticipate costs and higher tax rates from growth, make up the emerging antigrowth coalition; these people develop an ideology in favor of environmental quality and against purely quantitative concepts of collective goals.[40] Similar ideological commitments have appeared among environmentalists and young middle-class activists.[41] Having been thoroughly exposed to a culture in which the pursuit of material gain has dominated local economics, a part of the middle class has turned its attention to a collective search for qualitative goals. This search has at times focused on environmentalism, regionalism, and nationalism as well as more specifically issue-oriented projects, for example antiwar or anti–nuclear power movements. These general and specific movements and activities are locally and territorially rooted by nature.

Contributing to local capacity *may be* the relative presence or absence of cultural differentiation. Most typically this appears as a marked distinction between indigenous and nationally linked populations. Such a distinction appears in Wales and Appalachia. In Wales it is most apparent: part of the population has Welsh roots and part has English roots and connections, with associated differences in language, religion, social network. In Appalachia there is a similar distinction in roots. An indigenous Appalachian does many things and gets access to things impossible for one with outside roots, and the reverse is true: outsiders may have some access that also cannot be gotten by the others.

Whether cultural differentiation reinforces or detracts from local capacity is not easy to discern. On the one hand, the splits between insiders and outsiders can cause a paralysis in local capacity as the different groups disagree and block each other's initiatives and programs. These splits can also be a means of external control. Cultural characteristics, such as language, can be used as criteria for exclusion or inclusion in important jobs, and large employers can manipulate jobs to reinforce local prejudices so as to defuse any concerted local pressure on themselves.

But cultural differentiation also can reinforce local capacity. Resistance to external control, whether the resistance is organized by the local bourgeoisie or by some other group (such as the antigrowth coalition), requires a positive motivation and a set of symbols around which to develop a program. Nairn's "state history" can be interpreted as providing this, as can language, local custom, and attachments to the environment learned at an early age. Moreover, things may occur to reinvigorate a local culture as it borrows and responds to ideas developed elsewhere.

Interaction between Center and Region. Uneven spatial development—an uneven distribution of resources among regions—works to the disadvantage of workers in the poorer regions, thus providing a motive for political mobilization.[42] However, this motivation is not a *sufficient* cause for mobilization. Uneven development, in addition to being a distribution of resources and access, also is a system of external control, including ideology, political support, and technical capacity. Thus if a central government or a ruling central regime of private interests can mount other incentives, it can keep control of a deprived region and defuse mobilization, despite relative poverty there. To have political mobilization within a region against a central regime, this control must be relaxed or broken, and an adequate theory must specify how this relaxation or break occurs.

This interaction of control and response, while it is affected by the transitions in external control systems described above, is expressed through the interaction of centrality and local capacity as specified above. These two factors are not simply additive, but interact to cause regional mobilization. Under technocratic capitalism, central regimes develop enhanced access to all regions. Thus centrality develops independent of local capacity, as professional and technical elites become established in regions alongside market-capital institutions, building enclaves. But regions vary, and in some cases technocratic penetration is particularly enclaved and narrow, while local capacity is strong and reinforced by culture. Under these circumstances, the conditions for regional mobilization are met.

Popular Regionalism. The preceding summary, while it gives an account of how regionalism might develop under some circumstances (the transition to separatism case) leaves out several factors, including particularly some that might be expected to bear on the development of popular support. In general, popular participation in regional movements can be tied to the amount of overt support available from the central government and possibly to the manner of implementation as the government carries out its policies. The first factor is simply the direction of official policy, for example, rules of "maximum feasible participation" for poor people, and "affirmative action" rules imposed by the United States federal government on regional planning boards. The second factor concerns implementation of policy, where procedures may be so involved as to preclude popular participation regardless of policy. To the extent either of these factors are predicted by our formulation, we have a model for popular as well as indigenous regionalism.

Strong working-class representation in a national government makes it easier for the workers to participate in the regions, but it is only one factor. The initial populism represented in TVA was due in part to the working-class representation in the federal government in Roosevelt's first term, and, for peripheral regions generally, a strong worker movement in the cities helps make populist alliances possible.[43] In general, it would seem that liberal central governments would make it easier than conservative ones for workers on the periphery, while social democratic central governments would make it easier than would liberals.

Other factors can subvert central support for workers at the periphery. One is the use of market exchange as a means of external control. In liberal and social democratic regimes (as in the United States and Great Britain), the market-system framework, which implies exchange as a way of controlling peripheral regions, has the effect of splitting the working class from regionalism. Under market conditions, workers in the more productive jobs and industries get rewarded highly even if the population of the region generally is suffering in various ways. The market thus splits organized from the unorganized workers, making organization of the working class as a whole more difficult, and making it more difficult for them to exert influence in a regional movement.

Implementation of the procedures of external control through government is a second factor in opposition to official policies favoring popular participation. Selznick presented the classic case of this effect in his study of the TVA: overt populist policies declined as the agency found it easier to cultivate support from the more conservative forces within the region.[44] Diffuse bureaucratic systems allow much distortion of central policy by local elites and parties. This produces an "extractive" model of administration in the United States, where the bureaucracy is made diffuse by the federal system, and where central and local elites are resistant to populist ideologies. The conditions for populist administration, he argues, include *both* urban and peripheral support for populist policy *and* an integrated bureaucracy.[45]

Both O'Connor and Beer suggest that the development of the state under modern capitalism might result in a highly technocratic, centralized administrative system within the regions. Beer's suggestion of a developing scientific-technical elite occupying state and regional agencies would seem to leave little room for popular control or for the development of local capacity below the regional level (where workers might have more influence). O'Connor's formulation of a social-industrial complex creating regional administration for social programs in concert with monopoly capital and monopoly-sector labor, in effect, elaborates this picture. Thus the effect of technocratic federalism, while it redistributes resources to the regions, may also redistribute them within regions, toward the larger centers and away from smaller places.

Local Elite Policy. In general, *any* regional mobilization would seem to incorporate all local classes and groups, as it is in the nature of political mobilization to seek allies widely. As a matter of practice, however, popular participation in the regional movement is affected by the ability of other social classes to resist incorporation by central regimes. If it is easy for industrial and landowning and mercantile elites in the region to form alliances with the center, and if they have no ability to resist such alliances, then these elites will not be so motivated to respond to demands for popular participation. At the extreme, they may play a role like that attributed by Gramsci to the Mezzogiorno intelligentsia: supported by jobs in public administration by the regime that preceded fascism in Italy, they become "a kind of auxiliary private police" by supporting the regime ideologically, while overt police measures repressed mass movements with periodic massacres.[46] If, on the other hand, regional elites are blocked from national roles and support, and if they have resources to resist, the middle classes may see popular participation in a different light and even come to depend on it.

For more narrowly defined groups outside of the working class, this latter possibility seems realistic. First, small businesses may react to their systematic exclusion from the large-scale corporate economy, forming coalitions against particular policies: they may demand transportation subsidies for their areas, for example, in concert with unions. The antigrowth coalition I mentioned earlier could possibly include major participation by workers. The possibility of such coalitions has been pointed out before by theorists who see a "new working class" developing out of the increasing concentrations of economic activity in the service sectors.[47] It remains an issue, however, what proportion of these "workers" can be expected to ally with the traditional working class.

The propensity for such interclass alliances to form must be related strongly to the resources for them that may exist: both material support and organizational and cultural tradition. Nairn's concept of "state history" is pertinent in this respect in that it suggests both symbols around which groups can rally and a store of experience. Much research has suggested the importance of such experience in the success of progressive coalitions. In the United States, many successful movements of the 1970s are demonstrably built on the antiwar organizing experience of the 1960s. Community researchers have found the successful adoption of redistributive policies to be associated with a history of previous experience with other such programs.[48] The antigrowth coalition built on experience with antiwar activities and material independence from a need for local growth.[49]

Chapter 3

Planning in the Context of Welsh Separatism

A dominant theme in Welsh history is the long process of incorporation into the British economy and British politics and administration. Wales was, after the fifth century, the main locus of Celtic culture and resistance to Saxon intrusions, celebrated in the Arthurian legend. It was maintained as a separate state until 1284, and British rule after that time was punctuated by periods of dissent and, occasionally, rebellion.[1] There have been various methods used to achieve incorporation, but since at least World War II, a significant one has been regional economic policy, in which planning has played a major part. This chapter presents a description of these methods and the response to them.[2] As will be seen, in regional policy as in other modes of incorporation, the themes of Welsh acquiescence and dissent reassert themselves. First, I provide a brief summary of British policy toward Wales in the context of Welsh politics and overall regional policy in the United Kingdom. Second, I describe the establishment of regional planning in Wales by the British. Third, I provide description of the local response to official regionalism and planning.

Welsh Institutions and the British State

Welsh national identity survived its incorporation in the United Kingdom. The Welsh language was spoken by the majority of Welsh people as late as 1900, a substantial literature continues to be published in Welsh, Welsh nonconformist religion represented a national movement against the Church of England in the nineteenth century, and national consciousness supports numerous local community institutions including the Eistedfod—festivals of poetry and song in the Welsh language.[3] Periodically, Welsh nationalism has resulted in a political movement. In the late nineteenth century, Tom Ellis and Lloyd George led Cymru Fydd (literally, Young Wales) in a campaign that included disestablishment of the Anglican Church (successful) and home rule (ultimately abandoned). The Labour Party found its early strength in the industrial South Wales valleys, and while it was dominantly centralist, it still contained elements of nationalism. Plaid Cymru, the Welsh nationalist party, was founded in 1925 and, after marginal existence for forty years, became a significant threat to Labour Party dominance in the late 1960s.

This persistent Welsh national identity made for an uneasy relationship with London governments, and incorporation within the United Kingdom, while seldom in doubt, has frequently been a matter of controversy. It is useful to describe this uneasiness under two headings, the cultural and the economic. In Wales, nationalism is particularly rooted in culture, and is fundamentally different from national movements with more developed economic motivations. In Scotland, for example, while little of the Gaelic language remains, there is a more developed economy and with it more governmental apparatus. In Wales, the cultural emphasis has made politics distinctive. On the one hand, cultural issues have been argued strongly and with sophistication. The main issues that stimulated the revival of Welsh nationalism after 1850 were the teaching of Welsh in the schools and the campaign for disestablishment of the Church of England in Wales. It was these that formed the motivation for the Cymru Fydd home-rule campaign.

The *dominant* goal of Plaid Cymru was the preservation of the language, with the establishment of the separate state seen as a means. Other objectives became equally important only after the 1960s. Violent and nonviolent protest has always been at the fringe, at least, of the nationalist movement, but has always focused on cultural issues, such as bilingual road signs or the threat to communities posed by reservoirs, or the establishment of an R.A.F. bombing school. These were not economic issues. Numerous organizations and pressure groups were organized around these and other cultural issues. Concern about these issues was not confined to the nationalist political party. In fact, as Plaid Cymru began to become a more serious political presence in the 1960s, nationalist groups outside of the party also grew. Most important, perhaps, was the Welsh Language Society, among a number of others.

The predominance of cultural goals among Welsh nationalists, and in Wales generally, has at least confused the issue of political autonomy and the cause of a separate state. Autonomy was always advocated as a means to something else. But when British governments offered alternative means, the objective of autonomy became less important. Thus when the Liberal Party adopted Welsh disestablishment as a part of its party program in 1891, it made an independent Welsh party seem less necessary.[4] Similarly, Tom Ellis and Lloyd George, upon receiving posts in British governments, were removed as forces for an autonomous Welsh government apparatus. Kenneth O. Morgan, in comparing Welsh and Irish home-rule demands commented: "The ideal of Wales was to be recognized as a part of the British political and social structure; the ideal of Ireland was to be served from it."[5] The idea of a separate state only became a significant minority movement in the 1960s. Even then, as Plaid Cymru was on the verge of winning parliamentary elections, Saunders Lewis, its founder, led a movement away from electoral politics and toward the founding of the Welsh Language Society.

There was also a set of economic conflicts and reactions marking incorporation into Britain. These resulted in a different set of interests and alliances being mobilized, not overlapping very much with those concerned by cultural issues and not supporting nationalism. First, it is often noted that the industrial revolution came to Wales in a way different from what happened in other parts of the British Isles. Wales was developed by outsiders. It remained a country of villages, interspersed with estates and towns controlled by Anglicized gentry and administrators. While Scotland produced Adam Smith, Hume, and Watt, Wales had no comparable achievements. Even its literary revivals waited until much later. There was no bourgeoisie-led nationalism rooted in industrial interest. Development was largely financed from London or by merger with English firms, industries were often owned in England, particularly after 1900, and the managers often came from England or, following the pattern of the gentry, found that the way to success was through a British rather than a Welsh ladder of upward mobility.

Industrial development did occur early in Wales. Coal and iron production began in the South Wales valleys around 1750, and latter-day politicians could make at least half a claim that the industrial revolution "began" in Wales. Later, population soared in South Wales: first in Merthyr Tydfil, then coastal towns like Cardiff, Newport, and Swansea. The total Wales population went from 0.6 million in 1801 to 1.2 million in 1851, with most of the net growth in South Wales, which led Britain in iron production. From 1851 to the 1920s, total population more than doubled again as iron and steel were surpassed by coal, again in South Wales (by this time North and West Wales were suffering net losses).[6] The effect of this industrialization was to produce a concentration of working-class people in South Wales that was a peculiar amalgam of Welsh and immigrant. While much of the growth in South Wales came from a migration out of rural Wales, there was also a large in-migration of English and other non-Welsh workers, so that the culture of South Wales became even more different from the rest of Wales than it had been.[7] Second, the base of industrialization was much less diversified than in Britain generally, concentrated mainly in coal and steel production. After 1920 this made for extreme vulnerability to world market fluctuations, and, in the depressions of the 1918–39 period, Wales suffered unemployment much higher than the average in the United Kingdom.[8]

While rural Wales suffered its own kind of economic pressures, resulting in agricultural and village depopulation and feeding a kind of liberal and religious radicalism, South Wales produced a working class that, while tinged with radicalism, was by the late nineteenth and early twentieth century becoming the stronghold of development of the Labour Party. This meant organization on the basis of common working-class interests, to be fought in alliance with the working class in all of Britain, through the party and trade union organization. Peculiarly Welsh interests did get expressed through Labour party and trade union organization, but the dominant organizing concept was class, and alliances with the British were the dominant way these could be fought. This strategy had confounded any simple nationalist program for a long time. Chartist uprisings, which had been as strong in South Wales as anywhere, were more on a class than national basis, and even the rural Rebecca movement of the 1840s, which focused on landlords, found hope in intervention by London, finding the British less antagonistic than the Welsh gentry.[9]

Twentieth-century Welsh Labour attitudes are perhaps typified by Aneurin Bevan, creator of the National Health Service in the postwar Labour government. Bevan hoped to see national institutions develop, but without what he thought were parochial characteristics, particularly the tendency to define Welsh culture as belonging exclusively to Welsh speakers. He argued that part of Welsh culture, "as rich and profound," existed among the English-speakers of South Wales. He was willing to advocate a "considerable devolution of government" for Wales and to support the retention of the Welsh language, but would not support the creation of a Welsh Parliament or any view of a Welsh solution to economic, as opposed to cultural, problems.[10] Upon the establishment of a Welsh "day" for parliamentary debate, he denounced it as a farce: "My colleagues, all of them members of the Miners' Federation of Great Britain, have no special solution for the Welsh coal industry which is not a solution for the whole of the mining industry of Great Britain. There is no Welsh problem."[11]

Bevan's solutions were socialist and centralist, not only his own National Health Service, but the programs of nationalization carried out by the Labour government of 1945–51, which were designed to place strong working-class representation at the heads of key industrial sectors and institutions. But Welsh

Labour support of these programs represented an added dimension of incorporation of Wales into Britain.

The Growth of Central Control. After 1951, moreover, Labour went out of power in Britain generally, and in the thirteen years of Conservative governments new policies emerged that added new layers to the administrative paraphernalia. The Tories claimed that they could provide better leadership while dismantling few of the 1945–51 Labour innovations. After 1960, Labour formulated a program that countered this by claiming to be more modern and technically advanced that the Conservatives. Their program emphasized economic planning, technological innovation in industry, and administrative reform.

This new thrust toward economic planning and management (that had also had significant beginnings within the Macmillan government after 1960) had a strong regionalist component that affected Wales and other peripheral regions of Britain. As in the case of the new emphasis on national economic planning, the attraction to regional policy had been building up for a long time.[12] First, the development of government authority had been building up so that there were many policy instruments in place, before there was a policy. The nationalized industries, the health service, the increase of government employment generally, and the development of tax and credit instruments affecting the private sector were all in existence by 1960. Second, with the growth in central government bureaucratic machinery, there became apparent a need for some way to deal with decision-making bottlenecks in London, and some sort of regionalization began to seem imperative by the 1960s. There was certainly ambiguity in this, but at least superficial support to decentralist aims began to appear. Third, a rationale for regional policy already existed. The Barlow Report of 1940 had set the terms by which population policy and industrial policy were brought together. Both unemployment at the periphery, and congestion at the center, were caused by a drift of population and industry to the South East, and they recommended measures to reverse or slow this drift: "(a) redevelopment of congested urban areas; (b) decentralization and dispersal of industries and industrial population from such areas; and (c) encouragement of a reasonable balance of industrial development, so far as possible, throughout the various divisions or regions of Great Britain, coupled with appropriate diversification of industry in each division or region throughout the country."[13]

Regional policy in the United Kingdom, as in other Western countries, consisted of an uneasy alliance of these population-oriented and employment-oriented policies through the postwar period. They were never brought together in one ministry, though they were subjected to some amount of coordinated scrutiny. The most important thing that brought them together, and that also resulted in an added degree of central government involvement in Wales and other parts of the United Kindgom, was the great interest in economic modernization that began under the Conservatives and culminated in the Labour government of 1964. Around this theme there developed (1) increases in the attention given to regional employment and industrial incentives for the "special areas," (2) the development of a series of measures for participation, administrative decentralization, and government reform, and (3) a new prominence for planning at the regional level.[14] This impetus—initially after 1964 receiving a large boost from the general expectations of economic growth—spread from economic policy to embrace issues of bureaucratization and reform in other ministries.

Wales was included in this, but in a special way. From the standpoint of regional initiatives by the central government, Wales got, a little later, treatment that had begun in Scotland and northern England. The measures in force up to 1964 included a system of permits for new industrial operations, designed to limit development around London, together with a set of "development districts," including parts of Wales, Scotland, and northern England, where industry was encouraged to locate by means of subsidized factory construction, and a system of negotiable grants and tax incentives. In addition, the Macmillan government had given special attention to Scotland and the North West and began work in other high unemployment areas, including Wales, through the creation of the new ministerial position of Secretary of State for Industry, Trade, and Regional Development. In this position Edward Heath had gotten the participation of local business and political leaders in special surveys and reports.

The new Labour government of 1964 made modernization, including planning, management, and technological development, its major theme, and one of its first moves was the creation of the Department of Economic Affairs (DEA), called a "superministry" under the Deputy Prime Minister, George Brown, which was to have the leading role in national economic planning and management, and which had as a prime mission the establishment of regional planning machinery throughout Britain.[15] Under DEA, regional policy was greatly expanded. Industrial development certificates were restricted further in the South East, and made to apply to office projects. The development districts were expanded into new "development areas," which now included all of Scotland and Northern Ireland, the northern England areas, Cornwall, and almost all of Wales. The 1966 Industrial Development Act established a policy of subsidizing industrial investment throughout Britain by means of a 20 percent cash grant, but the figure was 40 percent in the development areas. In 1967 the government established the Regional Employment Premium, a payment of £1.50 per week per adult male employee that, together with a smaller tax rebate program, amounted to "something like an 8 percent reduction in the average firm's wages bill." Other subsidies were also employed. In total, the subsidies increased by over 400 percent, from £69.2 million in 1966–67 to £302.0 million in 1969–70.[16]

The regional planning efforts under Brown included not only an expansion of the centrally directed subsidy machinery but also regional economic planning councils consisting of industrialists, local officials, and others appointed in eight English regions, plus Scotland and Wales. They were charged to advise DEA on the needs and aims of the regions and to work out the regional implications of the national plan.[17] The new regional bodies, like the other efforts of DEA, involved great amounts of consultation between government and private sector, behind which Brown was the driving force and catalyst. For a short time, large numbers of persons who would not normally have participated actively in government did so, and part of the effort was in the regions. All this reflected and created expectations, in Britain generally, that there would be further delegation and devolution of authority. The new regional machinery was put forward as the first step that would lead eventually to regional-level elected assemblies.[18]

The economic planning councils themselves, after a year or two of activity and after much publicity, began to fade. They had been set up on the premise that they could advise on the national plan; but in 1966 the Government dropped the idea of a national plan, and in any event it appeared that DEA could not provide either the policy guidance or staffing that most of the councils needed. But the idea of regional institutions in some form was, by the late 1960s, stronger than ever in Britain generally, and it is worth asking why this was so.[19]

There was a general dissatisfaction with central institutions, in particular with government bureaucracies. On the one hand there were complaints from local governments focused on the difficulties of dealing with the central ministries. This was perhaps most acute in the area of planning and housing, with public and private construction subject to a cumbersome decision process centered in London and a rising wave of protest against lack of participation by affected neighborhoods. There were also complaints against other ministries, and the administrative systems for planning, health, and water and waste treatment, among others, were all under review or altered by 1970; and the lodging of more foci of decision at the regional level was one of the steps considered.[20] There seemed to be, nevertheless, a general optimism. Many people and interest groups made at least tentative commitments to participate in the studies and new institutions that were being tried. Even the ferment and protest of the period, such as that surrounding planning, occurred not because of rigid polarization between interests, but because new groups were drawn into politics, and because established power centers, while perhaps resistant, were less than monolithic. The new interest in regional organizations was a part of this situation.

Second, the reform or reorganization of local government had been under study by a Royal Commission under Lord Redcliffe-Maud and it had been discussing the creation of provincial (regional) councils. Its report, in 1969, proposed the creation of eight provincial councils for England and Wales, with physical and economic planning functions, and the amalgamation of the existing local governments into fifty-eight unitary councils plus three metropolitan-areas councils (its recommendations excluded London).[21]

There was, in addition, the Royal Commission on the Constitution, which the Wilson government appointed in 1969 under Lord Crowther to examine in the broadest way the issues raised by nationalists in Scotland and Wales: for all the "countries, nations and regions of the United Kingdom," to consider whether there should be changes in the functions of the central legislature, administrative, economic, or constitutional relationships.[22] This served to keep speculation alive, while putting off any definite government initiatives, and allowed the Government, while considering the Redcliffe-Maud report, to decide not to deal with the regional proposals until the Crowther Commission reported.

For Britain generally, many of these decentralist initiatives were in the end contained. Local government reform was eventually implemented by the Conservatives in a form that involved little or no delegation of parliamentary authority. Decentralization of civil service offices was achieved without relinquishing much central control.[23] As far as the economic planning councils were concerned, Brown intended that their functions remain advisory and technical. "I wanted them to leave the politics to me," he said.[24] The Royal Commission on the Constitution suffered the death of its chairman, Lord Crowther, and it did not finally report until 1973, by which time the government was too preoccupied by economic crisis to do much about it.

Many of these discussions of decentralization or devolution

did not primarily reflect the demands for reform from people at the local level, but the views generated from within the central government, in which civil servants saw a more regionalized structure as a more efficient way to govern while maintaining a centralized structure. As it is often noted, Britain is a unitary state, in contrast to the federal structure of such other Western countries as the United States, Canada, and West Germany. Formal authority derives effectively from Parliament, which is led by a cabinet consisting of the leadership of the majority party, all of whom owe their position to the election of the national party, not to local campaigns, as is much more the case in the United States. The civil service departments are headed by cabinet ministers, but the civil service is also centralized in London by a career system that emphasizes status in an integrated national system. One former cabinet minister described it this way:

> It is a peculiarity of Britain when you go into Parliament that by the time you are forty you know the people who are going to be senior ministers and even Prime Minister for the next twenty, thirty, forty years. In the Civil Service any particular grade of assistant principal entrant looks around to see who will be the Permanent Secretaries of the future on the same course as himself, even though they will not get the job for the next thirty years. This is a highly inbred, highly unsatisfactory business and inherently seems unlikely to produce the best talent and responsiveness, particularly in the rapidly changing situations of professionalism and problems we have today.[25]

This sort of concentration in Parliament and civil service was reinforced by a class structure and value system that both integrated this leadership and helped ensure that it was respected and followed by nonelites. Over the years both Conservative and Labour parties made use of these integrating factors. One result was a general consensus between the parties as to what issues should be fought about openly, thus making it easier to govern. In addition, the organization of universities and of business reinforced the unitary system. The status ranking among universities had had Oxford and Cambridge at the top for a long time, with pervasive effects on the structure of research, political advice, and influence. Business was also an integrated system that reflected both class integration and, increasingly, geographic integration centered in London.

This system of government had, from time to time, been the subject of complaints from the periphery. Ireland had always been a violent problem, but there were also complaints from Scotland, Wales, and some of the English provinces like the North West. Opposition parties would talk about some modification at least of administrative centralization, a promise that tended to be forgotten once they got in office. During World War II there had been set up a skeletal provincial administrative apparatus. In Wales the central ministries needed some form of regional office, and as their functions grew, the needs increased. By 1945 there were fifteen regional offices in Wales, with some provision for operating coordination among them. The office of a Minister of Welsh Affairs was established in 1951. This was held by the Home Secretary until 1957, after which it was transferred to the Minister of Housing and Local Government.[26] This was the situation until the creation of the Welsh Office in 1964.

There were also advisory bodies. The main institution representing Wales in a general way was the Council for Wales and Monmouthshire, which was appointed in 1949 to see that the Government was "adequately informed of the impact of government activities on the general life of the people of Wales."[27] As originally constituted, the council consisted of representatives from local authorities plus three appointed by the Prime Minister. During the 1950s, the council produced a number of reports criticizing Government policy toward Wales, one of which, a set of proposals on government administration in 1957 that included a Secretary of State for Wales, resulted in a "bitter row" with the Prime Minister,[28] and led to the resignation of several members of the council. After that, the Government established more coordinating machinery within the regional civil service departments, and the council became less vocal.

The council reflected a pattern of response by Government to demands for devolution that persisted in subsequent decades. The atmosphere in which it was created consisted of two kinds of demands. One was for more government attention to Wales. The other was for institutions more responsive to Wales than the Parliament and ministries. The council was a compromise designed to provide a little of each. The difficulty was that the more it got into the first task, the more aroused people became about the second. Each of the problems it dealt with did involve some kind of advice to the Government and in most cases on a substantive problem the Government could act on. But the methods it used aroused opposition. The Welsh demanded an open process they could participate in, the more so, the more the council dealt with significant problems. The Government, on the other hand, demanded a secret advisory process. This was inherent in its structure as a unitary government with a hierarchical civil service. When the council pressed its claims openly or when it proposed changes in this unitary structure, it met resistance from London. When it operated in secret, it got criticism in Wales. This dilemma persisted, yet the Government continued to establish advisory bodies.

There were other institutions established in London that had a specifically Welsh basis prior to 1964. Parliament established the Welsh Grand Committee—consisting of the Members from Wales, in 1960, which was to meet and consider bills pertaining directly to Wales—and had established one day of general debate on Welsh issues per session. Other administrative bodies with at least some central government sponsorship were established in Wales by the mid-1960s. the Development Corporation for Wales had financial support from central ministries. The Confederation of British Industry had also been set up with government encouragement and had an active office in Wales by 1965.

All of these measures fit rather well into the concept of the unitary state. They disturbed neither the hierarchy of administration nor the power of the parliamentary parties to define issues and mobilize consent.

Both the demands for political access and for subsidies to

maintain employment in Wales could be met in theory through the operations of a unitary government—that is, one without the territorial division of constitutional authority characteristic of federal systems—with its center of power in London. Neither subsidies nor the granting of administrative attention, nor even the establishment of branch offices of central ministries in Cardiff really violated that principle. It was possible for British governments, at least through the mid-1960s, to keep Welsh issues from an attack on the most basic questions, to focus instead on how much subsidy, how much access. The basic structure of the relationships between central power and Welsh power did not arise as long as these issues were in the foreground. The way this was maintained, and the way it then disintegrated after 1964, are equally stories of the nature and transitions of British government and economy, and of Welsh politics and economics.

Wales presented a different kind of problem from that of the English regions and, for that matter, Scotland. While the agitation for devolution diminished or changed direction in England, in Wales it gathered momentum. Reasons for this can be found both in economics and politics, and in underlying cultural factors. First, Wales had many of the characteristics of peripheral regions: poor communications, cultural distinctiveness, a common rural background, and a combination of some national institutions with a pervasive penetration by central institutions. With regard to physical features and communications, Wales was divided into three parts by mountains: North, Mid-, and South Wales. There were no rail links or motorways linking these parts directly, and the main access of each is to England to the east. Second, Wales had a distinct culture. It had a language spoken by an overall average of 19 percent of the population (down from 26 percent in 1961), much more in some parts of Wales. Most of its land areas was rural and depopulated, and a tradition of small villages and towns pervaded the more urbanized counties of South Wales, where most of the population lived. It had a collective sense of national identity. Third, Wales had many institutions organized on a Welsh basis. These included the Confederation of British Industries and the Trades Union Congress and other trade and voluntary associations.

Finally, Welsh institutions were polarized, the most important cleavage being between those who had English and those who had Welsh roots. The former dominated business, were identified with a growing second-home and retirement element throughout Wales, with South Wales and other areas linked to English metropolitan areas, and to some extent with regional offices of central ministries in Wales. The latter were more prominent in education, the clergy, relatively more involved in local government, resided in the more rural areas, and included a number of persons with English roots who had adopted Welsh culture.

In the period before 1964, this polarization began to take on new forms, and the underlying cultural schisms were developing political manifestations that governments in London had to be concerned about and adapt to. There were several such developments. First, nationalism in Wales, which in making language the main issue had not effectively addressed economic issues, began to integrate economic goals into its program and, for more people, to take on new meanings, including separatism. Second, after the 1961 census, which showed the proportion of Welsh speakers dropping to 26 percent, the Welsh Language Society was organized and carried on a vigorous campaign for official bilingualism. The society was successful in raising the general awareness of the cultural issue and transforming it from one felt by a shrinking proportion of older persons to a cause shared by the young.[29] Plaid Cymru, the nationalist political party, still had never won a parliamentary seat, but would soon be in a position to take advantage both of the increasing nationalist sentiment and of the effort at economic management that would soon emerge with the Labour victory.

Because of the background of nationalist institutions and because of the polarization just described, the development of central government-initiated Welsh institutions had taken a precarious course. The clientele for these was polarized. In other parts of Great Britain, labor unions, local officials, and industrialists were predisposed to accept government-sponsored regionalism. Their expanding cities created occasions for them to interact, and the regional bodies offered better access to ministries of the central government to obtain funds and subsidies to help deal with these problems, so the coalition between industrialists and local public officials mobilized effectively.[30] In Wales urbanization was less a factor, and the localities were more likely to be motivated by nationalist issues like devolution and the language.[31] Industrial participation in regional bodies was not vigorous for different reasons. Many more major industries were absentee-owned and not rooted in Wales. While they wanted very much to press, through regional bodies, for government regional subsidies, they felt the need to be cagey about it, since all around them, and to an increasing extent, there were others who would press not only for subsidies, but for Welsh control. Thus they could not as easily (compared to their counterparts in England) team up with the local authorities, and the government in London found itself dealing with a relatively fragmented constituency in Wales.

In this situation, the balanced bargaining position of labor union, local government, and industry, which had achieved a temporary consensus on regional issues in Britain more generally, broke down. In Wales, more so than in other parts of Britain, there was less willingness to accept compromises founded on expectations of growth, and more of a tendency to criticize government policies that did not produce growth. This problem, when it appeared in other places, took more of a form of quantitative wage demands by the unions. In Wales the territorial demands complicated matters, leaving ministries of the central government in a more defensive position. This problem is illustrated by the history of the major central government–initiated Welsh institutions that formed around regional policy after 1964.

Centrally Initiated Regionalism: 1964–75

Government-sponsored attempts to solve specifically Welsh problems entered a new phase with the Labour Government in 1964. The creation of the Welsh Office in Cardiff, headed by a cabinet-status Secretary of State, was the major part of this. Another development was the replacement of the Council for Wales and Monmouthshire by the Welsh Economic Council (WEC).

Previous governments had kept a low profile in Wales, conducting administration through the ministries in London and making policy in Parliament with Welsh considerations integrated into bills devised with Britain as a whole in mind. There were regional offices of the ministries in Cardiff, but this did not change things much, as no one in them was of very high rank. Advisory bodies deliberated in secret as a rule—when the Council for Wales and Monmouthshire made public its recommendations, it was rebuffed in London. In contrast, the new institutions gave the Government prominence in Wales, and it was no longer possible for the Welsh to complain that they had inadequate access to the ministries or to the cabinet. On the political side, there was, starting in 1964, a Secretary of State who would divide his time between cabinet affairs and the Welsh Office. There would also be two additional members of Parliament with special executive responsibilities: a Minister of State and a Minister for Welsh Affairs, not of cabinet rank but responsible to the Secretary of State and with other functions in the Welsh Office. On the civil service side, the Welsh Office had by 1967 a permanent Secretary, four undersecretaries and several assistant secretaries, each responsible for functional or administrative divisions.[32] Much was made of the increase in civil service rank now represented in Cardiff, since the offices combined under the Secretary of State would have new access to policy-making committees in London.[33] Another source of influence was the communication now possible among departments in Cardiff. This would give a Wales-based civil servant an advantage compared to his counterpart in an English region. The functions initially assigned to the new agency were housing, local government, and roads, but its responsibilities grew steadily. By 1975 it had taken over responsibility for forestry and agriculture (jointly with the Ministry of Agriculture), ancient monuments, tourism, health care, child care, primary and secondary education, and financing the National Museum and National Library of Wales. The staff increased from 225 in

1964 to 990 in 1972, and "nearly one half of the identifiable expenditure of government departments and local authorities in Wales in 1971–72 fell within the responsibility of the Secretary of State."[34]

Thus it is arguable that the demands for a Welsh voice in the cabinet, which caused the creation of the Welsh Office, had been met. There is some evidence that the Secretary of State was, at least to some extent, performing this function. The Welsh Office seemed to have the support of the business community, and the actions of the Secretary of State in saving rail service in central Wales and in stopping the construction of a reservoir in the Dulas Valley have been cited as examples of this effectiveness.[35] Nevertheless, the Welsh Office did not satisfy the demands for devolution in Wales, and to large segments of the population, appeared as a major disappointment.

The 1967 White Paper, Wales: The Way Ahead. An analysis of this might be made by examining several issues, but the focus here will be on the regional planning process. Because of the establishment of the Welsh Office, the 1964 regional planning apparatus was set-up differently from that in the English regions.[36] Rather than an economic planning council appointed wholly from outside of the Government, the Welsh Economic Council was provided with the Minister of State as chairman. Rather than a loosely defined economic planning board gathered from regional offices with few or no high ranking civil servants, the WEC was immediately presented with the new Welsh Office as its staff.

The WEC consisted initially of twenty-five members, whose backgrounds were as follows: local authorities (7), trade unions (4), industry (4), commerce and finance (2), agriculture and rural industries (2), universities (2), research (1), tourism (1), construction (1), transport (1). Its main formal responsibility was to give advice to the central government. In theory, it was to have a free hand in this. George Brown, addressing the first meeting of the WEC in 1965, said in response to a question that they were not required to simply work out the implications of the national plan, but that the national plan would be responsive to their conclusions for Wales. On the other hand, the Welsh Office, with its Minister of State sitting as WEC chairman, and its staff charged with any technical work to be done, effectively set the agenda for the WEC, and in the end constrained what it could say. The Welsh Office and its ministers, including the successive chairmen of the council, were not in a position to be independent of central government policy. Anything the Welsh Office did or said had to be justifiable as consistent with goals set by the cabinet. The WEC, which could hardly speak other than through its chairman, thus was confined to providing advice in private, or to following the lead of the Welsh Office and central government in any public utterances.

The role of the WEC and the Welsh Office in any regional strategy for Wales was associated in the public mind with an official planning effort published in 1967 as *Wales: The Way Ahead.*[38] As an effective policy statement (that is, one that could win support or stimulate alternatives that could win support), this effort was largely abortive. The details are revealing of the position that the WEC and the Welsh Office were in.

First, the plan was oversold. The development of an economic strategy for Wales had been an important component of the policy of the central government beginning in 1963 when, as part of a move in this direction by the Conservative government in several parts of Britain, an Economic Intelligence Unit was set up to gather data for Wales. No report emanated from this, but with the establishment of the Welsh Office and of the Welsh Economic Council, the production of an economic plan for Wales was taken up publicly as a major task. Ministers promised the plan for a long time before it finally appeared in July of 1967. The creation of the WEC also contributed to the development of expectations for planning in Wales. The Council for Wales and Monmouthshire had been in eclipse, but the adoption of the DEA strategy for regional planning in Wales dictated a new advisory council, despite the recent creation of the Welsh Office, and this helped to stir expectations.

Second, the way the plan was produced led to criticism. The Welsh Office operated in secret using only its own resources and those it could borrow from other ministries, it was slow in production, and in the end an outsider from another ministry was brought in for the final draft. The newly created WEC was not used as a resource for producing the plan, and was brought in for review purposes only in April of 1967, as the document was ready to go to press. When some members of the council asked that the document be substantially revised, the Welsh Office refused to do so. Observers found it difficult to account fully for this style of operation. One factor was the hierarchical responsibility of the civil servants and ministers to the cabinet. Direct command prevented the revision of *Wales: The Way Ahead.* One informant reported the failure to respond to the council's demands for revision occurred immediately after consultation with the cabinet. But a more pervasive hierarchical structure constrained analysis at the technical level. Privately, Welsh Office analysts indicated that the problems of making a comprehensive policy for Wales were politically very touchy and technically difficult, and since the responsibility of the Secretary of State to the cabinet forced him to be very careful in making policy statements (or plans), this made the Welsh Office planners basically conservative rather than plan-minded. In addition, others argued that the difficulties in producing *Wales: The Way Ahead* were due to a lack of expertise, attributable to an early policy of favoring Welsh speakers in staffing, and to the fact that most of the bright young economists were attracted to the DEA offices (outside of Wales) over the Welsh Office.

Third, *Wales: The Way Ahead* had substantial flaws. The most prominent—the flaw that occasioned the criticism from within the Welsh Economic Council—was the manner in which its employment forecasts were made. The report itself simply presented estimates of 1971 labor force and employment in narrative form. No basis for these estimates was given, nor were there tables indicating the procedure that yielded the estimates.[39] The actual figures were hedged carefully, but suggested that there might be an excess of fifteen thousand persons in the labor force, over jobs available in Wales. This figure itself came under attack, since an independent analysis, earlier commissioned by the council, had used much more sophisticated methods and had come up with much higher estimates of the 1971 "job gap."[40] Some persons interviewed felt the Welsh Office had simply doctored the forecast so that the job gap would appear about equivalent to the number of new jobs projected to result from the Labour government's new regional policy instruments being introduced at about that time. Whatever the motivations and procedures, the estimates "soon proved foolishly optimistic."[41] By 1969 unemployment had mounted to thirty-five thousand.[42]

The plan was also criticized for a lack of coherence. There appeared to be no overall strategy linking its proposals, and so *Wales: The Way Ahead* amounted to a list or inventory of proposals, most of which had been previously announced by the Government. The most important of these dealt with growth-point strategies. With the establishment of the Welsh Office, two major new towns had been considered for Wales: at Newtown in Mid-Wales, and Llantrisant near Cardiff. The report proposed a drastically scaled-down proposal for Mid-Wales, and a population increase in Newtown to only eleven thousand, rather than the seventy thousand that had originally been proposed by consultants. It did propose to move ahead with Llantrisant, a proposal whose fate is described below.

Prior to the publication of *Wales: The Way Ahead*, the Welsh Economic Council had been used to comment on and approve a number of specific policy issues and proposals, which it did by means of smaller working panels. Subjects included Mid-Wales development policy, comments on the national plan, advice to the government on employment and redeployment in industry, and numerous other schemes and proposals.[43] But the general plan being prepared by the Welsh Office staff was the crucial missing ingredient during this time, as council members found it difficult to deal with specialized topics without an overall policy framework.[44] After the plan was published, the council was largely vitiated as a policy-making body, it being obvious that it would be dependent on the Welsh Office for whatever role it might play. The old criticism of the "nominated" (appointed from London) advisory body, made earlier for the Council for Wales and Monmouthshire, was repeated on many sides: particularly directed at the use of the Minister of State as chairman. After the decision to publish *Wales: The Way Ahead* in 1967, one member of the council "resigned in disgust," and it was partly to restore the usefulness of the council that the Government disbanded the original council in 1967 and appointed instead a new Welsh Council.[45] This had an expanded membership of thirty-six and its chairman was independent of the Government. Upon taking office he suggested ways the new council could assert its independence from the Welsh Office: "I enjoy an independence which the minister of the state lacked and can use my relations with the media to the advantage of the council—and to the disadvantage of intractable politicians should the need ever arise."[46]

Certainly, the volume of published material disseminated to the public increased over that produced by the WEC. The new council's proposals included positions on devolution, a proposal for a separate Welsh Water Board, proposals for rural Wales, and a critique of regional policy.

Later, the Welsh Council seemed to be steering a course somewhere between the independent style of the old Council for Wales and Monmouthshire, and the WEC's role as a rubber stamp for the Welsh Office. Sir Melwyn Rosser, its second chairman, advocated a moderate approach. Feeling the political base of the Welsh Council was inadequate to deal with "hot" political issues (for example, the closure of coal pits by the nationalized coal industry), he saw "forward thinking as the best role" and, in a series of reports, had focused the work of the new council on topics of long-range importance: water resources, health, rural Wales, aviation, road and rail transport, the Common Market, and an assessment of regional policy. Rosser felt these activities would have a long-term, if not a short-term, impact on Welsh affairs. The water report helped influence the creation of a Welsh National Water Authority with a wide range of powers. On the issue of devolution, the council had supported an elective assembly with limited authority that would gradually assume control of the functions of the Welsh Office. Too fast an assumption of powers by the assembly would lead to conflict between central ministries and local authorities. The lesson, he thought, of the gradual evolution of the Welsh Office was that gradualism did not result in such conflicts.[47]

But the Welsh Council in 1975 was, despite these attitudes that were independent of the central government line, seen generally as anything but an independent body. Like its earlier models, it faced a dilemma: its natural constituency was polarized. Businessmen and civil servants, to which it was most connected, saw it as a possibly constructive force representing them in solving problems within the framework of a unitary government. Others, quite vocal and often representing local government interests, saw the unitary framework as unworkable. Moreover, many constituents were stung by the way the council had been set up. There had been a campaign both by Plaid Cymru and by elements in the Labour and Liberal parties to establish an *elected* "Welsh council" with a role in administration. The purely advisory, appointed body that was set up was thus a disappointment. And the situation had evolved from that which affected the earlier council. Then, its main purpose had been to increase Welsh participation in a unitary system that needed some minor tinkering. Now there had been a decade of experience with the Welsh Office and an increasing number of people had concluded that more drastic changes were necessary.

Devolution. After the publication of *Wales: The Way Ahead*, organizational developments in the Welsh Office and in government administration generally became an important aspect of regional policy. In 1965 the creation of the Welsh Office and the Welsh Economic Council (along with the regional planning that had already begun in other places) helped focus attention on the regional plan. With a new administrative body, planning seemed more relevant, more susceptible to enactment. This had resulted in the intense scrutiny of *Wales: the Way Ahead* and partly explains the disappointment in it. And then, despite the plan's inadequacies, more organizational machinery developed. This was partly a matter of maintaining the momentum that began with the establishment of the Welsh Office, as it had been expected that it would increase its functions over time. But there was also a new momentum generated after 1965, commonly attributed to the Plaid Cymru gains after 1966, similar victories for the Scottish nationalists, the appointment of the Royal Commission on the Constitution and the long process of consideration of Welsh and Scottish assemblies that would have legislative power.[48] The latter proposals, called "devolution," would have changed the basic structure of British government, and it was not until 1979 that they were finally defeated in referenda. But while they were being considered, significant development of the administrative apparatus of government went on, largely by executive action, occasionally as the result of legislation.

One major change, not strictly subsumed under devolution but, in the end having effects on it, was the reorganization of local government. This, after a long period of gestation, emerged in legislation for England and Wales in 1972. Its effect was to transform a Welsh local government system that had consisted of 165 localities and 13 counties into one with 37 localities and 8 counties. The practical outcome was that the new counties, because of their relatively large size compared to any local governments that had existed previously, took on important new administrative and overview functions, including "structure planning." Local planning had, in the past, been largely consumed by the problems of controlling land development. The new structure planning adopted a vogue that had developed among planners in the 1960s for "strategic" planning looking not only at land use but also at the rational organization of all local government functions. The chief executive officers of the new counties began to see planning as a way to maintain influence over operating functions in the municipalities, and also to bargain more effectively with the Welsh Office, and central government agencies. Their emergence as a strong lobby has been suggested by some as a source of opposition to the proposed devolution of powers to a Welsh assembly, which they saw as a possible obstacle to direct dealings with sources of funds and authority in London and the Welsh Office.

While devolution was being debated, new agencies responsible to Parliament were set up in Wales. Perhaps most important was the Welsh Development Agency, established in 1976, with authority to reclaim derelict land, build and operate advance factories, and to finance new enterprises and expansions of existing ones. There was also the Land Authority for Wales, set up in 1976 with power to acquire land for purposes of development and control, and the Development Board for Rural Wales with broad powers to promote economic and social development in Mid-Wales, established in 1977. Meanwhile, the Welsh Office itself was expanding functions and staff. In 1978, it received reponsibility for functions of the ministry of agriculture, and in 1979 for a large part of the department of industry programs in Wales. The Welsh Office staff had grown to 2500.

All of these new offices and institutions developed within the gradualist framework described by Rosser, and within which the Welsh Council operated. They were part of it and did not represent a break from the overall policies of the central government.[49]

Local Response to Government Policy

Despite these initiatives, by 1975 local or larger-scale responses in Wales had contradicted, modified, or preempted the cautious plans produced by the government. These responses included, but also transcended, the documents that opposition political parties would normally produce. In addition to political opposition, their basis included desires to protect and maintain Welsh communities, a general ideology of economic decentralization, and in the case of Plaid Cymru, the demand for a separate Welsh state. The following are the major, but not the only, examples of locally based regional schemes. Planning efforts by local authorities are not discussed.[50]

Mid-Wales Industrial Development Association. Throughout the 1950s, British governments had neglected Welsh demands for special consideration. An area that felt particularly neglected was Mid-Wales. This area, comprising the then counties of Cardigan,

Merioneth, Montgomery, Radnor, and part of Brecon, had by 1957 suffered a population decline of 100,000 from its 1871 peak of 275,000. The Mid-Wales Industrial Development Corporation (MWIDA) began operations in that year as the five counties joined together under the leadership of Arthur Beacham, an economist at the University of Wales.[51] Funds came from the counties, and Beacham obtained supplementary aid from the Development Commission, an agency that had been founded in London in 1911 to assist the development of rural industries. MWIDA then began to promote, and then build advance factories in the small towns in the area. By 1974, it had attracted 110 firms and was operating with a professional staff and a budget of £20,000 and had established itself as a successful and widely known operation.

MWIDA's strategy for economic development emerged as a compromise between an urbanization or growth-point strategy of the sort that came into vogue in Europe during the 1960s and a policy maximizing the retention of small-scale village life that was more favored politically in the area. Until about 1960, MWIDA had been attempting to promote manufacturing development wherever it could in Mid-Wales, and had located perhaps twenty firms in scattered locations. It then developed the idea that such development might not be effective in reducing depopulation, which it began to see as a function not solely of employment opportunities, but the concentration of employment and accompanying stores and services in larger places. Instrumental in this thinking was a large-scale study of the Mid-Wales situation under government auspices, the Committee on Depopulation in Mid-Wales, which was chaired by Beacham. The resulting document suggested the value of concentrating new employment, and helped move the Government toward a position of investing resources in a large new town project in the area.[52] In the meantime, without government policy support, MWIDA itself had begun to concentrate its own activities. In the early 1960s it was confining its new factory locations to fourteen of the larger towns in the area, and apparently it was preparing to participate in the large new town development if the government supported it.

Local governments in the area were, on the other hand, cautious about the idea of concentrated development. Subsequent to the Beacham report the Welsh Office commissioned a consultant to do a report on a new town, but when this appeared, proposing a community of 70,000 population in the valley between Newtown and Caersws, there was a strong reaction.[53] First, the new community would be grossly out of scale in the region, for there were few places with population greater than 5,000. Second, development on the proposed scale would have many side effects that seemed undesirable: it would put a great burden on social and other services and would mean the immigration of most of the population from England. This would make it even more difficult to preserve the Welsh language; and increasing the services required would mean changing the ways in which they were organized. something most persons did not want to do precipitously. Finally, and apparently most decisively, the development would cost a great deal. Faced with this, plus opposition to the scheme, the Welsh Office backed away from the 70,000 figure and, in *Wales: The Way Ahead*, advocated a more modest increment of 5,000 persons in Newtown, while designating an additional six towns as minor growth centers.

MWIDA itself did not take part in the opposition to the larger new town, but it proceeded to advocate and promote vigorously the smaller-scale development in Newtown and the other designated places. When the Newtown development was funded under the new towns legislation, MWIDA supplied staff for the new corporation responsible. It took an economic, rather than a cultural orientation to its work. Its main aim continued to be to stem depopulation, not to maintain Welsh culture, though in its pragmatic pursuit of small-scale industry and the development of village-level economies, it was decidedly not a threat to Welsh culture in the way a large-scale development strategy might have been.

Heads of the Valleys. South Wales includes an urbanized part near the Bristol Channel and along the main rail and road lines, including such places as Newport, Cardiff, Port Talbot and

Swansea, and a number of coal mining and steel-producing towns in narrow valleys to the north: Merthyr Tydfil, Ebbw Vale, Aberdare, and the Rhondda are examples. The more obvious places for new industrial growth are in the first group of places. They have more land and easier transport connections. For a long time planners had proposed a major new town in that area as a means of facilitating industrial growth, and the Welsh Office had proposed this in Llantrisant, just to the west of Cardiff, justifying the proposal partly by the claim that it would supply jobs that surplus labor in the valley towns could fill. Other areas adjacent to the main South Wales cities were, similarly, proposed for industrial development in the plans of those places.

When, in 1971, it appeared that the Welsh Office would go ahead with the Llantrisant proposal, the local authorities in Merthyr Tydfil and Ebbw Vale began to seek ways to object to this coastal emphasis, and together with fourteen other valley towns they formed the Heads of the Valleys Standing Conference. A standing conference has no formal authority, but the Valleys unit was a natural one, since all the towns felt a threat to their continued existence in what they perceived as a Welsh Office policy that neglected them and favored the coastal areas. In 1972, the Welsh Office took the first steps to designate a new town in Llantrisant, and in the ensuing public inquiry the opposition was given a chance to present its case.[54] The groups against the coastal development included (1) the valley towns, (2) coastal authorities in a position to compete for industrial development with those nearest to Llantrisant, and (3) private individuals and organizations who considered the proposal unsatisfactory for ideological or political reasons. The main arguments presented at the Llantrisant Inquiry were the following:

First, the valley towns argued that the coastal development represented not only a neglect of their needs, but would result in positive harm to them. While it had been presented as a stimulant to employment in South Wales generally, they argued that it was located too far away from the Valley towns for them to benefit. People would not be able to commute from the upper valley towns, particularly since rail service had been allowed to deteriorate, and so if Llantrisant were allowed to develop with large quantities of new employment opportunities the result would be further out-migration from the Valleys.

Second, they argued that sufficient land for industrial expansion existed in the valleys themselves, and the selection of Llantrisant was based on an inadequate survey of available sites.

Third, the beginnings of a theoretical argument against concentration of the development on the coast emerged. Professor Harold Carter, a geographer at the University of Wales, suggested that the Llantrisant development represented a crude growth-pole theory. A more appropriate conception, he said, would include a larger number of smaller poles, thus giving the valley communities a share of development.[55]

After the inquiry, the examiner found against the Llantrisant proposal, and the Welsh Office withdrew its case. Whether it should have withdrawn was a matter of debate. Many economists felt that large-scale development on the coast was the most obvious strategy for the economic development of Wales, and that the problem simply was that the Welsh Office "lacked nerve" to proceed with a coordinated strategy. But there was no consensus for this view, either at the political level of short-term self-interest of the communities that comprise South Wales, or in academic or ideological argument. There were a series of proposals for economic development along the coast following the Llantrisant dispute, which mainly served to sharpen and draw out the lines of debate without resulting in the emergence of any clear strategy for economic development. These included proposals near Newport and Cardiff in 1975 and 1976. In each case, the standing conference presented opposition, including expert testimony and elaborate consultant-prepared reports. These representations continued through the Examinations in Public carried out for the structure plans of the individual counties concerned, which occurred in 1978 and 1979.

These activities of local governments in the valleys took place in the context of sometimes intense community organizing. The most regionally oriented group was the Call to the Valleys, a community organizing project embracing a range of valley communities, which developed out of a smaller group in Aberfan in 1972. The project went on through most of the decade, consisting of a series of meetings and conferences. Impressions differ on their practical effects, but what is clear is that they provided a forum from which, among other things, planning policies for South Wales were once more examined, and the policy of focusing growth at the valley mouths was again questioned. These meetings, which attracted both the resources of academics and professionals and the representation of large numbers of local people, provided a background of information and personal contacts for the Standing Conference.[56]

The Heads of the Valleys Standing Conference represented a defensive style of organization: it was held together by a common sense of threat and was attacked for having little in the way of a positive program for Welsh development. Its spokesmen replied that it had made a positive contribution, for example, the report on industrial sites in the valleys. To call it a defensive organization with a negative program implied that South Wales lacked a positive program. Without a legitimate plan for development in South Wales, they said, the Welsh Office had provided no more support for development than the Standing Conference and deserved to be seen in no better light.

Standing Conference on Regional Policy in South Wales. Much locally initiated regional organization developed from a common commitment to local problem solving on the part of elected and appointed officers. They might have few "substantive" policy agreements of the sort that united the valley communities, but instead an interest in maintaining their prerogatives and authority as occupiers of a particular level of government. These kinds of interests were motivations for the maintenance of standing conferences in England. In the North West the Standing Conference was concerned to watch out for the interests of local government against the Economic Planning Council and then the Strategic Plan Team. This motivation was relatively stronger in Wales, where both local government reorganization and devolution were live issues that made the authority of local government problematic. The main example of this sort of regionalism in Wales was the Standing Conference on Regional Policy in South Wales.

The Standing Conference had existed prior to the 1974 reorganization, but had not been effective. After reorganization there were four, larger counties: West, Mid-, and South Glamorgan, and Gwent; and the chief executive offices gave the Standing Conference increased importance. Whereas previously the Standing Conference had been dominated by planners and had suffered from the antagonism of the clerks in some cases, after 1974 the chief executives supplemented the planners with their own staffs, and broadened the agenda to include numerous items of day-to-day interest. A 1976 agenda, for example, included such items as legislative developments in the creation of the Welsh Development Agency, Dutch Elm disease, rail service cuts, the creation of a fire training center, gypsy sites, and the prospects for influencing the British Steel Corporation to continue operations in the area. The importance of this breadth of concern was that it gave the executives a forum for information exchange that would increase their leverage on the Welsh Office. This would hold both in individual dealings, which would count for more if participants were well-informed, and on subjects on which the counties chose to go to the Welsh Office together.

Planning became a major concern of the standing conference because the new counties were mandated to draw up structure plans. These were county-wide expenditure programs and were crucial to the development of new public spending or the attraction of industrial development to the counties. For structure planning, the Standing Conference was a vehicle for the counties to jockey for control of their own decision making, chiefly against the Welsh Office. They had a common interest in getting the best possible technical projections and in maximizing the exchange of information about what each county planned and what public and private bodies planned to do in South Wales. When the Welsh Office seemed unsatisfactory in any respect for these ends, the Standing Conference was in a position to suggest alternative procedures of research and to try to take the lead away from the Welsh Office in whatever aspect of planning seemed unsatisfactory. But since the Welsh Office was armed only with the discredited 1967 policy document, it was in a weak position. In 1976, county planners were claiming that regional strategy for South Wales would emerge from the counties, not the Welsh Office.

Opposition under a Separatist Program: Plaid Cymru

Wales: The Way Ahead, and the subsequent failure to improve upon it, left a planning vacuum in Wales. Partly, this was a matter of lack of program ideas emanating from the Welsh Office, for the official document failed to provide the structure of major government projects and policies within which local authorities could begin to plan smaller projects. Planners in Wales tend to think in terms of policy hierarchies. Local or sectoral planning, in the absence of overall policy, tends to stop. At least as important, however, was the situation of ideological controversy within Wales. There were differing attitudes toward the underlying principles of any government plan, so that even if a plan and investment program had existed, there would have been opposition to it—as occurred in the case of the Newtown-Caersws new town and Llantrisant—on grounds that the policy served British, not Welsh interests. Thus at best, the price of planning in Wales would be high. The only way to avoid a vacuum would have been to have an extremely strong plan, backed by the commitment of major investments—something it was not possible for the government to provide in the late 1960s.

What gave the opposition an added measure of importance, and what gave them a measure of ideological coherence, was the emergence of Plaid Cymru as a separatist political party with increasing credibility after 1966. Its program included not only separation from Britain, but also a model of economic organization and political relationships distinct from those of the other major Welsh parties. The model included (1) decentralization of political authority within Wales, and (2) preservation of Welsh culture, a goal that they felt depended on the maintenance of local community life and bilingualism.

Plaid Cymru was widely regarded as a fringe group at the time of the 1964 election and the new government had little reason to take it seriously. It had run parliamentary candidates in twenty-three of the thirty-six Welsh seats, had won none, and its total poll was 4.8 percent, behind Labour's 57.8, the Conservative Party's 29.4 and Liberal Party's 7.3. It had a reputation for taking extreme stands on cultural issues: it stood for the adoption of Welsh as the official language of instruction in the schools, for example, as late as 1959.[58] That all this changed during the period of the 1964–70 Labour government was due in part to the economics of Labour Party policy and support and in part to a substantial shift in the Plaid Cymru position and their elaboration of a new program of economics and planning.

The Rise of Plaid Cymru. Plaid Cymru burst into the consciousness of the British in 1966, when Gwynfor Evans won a by-election for a parliamentary seat previously held by Labour in Carmarthen. The party claimed to have gained one thousand new members soon after that, and was immediately the focus of public attention.[59] From then on, Plaid Cymru gained steadily. From 1967 to 1970, local councilors increased from 36 to 48, and the numbers running in the local elections increased from 102 to 202. While Evans lost his seat in 1970, he soon regained it along with two other parliamentary candidates. In 1976, Emrys Roberts won control of the Merthyr Tydfil council, a major victory at the local level.[60]

For the most part, these gains were made at the expense of Labour, and reflected a change in the composition of Labour support. On the one hand, the Labour Party organization had deteriorated and stagnated during years when a Labour dominance was automatic. In addition, structural factors contributed to a decline in both union and Labour Party membership. This, according to Rawkins, was due, first, to the collapse of heavy industry in Wales and an increasing heterogeneity of manual labor resulting from technological change: coal production, for example, no longer involved as many workers doing similar jobs at the coal face; rather there was more use of sophisticated machinery and a greater variety of jobs.[61] There developed generally an increase in the militancy of labor, but a decrease in automatic support of the Labour Party. On the other hand, the Labour Party was controlled by older party functionaries who were unattractive to the 1960s generation of working class. Rawkins also attributes the decline of Labour to ideological changes that made Labour an elitist, technocratic party under Wilson and removed class issues from debate. Thus the national plan and other economic programs forced labour into a position where it had to deliver jobs and prosperity, which left open some territory for an opposition to exploit, if Labour failed to deliver. What happened, after 1966, was that both major British parties were increasingly unable to deliver.

Plaid Cymru moved from its position of cultural nationalism to much greater emphasis on economic issues after 1966. One element in this move was a change in policy from advocating the use of the only the Welsh language in schools to advocating bilingualism, which was finally adopted in 1968.[62] Perhaps more basic was a change in composition of party membership. The party, which had in the past drawn its principal strength from the Welsh-speaking counties of the north and west of Wales, now began to recruit members more heavily in the industrial areas of South Wales. Rawkins, who conducted extensive interviews with ninety-two Plaid Cymru activists in 1972–75 identified eleven of these as "modernist" in orientation, a group largely attracted to the party from South Wales after the Carmarthen by-election in 1966.[63] In contrast to the cultural objectives of most other party members, Rawkins described this group as combining "a firm conviction in the importance of grassroots political work . . . with a radical political commitment to economic and social justice."[64] Of Rawkins' sample, which included "the vast majority of the leading figures in Plaid Cymru," most were from middle-class families, a number from relatively Anglicized families, and they were professionals or managers. Two were factory workers. At the ordinary membership level, however, Rawkins reports that working-class representation easily exceeded 50 percent in a number of South Wales constituencies.[65] The impact of the modernists was apparently crucial in the reorientation of the party after 1966, when its sudden prominence in Parliament forced it to address a wider range of issues. One important move was the establishment in 1966 of the Plaid Cymru Research Group, which began to produce position papers on economic issues.[66] From then on, the party began to develop an economic policy to complement its concerns about language and community, and the modernists increasingly dominated the public pronouncements made by Plaid Cymru.

Plaid Cymru Economic Policy. Within a decade the research group had produced scores of position papers, but the most important work during the 1960s was *An Economic Plan for Wales*, which was produced both to fill gaps left by *Wales: The Way Ahead*—so that there would be some statement on the Welsh economy—and also to establish a more identifiable party position distinct from that of other parties.[67] In addition, it was presented to the Commission on the Constitution in 1970 as an official submission "to show how a responsible Welsh Government could proceed to develop" the economic potential of Wales.[68] That is, it was in some respects a demonstration of how planning might be done under conditions of independence.

The central point of *An Economic Plan For Wales* was that, instead of taking the central government's regional policy as a given, it started from the projection of the number of jobs that would be needed to maintain Welsh communities, then keyed its proposals to this projection. This contrasted with *Wales: The Way Ahead* and the thinking in the Welsh Office. Government regional policy would be shown to be inadequate for Welsh employment needs under this assumption and, implicitly, to favor out-migration to England. Phil Williams, who coauthored the plan, said:

> The Government wants to maximize the mobility of labour to solve economic problems which they see from the point of view of Britain as a whole. We on the other hand want

> stable communities in Wales and so we are against labour mobility and in favor of the direction of industry. We want to limit the migration of Welshmen out of Wales to the natural level which would match the number of Welshmen returning to Wales or indeed other young people coming to Wales to find employment. For the last fifty years the tendency has been for a very large number of young Welshmen to be forced to leave Wales, and in return only an aging population come to Wales to retire, and this we feel is a totally unnatural development of our national community.[69]

Such a viewpoint turns regional economics and British regional policy inside out. The usual idea is to use regional policy only to cushion the sharper blows of labor mobility on communities and regions. *Wales: The Way Ahead* made its *projections* of employment in part on the "basis of the existing plans of the industries" in coal and steel, and in part by extrapolating past trends. The Plaid Cymru plan, rather than make projections, sought the reasons why employment was declining or not increasing fast enough, and tried to act on these.

This led the Plaid Cymru planners to take a closer look at the organization of production in Wales, while the Welsh Office tended more to examine demand and to adjust its proposals accordingly. Because they were proposing a separatist program in general, Plaid Cymru had open to them options for a production orientation that were not available to the Welsh Office. Most important, they proposed that the existing regional policy instruments that emphasized direct subsidies to manufacturers be replaced by subsidies for infrastructure improvements, including roads, public services, and industrial parks operated by local governments or public bodies. These improvements were then to be used and directed in ways much different from what the Welsh Office had proposed. First, they were to be concentrated in twenty-three major and secondary growth centers spread throughout Wales, in contrast to the Welsh Office plan.[70] *Wales: The Way Ahead*, insofar as it had a policy of geographic concentration, limited itself to the Mid-Wales proposal and the Llantrisant plan, though, by leaving location largely to market forces, it was implicitly favoring the South Wales coastal area. A second infrastructure priority of Plaid Cymru would have allocated relatively more to the improvement of roads and of links within Wales, as opposed to links from Wales to London and other parts of England.[71] Another would have been an increase in the subsidy for housing.[72]

In addition to infrastructure, the plan proposed other intervention in the organization of production: an easing of incentives to concentrate agriculture (to retain some employment), and a National Development Authority. This would manage the installation of industry and other aspects of the growth areas, create a national roadbuilding company, operate a Welsh regional policy, and, where private enterprise failed to set up a business, launch subsidiary production companies. There would also be a new Bank of Wales to supply capital.

Plaid Cymru was in effect proposing a series of trades with England, the net effect of which would be to increase Welsh control and community control over their economy. They were prepared to give up all British subsidies to Wales, including capital improvements and the regional policy subsidies. In return they asked for control of the way they spent their own tax moneys. They differed with the British over whether they could afford to do this. Williams was sharply questioned on this before the Commission on the Constitution in 1970:

> Lord Crowther: Surely, Dr. Williams, you are being very simple-minded . . . the reason why the Government . . . provides this money for Wales, Scotland and other places is because there are Welsh and Scottish Members of Parliament at Westminster screaming their heads off about it . . . Is it not likely that much more money would be provided for Welsh development by a political solution that went only part way, but still left the financing of public expenditure throughout the United Kingdom as a burden on the Treasurer?
>
> Williams: This has been a political issue in Wales over the last few years . . . one of the few things that really divide our policy from the Liberal Party policy . . . We have acted

> on the assumption that a Welsh Government . . . would have total responsibility for raising revenue in Wales and for meeting all government expenditure in Wales . . . Under the present system Wales has never benefitted economically to the extent that one might objectively have thought possible.
> Crowther: Why therefore jump to something that would be worse?
> Williams: This is what we are here to debate. But it could hardly be worse, and we assume it would be considerably better. This is our confidence in Wales.[73]

The plan had made a detailed financial case, though, and had put prices on its proposals. It was clear what they gave up and what they got. Their economics made as much sense as those of the Welsh Office and the British government. A quantitative comparison of expenditure allocations under the British, and under the Plaid Cymru program, is easily constructed from the document. The planners estimated total British revenues from Wales at £540 million for 1967–68. Against this, they estimated central government expenditures in Wales at £457 million, exclusive of the Welsh portions of defense expenditures and national debt retirement. On a per capita basis, these would be £70 million and £50 million, respectively, so that expenditures would total £577 million in excess of revenues. The Plaid Cymru proposal was to reduce the local defense and debt retirement contributions drastically, a political decision that an independent Wales might make. Thus the planners projected contributions of £22 million to defense and £25 million to debt retirement. This would leave a surplus over revenues of £36 million, which they proposed be spent on the proposed additional road program, the national development authority, and other internal purposes.[74] With this kind of research, particularly if one made comparisons to *Wales: The Way Ahead*, it was difficult to attack the Plaid Cymru program as economically unsound. The funds for new Welsh domestic spending were to come from reductions in contributions for defense and for the British national debt, both based on reasoned argument from a Welsh point of view. There was not a clear technical argument to be made, and the debate turned into a political one.

In fact the plan was not as radically decentralist as some of the party's other pronouncements have been.[75] For its basic purpose, it was just about right. It was a sane, levelheaded demonstration that an independent Wales could produce a competent economic plan following from a shift of the key premises noted above. Other statements went much further on many aspects of their economic policy. The party manifesto took a position on worker management—the creation of Welsh coal and steel boards would make possible greater worker participation:

> The workers themselves must have much more to say in the running of industry, leading towards a system of co-ownership. Worker participation should start first in the Nationalized Industries . . . Labour's policy for a National Enterprise Board (based in London) and its regional arm, the Welsh Development Agency, to further extend public ownership, is centralist. It will defeat the objective of ensuring a wider distribution of responsibility amongst the workers. Nationalization, as we have experienced it, although changing the nominal ownership of industry, has increased rather than decreased the power of existing vested interests.[76]

Party proposals for worker control and community control of production received modest elaborations.[77] But there were certainly statements of intent in this direction, one by Emrys Roberts, who would later win the Merthyr Tydfil borough council presidency.

> Plaid Cymru wants a parliament for Wales . . . but not as an end in itself. The party has very detailed economic and industrial policies, not merely for Wales as a whole, but for each part of Wales. Parliament is seen as a means of implementing the socialism which Welshmen have been preaching for so long. The emphasis, however, is not on bureaucratic state control, but on local control and worker's co-

ownership. Indeed Plaid's definition of a nation is a community of communities. This emphasis on community is the rallying point for a new radical movement which will not be confined to Wales and Scotland, but is relevant to Britain as a whole . . . It's the logical next step forward. All over Britain, communities are rebelling: the national communities in Wales, Scotland and Ireland; urban communities aginst unthinking urban renewal . . . rural communities against their destruction to make way for a reservoir, a motorway, or an airport; working communities against the destruction of their industrial units; students' communities against the paternalism . . . which treats them as educational units to be processed.[78]

Conclusion: The Role of Planning

In Wales, regional policy and planning together were a major political issue between 1964 and 1979. They were major, not only in the usual way that issues attract the attention of interest groups, but also in the sense that they helped form the agenda of issues and helped bring new interest groups to prominence: not only Plaid Cymru but also the Heads of the Valleys Standing Conference. There are some further observations to be made about this: how planning had this effect, what of substance was raised and not raised by planning, and what limits existed on what might be raised.

With an inexperienced, newly established Welsh Office, under conditions of long-standing polarization in the area, with a number of relatively expert critics expecting a substantial document, *Wales: The Way Ahead* created a policy vacuum. In this situation, alternative plans were bound to get a hearing. The Plaid Cymru plan was profoundly different from government plans in several ways, and so it made an impact on Welsh opinion. It might have been superficially different. It might simply have suggested a major growth center at another coastal site, rather than at Llantrisant, or it might have suggested a different level of regional subsidy, asking London for more than it had been prepared to give. This might have gotten it more attention in the short run, as its fundamental premises would have been more familiar and easy to follow.

As it was, *An Economic Plan for Wales* expressed a set of ideas that came to be repeated later in many different contexts. Typically, the ideas were presented without attribution, and we cannot be sure whether the plan's authors originated ideas that were adopted by others, or whether they simply stated ideas that were in the air at the time. The point is not who was responsible, but that a set of largely similar propositions opposing those stated by the Government came into currency during the period. This helped to raise an opposition consciousness and to change the agenda of issues the government could discuss in Wales. The most important of the issues raised in opposition plans were their supply orientation—including their insistence that any employment projections start from the present population distribution and its needs—and their multiple growth-points strategy, which in effect opposed the policy of concentration in the coastal plain. The first of these ideas was implicit and the latter was worked out in much more detail in the proposals of the Heads of the Valleys Standing Conference. In general, the existence of this opposition not only produced pluralist debate among planners around regional policy issues, it also helped sustain the emergence of interest groups and political parties that would be able to contest a much wider range of issues.

Still, not all the possible issues got raised, and in some respects the most important ones were obscured by the way government planning and its opposition worked things out. As Rees and Lambert point out, what actually happened in South Wales was a "regionalist consensus" developed, involving not only the Welsh Office and government-induced agencies in Wales, but also the Plaid Cymru proposals.[79] The point they make is that, whatever the controversies that existed among the various factions, in a number of respects they all agreed in supporting certain policies, and not supporting others. They supported a kind of palliative policy toward the valley communities, emphasizing social services and housing while letting employment move out; in general they did not address the fundamental effects of relationships of production—i.e., income inequalities between owners and workers—upon social relations.

This criticism certainly is true in general, particularly if one looks at the way the regional debate of the period seems to have turned out in the minds of most informed people. What happened, in the event, was a process of absorption. Welsh Office planners, in particular, simply did not respond to criticisms or to the alternative proposals. Others felt free to come up with components of a regional policy, adapted to their own interests. The resulting compromise was a "consensus" of sorts, at least on the kinds of issues singled out by Rees and Lambert. Another factor pushing issues toward a consensus on substantive points was the developing devolutionary administrative structure. Over the period from 1964 to 1979, the number of government officials and their authority to implement actions increased enormously in Wales. Indications are that, with this, a modus vivendi developed among these officials and agencies.[80] One aspect of this was the relationship between the chief executive officers of the counties and the Welsh Office, partly by means of the Standing Conference of South Wales. What happened was the planning vacuum, ostensibly filled by plans and counterproposals, was really filled by new pieces of implementing machinery. It may be that this machinery, piece by piece, diverted attention from substance of regional policy. Each new move allowed Plaid Cymru to claim another victory but in the end Labour could claim them too.

Could it have been otherwise? There seem to have been two kinds of limits on the kinds of questions raised by planning: those in the content of the plans themselves, and inherent limits in planning per se. On the first point, one might ask whether Plaid Cymru might have raised different questions or elaborated its points more fully. My own impression is that the supply orientation in the Plaid Cymru plan stood for a much wider range of issues that the authors never fully worked out. Many planners were thinking about the organization of supply during the 1960s. Shonfield described the issues this began to raise at the national level in a famous book of the period.[81] In regional planning, where the planner is much closer to the industrialists he is planning for, one quickly gets to problems of the organization of factors of production, not in terms of industrial sectors, but particular firms. The typical "supply" issues of the 1960s was how much investment in new technology and equipment an industrial sector might be induced to make. The next questions would be, how does the firm organize itself more generally? and what should be the shares in authority and incomes between levels of the organization—i.e. between owners and workers? Part of the pulling back from supply-oriented planning at the end of the 1960s was a pulling back from these questions. The Plaid Cymru plan did not pull back from it, but it did not explore it fully, either. If it had been able to, the "regional debate" in South Wales might have persisted longer.

Another kind of limit on the issues raised by planning may be inherent in planning: the issues in regional planning seemed to be exhausted by 1979. All the plans, starting with *Wales: The Way Ahead*, were breaking new ground in that, for the first time, they were stating policies that related population, employment, and location; and they all involved a concern with certain major public works. The first time could only happen once, and by 1979 all the actors had had their say. Any revisions would lack the impact of the first efforts. And concerns about public works were almost one-time issues, given the climate of retrenchment in government spending that soon set in. Thus, at least one cycle of planning seemed to be over. The issues that would be raised during the 1980s would be argued in a different way.

Chapter 4

Appalachia

Appalachia is the best-known and the prototypical peripheral region of the United States. Geographically it is large, remote, and rugged. Its area, defined legislatively by the Appalachian Regional Development Act of 1965, extends from northeastern Mississippi to the southern tier of counties in New York, a distance of one thousand miles, while its width is three to four hundred miles for most of that distance.[1] Everywhere, travel is severely restricted by hills and mountains, and of the nineteen million persons who live there, very few live close to fast roads that would connect them with metropolitan areas. The region's economy is also peripheral. Despite gains during the 1970s, it has a history of lagging behind the rest of the nation in urbanization, participation in the labor force, and income. The most severe lags are in central Appalachia, an area defined by the Appalachian Regional Commission and containing 1.8 million people in parts of Kentucky, Tennessee, Virginia and West Virginia. There, per capita personal income was 52 percent of the average in the United States in 1965, increasing to 65 percent in 1974; in the early 1970s, participation in the labor force averaged about 33 percent of the total population, compared to 42 percent for the United States; and, while it began to gain population faster than the United States as a whole after 1970, for decades it had suffered from severe out-migration.[2]

Appalachia also is a subculture: rural, certainly distinct from metropolitan culture. There are many books, one could say a regional literature and history, attesting to this; there is active pursuit of preservation and articulation of folk songs and crafts. There is also debate whether the subculture is developing or declining. On the one hand there has been penetration of Appalachia by commercial and governmental agencies, from a few outposts to smaller cities in the form of public bureaucracies, shopping centers led by national chains, fast-food shops. On the other hand, there is evidence of reaction to these developments. Conscious regionalism was at least as strong in the 1970s as, say, a decade or two earlier.[3] And national survey data have shown that rural attitudes, which predominate in Appalachia, have become increasingly distinct from those dominant in metropolitan areas.[4]

Another thing that makes Appalachia distinct and peripheral is the massive intrusion of absentee capital and ownership. This has been most apparent in the case of coal mining, but has extended to other industrial sectors, including heavy and light manufacturing. An indication of this is patterns of landownership: one study showed that in twenty-seven of West Virginia's fifty-five counties, out-of-state interests owned more than 50 percent of the land.[5] Similar patterns have been found in other parts of the region, a phenomenon closely associated with the incidence of coal seams. Outside domination has profoundly affected the social and political organization of the area. There has been a history of militant unionism in the central and northern coal fields, combined with intense and intermittently violent union-management conflict—the more extreme as one moves from the relatively institutionalized unionism of Pennsylvania, through West Virginia, to the southern parts of Appalachia where unionization has been spotty and incomplete.[6] There also has been a history of subordination of local politics to manipulation by outside (and inside-owned) business interests. The advent of federally subsidized, but locally distributed, welfare programs in the 1930s made local politics in much of Appalachia an instrument of political control for business interests, a situation that largely persists today.[7]

Finally, Appalachia has experienced, since the creation of the Appalachian Regional Commission (ARC) in 1965, a kind of centrally initiated regional policy, parallel to that applied to peripheral regions in much of Western Europe, though with differences; and this has occasioned response and opposition on the part of local groups. ARC is worth extended attention, since its experience illustrates the strengths and the weaknesses of regional policy wherever it may be applied in the United States and illustrates the main characteristics of a federal system.

The remainder of this chapter describes the interaction of the national system—as evidenced in federal-state regional policy—and local response. It describes regional policy primarily as the programs coordinated by the Appalachian Regional Commission, though it touches on a number of other national institutions that have had enormous impact on Appalachia. It describes local response largely as the efforts of three groups that tried to put together an *aggregation* of local responses, i.e., regional responses. The purpose is not a comprehensive treatment, but an attempt to provide important examples of general processes at work in the region.

Federal Policy toward Appalachia

Regional policy in Appalachia occurs in the context of a federal system in which formal authority is divided among federal, state, and local governments and where the actual interplay among interest groups is more complex and less channeled than in such unitary states as Britain and France. This makes regional policy, as evolved in Western Europe following World War II, relatively difficult to adopt. In the first place, it has been more difficult to obtain agreement on special treatment for any one region or for a class of regions. The Tennessee Valley Authority (TVA) was an exception to this in the New Deal period, but it had no imitators. The Appalachian Regional Commission, perhaps the major case of special treatment for a region since TVA, has been characterized as a largely fortuitous occurrence, unlikely to be repeated.[8] What is more common than comprehensive national policy toward a region is widespread dispersal of subsidies and special treatments throughout the country, as Congress and federal agencies attempt to maximize political support among a large number of local interests who command legislative votes. The history of rivers and harbors legislation exemplifies this, in contrast to the more comprehensive treatment of a region made possible under TVA. Similarly, the efforts to enact a depressed-areas policy after World War II resulted first in the Area Redevelopment Act of 1961, a scheme that dispersed subsidies to as many as one-third of the approximately three thousand counties in the United States and that spread available funds so thinly that no one was persuaded of its relevance to any national goals.

The complexity of interests and levels of government also affects the administration of regional policy. Once regional legislation has been passed, conflicts with state and local interests absorb so much energy that the aims of programs get lost while local and federal administrators attempt to maintain their own organizational stability. Selznick described this phenomenon for the case of TVA in the 1930s and 1940s. The TVA's more controversial goals (e.g., land reform) were dropped to obtain modus vivendi with a conservative local constituency.[9] Similar things happened when the Economic Development Administration (EDA), which succeeded the Area Redevelopment Administration in 1965, attempted to establish multicounty regional planning agencies with significant representation of the poor and minorities. This kind of representation was, at least for a time, a national objective for regional policy, but it encountered local opposition to the extent that, if EDA were to have any effective local organizations, it needed to relax its requirements.[10]

Finally, local politics in the United States has relatively wide scope. Local politicians and administrators are formally free to undertake a wide variety of initiatives. There is little incentive for them to merely implement policies set by state or federal governments. In fact, their behavior varies: some choose to be passive rather than active and entrepreneurial.

The result is that little formal attention is given to regional policy by federal or state governments in the United States. Each region is presumed able to look out for itself. Coordination is notoriously absent compared to conditions in some other countries. Thus, while the 1970s witnessed increased interest in interregional shifts in resources, investments, and federal subsidies, and yielded new studies by such organizations as the Southern Growth Policies Board and the Conference of Northeast Governors, personnel or institutional resources to implement these studies has been lacking. Public servants in the United States tend to be entrepreneurial, rather than analytical, and so policies tended to stay within the obvious self-interests of the regions involved.

It is true that after 1960 Congress and federal agencies paid much attention, ad hoc or not, to regional and local affairs. Intergovernmental grants from the federal to lower levels of government increased exponentially: from roughly seven billion dollars in 1960, to twenty billion in 1968, to seventy billion in 1976.[12] Programs available to aggressive localities proliferated. This stimulated the development of a kind of local entrepreneurial capacity, commonly called "grantsmanship," and increased the pressure for planning and structural reform of local governments. The latter came from the federal government, which needed to legitimize its own programs as it lost control of them. No longer able to oversee its vast array of programs, unable to formulate rules to govern their application in a diverse set of localities, federal agencies resorted to a procedural device: if the local program was planned with participation by the local powers, the blame for failure need not rest solely on bureaucrats in Washington.[13]

This kind of development of the federal system, with a proliferation of programs and a stress on local entrepreneurship, was much more complete in cities than in rural areas. In the latter case, a series of distortions occurred in the system.[14] First, the system was distorted by a much greater frequency of local nonresponse in the rural areas. Local officials simply ignored the programs that became available, and so, in many places containing target populations (such as the poor), nothing was attempted. Second, state governments sometimes dealt with nonresponse by intervening to make moneys available for consultants, who would go into the town, do a report, deposit it, and leave. Third, the new agencies in Washington dealt with localities in standard, even moralistic, ways. A prominent attitude was that rural areas ought to "catch up" to metropolitan problems by "modernization," which usually meant hiring administrators and planners. VISTA, operating on the model of the Peace Corps, sent in community organizers. Community action programs, economic development districts, and other federally funded agencies were required to have representation of the poor and minorities, and in their operations they bypassed state and local power structures and elected officials. A decade or more later, many rural communities, traditional political officials still in office, still react to the shock of these initiatives.[15]

Appalachia was different from most such cases. In many states, rural areas got less attention than urban areas. What happened in the other states was that a good deal of tugging and pulling occurred around urban problems, with the rural places either being swept along or ignored. The core Appalachian states, in contrast, had a long history of this neglect, and the neglected counties were important constituencies, so that neglect itself became an issue, and by the mid-1960s the Appalachian counties received as much policy attention in the governors' offices as did the urban areas. The governors set up a counterforce to the federal initiatives, aimed at giving their Applachian counties special attention.

In summary, the following elements seemed to define the situation at the time of the establishment of ARC in 1965: (1) an administrative constituency and some public interest lobbies committed to modernization of state government in such states as Kentucky, Tennessee, and Georgia; (2) liberal reformers committed to changes in economics and politics through such instruments as a TVA-like authority; (3) a prevailing pattern of absentee-dominated industry interested in cheap labor and low taxes; (4) federal agencies—such as EDA, OEO, HUD—beginning to develop social and economic programs and seeking local constituencies; (5) private industrial interests and professionals who sought to extend the mandate of these federal agencies. What normally would have happened, what happened generally in the United States during the 1960s, would be for these interests to coalesce around national, *segmental* programs. In

Appalachia the first group, allied with the governors, got into the game early, made peace with the other groups, and created a different structure in ARC.

The Appalachian Regional Commission was created on the initiative of the governors, who had begun meeting to formulate a collective strategy for Appalachian development as early as 1960. President Kennedy, following his well-known exposure to West Virginia poverty in the 1960 primaries, later appointed the President's Appalachian Regional Commission to study the problem, with state government-oriented professionals in a preeminent position. The instrument of regional strategy that was proposed in the commission's 1964 report was a multistate body composed of the governors, who would share power equally with a federal co-chairman appointed by the president.[16] They ruled out a TVA-type agency, or measures to control the exploitation of Appalachia by absentee owners. They envisioned the creation of an institutional structure for planning that would coordinate state and federal programs, and carry out regional economic development activities at both the state and local levels. But the most important aim was to motivate the states to take a bigger role in development and to engage in more planning for the region than they had in the past. The incentive for this was simply that by exhibiting the capacity to plan and manage resources, they would be better able to extract commitments from Congress for monies that otherwise might be spent directly by the federal line agencies. The commission's scheme has been described not entirely in jest as "a collective raid on the federal treasury by the governors." The theory of those who invented ARC was that including the federal presence in the new agency as an equal voting partner would ultimately transform the states' and localities' approaches to development.

Some of the ideas considered by the commission were not adopted in the legislation. One proposal was for a federally chartered corporation, with bonding authority, able to loan money to local development districts. Others, which would have involved the commission in such activities as housing and poverty programs, were also dropped. Apparently, these proposals were dropped because of opposition from private business interests and from federal agencies jealous of their own program prerogatives within the Appalachian counties. According to several accounts, the proponents of ARC surrendered the more radical innovations in order to retain ones that seemed more possible. Patton says:

> The formulators of the program were consumed with the task of (1) securing a large amount of "preferential" federal money for Appalachia and (2) gaining support for permitting the Appalachian states to play a substantial role in allocating the money. In the process a program was molded that is innovative and potentially revolutionary in terms of intergovernmental relations . . . But to gain support to do this, other issues were compromised and the program was forced (1) to limit itself to construction of public facilities and to stay out of "individual"-oriented programs such as housing and the poverty program; (2) to avoid any program threatening the established economic position of coal and private power and utilities; and (3) to abandon any attempt to be an independent region commission TVA–style.[17]

This led to some constraints on the kind of planning that could be undertaken within ARC's mandate:

> Appalachian planning is most clearly an example of management planning. It is a tool to improve the governor's ability to manage state government and intergovernmental relations. In management planning the planners lose the ability for independent criticism and public advocacy of positions contrary to those believed by the governor to be in his best interest. The intent of management planning is to increase the political power and resources of the governor. It is the aim that has incurred the most ringing indictment of the Appalachian program and its planning. Planning becomes the tool of the existing power structure to enhance and perpetuate its control.[18]
>
> The planners, however, were not inclined to complete accommodation and, whenever possible, tried to cut a wide swath around the entrenched special interests and work in areas of political vacuum.[19]

Regional Planning under the Appalachian Regional Commission

The Appalachian Regional Commission, which was created to administer the program legislated in 1965, provided a forum in which state and federal representatives allocated special funds to the Appalachian states, and also a staff that planned and negotiated with federal functional agencies for the creation and expansion of special Appalachian components. By all accounts, the allocations among the states were best characterized initially as a pork-barrel procedure with no serious attempt at an overall rationale. ARC staff will admit as much, and there was until 1975 no overall plan that would justify particular distributions of projects among states.[20] There was instead a procedure of budgeting and program formulation, whereby the state representatives would approve a package put together from their own proposals for submission to Congress for special consideration as the "ARC" program. Most of the funds went for highway construction—$2.1 billion for the first six years of the program—with smaller amounts for health projects ($121 million), land conservation ($19 million), reclamation of mining areas ($33 million), vocational education ($91 million), and a general set of grants to subsidize local matching shares of other federal grant programs ($215 million), and a few much smaller programs.[21] The highway emphasis began with the earlier study commission, apparently at the insistence of the governors, and the locations of the highways were apparently set by the state staff members who worked on the original report.[22]

Thus the ARC staff had a complicated role to play. Was it to do planning, promote planning by the states, or just help lever projects into the states? They in fact did all these things, but the last received top priority. On the one hand, there were reasons not to get too technical. With thirteen governors constituting the predominant power on the commission, it was unlikely that there would be much consensus on goals, and so any planning the staff did was going to be difficult. Moreover, the governors themselves had varying commitments to planning. They needed planning to influence Congress to provide them with resources. There was, by 1978, evidence that a "new breed" of governors was beginning to take a more analytical, planning-oriented approach to state administration and to ARC, but this was much less in evidence in the 1960s. The result of this was that the ARC staff took a very project-oriented approach. Planning and analysis largely played a role of rationalizing and reinforcing the bagaining procedures of the commission, while encouraging the states to adopt some very general procedures and principles in their own planning. But ARC *does* claim to have caused changes in the behavior of the states.

Three main points have been made by ARC planners: the development of a growth-center strategy for concentrating resources in those cities with the most growth potential, a shift of emphasis from public works to services development, and an institutional shift of authority from state offices to multicounty "local development districts" (LDDs), closer to the local level.[23]

Growth Centers. ARC, like other economic development agencies in the 1960s, adopted the idea of growth centers as a strategy for concentrating investments within the region. Agency spokesmen are careful to emphasize the constraints that kept them from implementing a "pure" strategy. There was no growth-center prescription that would affect the allocations among states, for example, and many relatively small places were described as growth centers for limited purposes. But the argument, promulgated in the Washington offices of the ARC staff, had the potential to reinforce any state plans or attitudes toward restricting the kinds of investments that might be made in the rural areas and the smallest cities.

Shift to Services. There was a trend over ARC's history away from an emphasis on capital construction in ARC's infrastructure programs. The staff developed a belief that capital construction, such as public housing and water supply treatment facilities, could best be provided by other federal agencies and that the role of ARC should be to stimulate institutional innovation by providing services. Health programming, for example, shifted from constructing hospital space toward providing medical services in primary care centers. Growth centers began to be conceived as centers for service delivery rather than capital construction. This was a step beyond what might be termed a "crude" growth-center strategy, but it was still center oriented: service centers primarily for the people who lived in the centers or who were willing to travel to them. For the most part the idea of getting services to the people rather than forcing people to go to the services was alien to the planners.

Local Development Districts. The Appalachian Regional Development Act mandates that the states plan. Here, one supposes, is where a coalition of governors, if it is to have any collective effect at all, is most likely to make itself felt. Apparently the theory was that, with an enlarged role and responsibilities for the states and the governors in programming and project initiation, planning would have to follow. The ARC staff certainly did not prod the states overzealously. Its executive director gave the following instructions to his staff as the first set of state plans came in:

> The main criterion for judging any element of a plan is its logic, consistency, and effective use of available knowledge. The continual interchange of additional information and ideas between the states and the staff is essential if the plans are to be realistic and useful. *Remember:* The staff has as much or more to learn from the states in this process.[24]

But the capacity of the states to plan in 1965 was anything but promising. Some states had planning agenices, but most did little planning and had no connection to the budget decisions made by the governor's office. Others had planning staffs in the governor's office, but staffed them with persons with political, not planning, skills. In many cases the governor's office was institutionally handicapped by short tenure, prohibitions against self-succession, and by state constitutions that made large chunks of authority inaccessible to the governor by placing it in the hands of elected administrators. The "ideal" state planning set-up, from the standpoint of the administrators and state officials who were dominant in formulating ARC, would have overcome all these obstacles. The governor's staff would be politically competent to use planning to build an executive constituency, and analytically competent to lay out plans to bring federal and state programs to bear on problems whose solution would satisfy that constituency.

For state planning to be really established, it would need support at the local level. It was the judgment of all concerned, including those involved in the President's commission, that county and municipal governments could not provide such a constituency. Thus at an early stage the notion was to create some sort of multicounty body at the local level that could receive funds and undertake projects. Georgia and Kentucky had been perhaps the first states to invent such a unit, but other states followed, and by the time ARC was established, several federal agencies were promoting multicounty boards. ARCs approach, however, was to proceed slowly. ARC wanted to create a new kind of local unit, but not so boldly that it would be perceived as a threat to existing constituencies of the governors or, for that matter, of local officials.

ARC faced two general difficulties: First, local politics was a "problem" for the governors from the outset. In forming ARC, they had committed themselves to take an active role in the expanding system of intergovernmental grants rather than let local governments deal with federal program sources on their own. Yet they had to operate in states where local machines would be threatened by the feceral programs, even those mediated by the state ARC office. To bypass these local officials could be political suicide for a governor, who needed them to mobilize support in elections and in the legislature. Yet federal programs were often poor incentives, as far as the local organizations were concerned. Local politicians lived not by dispensing federal programs, but by supplying a slate of candidates with whom rural voters would identify personally and by dispensing public works jobs and welfare, neither of which were much under the governors' influence. Local politicians tended to get by through identifying with low taxes and opposition to strong government. This stance was encouraged, morally and financially, by local and corporate business. The following testimonial to this was offered in a commentary on a political boss in Mingo County, West Virginia:

> He was typical of local leaders who served not only their own interests but those of out-of-state corporations: Floyd was paid $6000 a year as secretary of the Mingo County Taxpayers Association, financed by coal companies and other large corporations, which in effect made him a lobbyist for those interests. Local politicians routinely received financial support from corporations concerned about the amount of local taxes that would be assessed.[25]

The second and more general difficulty for ARC was that local politics in Appalachia could be characterized as dependency politics. "Exploitation," observers say, "is the name of the game." Local officials would keep services and taxes low, while the economy stifled opportunity, and sufficient numbers of persons would be employed in political jobs or kept on welfare to man the machinery necessary for reelection. A governor, offering federal programs designed partially to break this kind of cycle, had little to offer this constituency in 1965.

The local development districts (LDDs) were potentially a means of bypassing this constituency of local politicians. They entailed, first, new organizations because they established a new level of administration. Thus county personnel practices could be avoided and professional staff hired at new wage scales on performance criteria. One former federal co-chairman put it this way:

> The ARC designers were extremely distrustful of the county courthouse crowd and the hope [in proposing local development districts] was to somehow finesse them. They hoped for coalitions of local people that would support the development goals of the region.[26]

On the other hand, the LDDs under ARC were at pains to recruit the participation of local elected officials wherever they could. States varied in what they authorized, and there was some change within states, but by the mid 1970s the predominant form mandated a governing board that included a majority of elected officials. This then became an artcle of faith with ARC personnel, who could justify LDDs because they were dominated by people who were elected. This fended off criticism that the LDDs were business dominated (unless one looked at business influence in elections) and the opposite issue: that the LDDs, like OEO-supported community action programs, were dominated by neither businessmen nor county commissioners, but by minorities, the poor, and outside agitators.

The district organizations were gradually established at the local level during the first decade of ARC's existence. They took different forms under different state-enabling statutes. The general picture was one of gradual development of organizational viability and financial support, an accretion of special-purpose federally mandated districts within the general-purpose LDDs, along with a general and persistent lack of visibility for the LDDs compared to county and local government agencies. Beyond this, different organizations have used different strategies. Perhaps the most typical LDD conceives itself mainly as a forum in which local politicians can discuss common problems. The leadership style facilitates this. Staff tend to be relatively nonprofessional and local, but competent to process paperwork for federal grants for the constituent counties and municipalities. The emphasis in this case is on the gradual widening of horizons and the education of the board members. A second LDD strategy is the professional style: a highly trained professional, ordinarily from outside the area, is hired. He hires a professional staff, and the agency moves very fast in attracting outside grants, building its budget, and then in spreading grants around the region. There is also a third strategy that defines professionalism not as technical expertise, but as the development of local-constituency participation and of political leadership within the region. Some LDDs practice this sort of strategy more or less openly; in others it can be practiced within an agency that overtly is dominated by one of the other strategies.

LDD evolution generally has been abetted by more general shifts in the federal grant system and its impact on localities, shifts that have forced increasing reliance on the multicounty organization. These include the simple increase in the number of available programs. An increase in the number of programs puts a premium on the capacity to initiate grant applications, which LDDs can supply and which are particularly needed in rural areas. There are also pressures of a regulatory nature that force localities to depend on LDDs. The first, obvious such pressure was for a regional review function, enacted through the federal Budget Circular A-95 in 1968, typically delegated to LDDs. This required that locally initiated projects pass through a screening procedure to determine if they were redundant with one another, in accordance with general policies, and so on. Other pressures have accumulated as federal and state legislation has begun to take a more intrusive role in local affairs. An example of this is environmental legislation. One component of this requires that open burning of solid waste be stopped, and small dumps be consolidated into county and multicounty disposal operations in accordance with a regional plan. The ability of state or federal agencies to seek injunctions against municipalities that violate the law forces elected officials to begin dealing with the multicounty organization to seek an alternative disposal system. Another example that appeared in West Virginia was a state law that required all ambulance service drivers and attendants to pass minimal training requirements. In order to meet these, it was necessary to provide for training, a function some LDDs, but few county or local governments could perform. Negotiations in at least one LDD then led to federal grants for emergency communications sytems linking the ambulances to the regional hospital, and a general consolidation of localized ambulance services under one regional system linked closely to the LDD.

This sort of squeeze seems to have occurred to varying degrees throughout Appalachia, thus ensuring the continued viability of the LDDS. In them, the governors have a stronger "planning" constituency than they would have without them. The questions in the late 1970s remained: was it just a constituency for grant-hustling? or was it in addition a constituency that would support rational state allocation rather than the traditional political calculus where the state house deals with each local political constituency one by one? No one claimed that a constituency for rational allocations had emerged, though some hoped things might be moving in that direction.

West Virginia was attempting to implement a new ARC-mandated procedure for a rational allocation among districts. Each LDD was to set priorities for projects, then the governor was to take these priorities into account in making allocations to counties. LDD staff feared that the governor would bypass the planning procedure. One director said "it would be interesting to see" whether his board would be willing to set priorities and present a package to Charleston; they generally did not believe this was the way the system worked, but believed that the way to win projects was in one-on-one bargaining with the state house. State planners insisted that LDD priorities would be considered, if not slavishly followed, though one acknowledged:

> As soon as a governor stops dealing with local officials individually he gives up power. As long as he deals one on one with the commissioner or mayor he has direct control.

Further, he said, the federal agencies reinforced this tendency to deal in ad hoc fashion. He once

> asked a HUD official who had a plan from him whether HUD would now follow it. The HUD man could not say. He had no procedure for setting the priorities the state had proposed. HUD, too, could only negotiate one on one.[27]

The ARC now affects the people in Appalachia, on three levels: in a remote way through the federal state commission, in a less remote way through the states, and in a more immediate way through the LDDs. It is a combination of grant-delivery-system and a planning system. But the emphasis has definitely been on the grants and programs, with plans used where they are needed.

It is worth noting that this tendency, which typifies an attitude that prevails generally among planners and local administrators in the United States, entailed for planners, if not for administrators, a new perspective. An ARC staff memorandum that assessed state planning in 1971 registered this new perspective: development planning by the states, the paper found, was largely irrelevant to decisions that had to be made; instead of asking what the ideal future should be, state planners should first look at the actions the governors could take, the choices they were actually facing; only then, should they analyze the plan.[28] An LDD director echoed this view:

> I've tried to fuse planning with action . . . I don't plan anymore in the long range. But you can't convince the commissioners and the mayors of the need for planning with the 1960s type plans. Instead, I make my planners be responsible for the product of their plans. They operate in each functional area with citizens' advisory committees . . . Hopefully once they get projects on the ground and the towns are administering them, then they'll demand regional planning.[29]

Opposition to ARC

Despite its success with state governments and local officials, ARC has been opposed by numerous grass-roots organizations throughout Appalachia. There have also been formulations of an overall regional strategy that poses a more fundamental challenge to United States policy towards Appalachia. This is true despite negligible opposition to the regions' political offices and the absence of an economic basis for a challenge. What has changed is the magnitude of some of the problems, the base for local activists responding to problems, and the relative sophistication of political consciousness. All have changed without much economic or political support.

ARC and almost all other governmental efforts to aid Appalachia have had to build an official constituency. ARC chose to work through the governors and state agencies, but other federal programs that in the mid-1960s chose to make end runs around the states to build clienteles at the local level found ultimately that they had to accommodate their programs to the needs of local officials. TVA in the 1930s and 1940s and the Office of Economic Opportunity in the 1960s were the most prominent examples, but this was also true of other programs.[30] In Appalachia this was particularly true because of the lack of strong local organizations outside of local government. But, if local governments in Appalachia adjusted to or perpetuated the lack of popular organization, there were thousands of communities that, lacking organization, offered a potential clientele of immense strength if anyone could build them up as viable organizations. This was the ground in which grass-roots organizing occurred in the 1960s and 1970s, and that ultimately generated an articulate opposition to official regional policy.

The history of community organizing in the region goes back at least several decades, but it has always faced great odds. Selznick noted the difficulties of developing organization in Tennessee Valley communities during the formative years of TVA. The United Mine Workers had organized in the coal fields in the 1920s and 1930s. Church-sponsored community projects had established a modest record of success. But by the 1960s, voluntary community organizing seemed to be losing ground. The UMW was decimated by the shift to machine technology in the mines and, with a highly centralized and corrupt leadership, offered no encouragement locally. Churches were not taking an active role in communities. The prevalent view was that the Appalachian culture was a handicap that kept the people from participating effectively in the national economy.[31] There was no questioning of local political institutions.

All of this changed after 1960. Part of the change was that the region began to import both problems and government-sponsored "solutions" at a faster rate. But most important was that large numbers of new kinds of people began to enter the region. Most well-known were the Appalachian Volunteers—organized by students and faculty members at Berea College in 1964—and the VISTA volunteers from the Office of Economic Opportunity, who began to enter Appalachia at about the same time. There were also church-sponsored missions that, reflecting a new social consciousness, sent many clergy and others, some from urban areas, into the region. In addition, with increased national interest in Appalachia, there was a general immigration of youngish professionals. Caudill cites the

> young men and women from across the continent who drifted back to the plateau country in search of their Appalachian origins, [and] . . . a host of young men and women who yearned to live lives of constructive service and to whom the acquisition of material wealth was secondary or, sometimes, nonexistent. From Harvard, Yale and Princeton to the University of California at Los Angeles, and from a hundred campuses in between, came inquiries. In the Appalachian coal fields, they supposed, they could dedicate a lifetime to teaching, the ministry, or some other important field.[32]

The vast majority of this new energy went to local activities. VISTA and the Appalachian Volunteers were structured in this way: workers were assigned to communities or counties and instructed to find ways to make themselves useful. The programs of the Office of Economic Opportunity, some of which involved organizing the poor, were necessarily local, and most of the activities that have been reported focus on very concrete, limited issues, whatever one might make of their broader implications.[33] Thus, one OEO-sponsored effort intended to restructure health care services in Floyd County, Kentucky, by giving more representation to the poor on a board of directors.[34] Community Development Corporations (CDCs) were started in several places: local people organizing collective production. Marie Cirrillo described (and organized) one such CDC in Clairfield, Tennessee, whose success helped stimulate other new organizations—health clinics, for example.[35]

Local organizing generated regional support organizations, but there was always a question of how much energy should be diverted from local causes.[36] The Highlander Center, originally a folk school, and the Council of the Southern Mountains, which earlier had devoted itself to the needs of religious groups, got OEO grants to provide technical assistance to community-action organizations. Berea College, the original source of the Appalachian Volunteers, got similar assistance. These organizations, in addition to providing training for community workers on federal contracts, served as communications facilities by holding conferences and publishing journals and newsletters. But two other efforts in the late 1960s and early 1970s were more ambitious in their attempts to articulate regional strategies and mobilize collective action, and they illustrate the limits of regionalism in Appalachia and the constraints under which collective action operates if its source is outside the constituency of official agencies like ARC. These are the Congress for Appalachian Development (CAD), which Harry Caudill and Gordon Ebersole tried to establish in 1966 and 1967, and the Peoples Appalachia Research Collective (PARC), which existed in Morgantown in the early 1970s.

The Congress for Appalachian Development.[37] When Caudill wrote *Night Comes to the Cumberlands* in 1962, he had attacked absentee-owned industries and had called for a "Southern Mountains Authority" vaguely similar to TVA, its authority and finances derived from Congress. He had not gone so far as to suggest local control over basic resources. Thus his major work, which made him the preeminent national spokesman for Appalachia and which was a major instrument for gaining the region national attention during the 1960s, did not clearly challenge the strategies of most Great Society programs, including ARC: added federal subsidies to localities, but no challenge to the most important power bases. In Appalachia, the most important power base is control of land and natural resources. This is largely in the hands of external corporate and financial centers and reinforces compliant local political machines. But during 1963 and 1964 Caudill became convinced that externally financed and controlled programs would not solve Appalachia's problems. Along with Gordon Ebersole, he began to elaborate a program for the establishment of a public authority that would take control of the land and exploit it for the benefit of its people. At first, he continued to advocate an authority on the model of TVA, but then, at Ebersole's urging, he adopted the narrower focus of the Public Utility District (PUD), a device that enables a publicly controlled body to issue bonds, acquire real estate by eminent domain, and construct and operate facilities that generate and distribute electric power. In the Pacific Northwest, where they had been employed successfully, PUDs generated revenue that supported other county services. There, many PUDs used hydroelectric power, and many simply bought power from federal agencies and confined themselves to distribution. In Appalachia, PUDs might not only generate hydroelectric power, but also utilize coal and acquire mining properties for that purpose.

By 1966 a number of prominent activists in the region had become attracted to the idea of a public authority and incorporated themselves as the Congress for Appalachian Development (CAD). Caudill was president, Ebersole was executive director. This group articulated a number of ideas. Caudill and Ebersole continued to develop the idea of the public utility district. Added to this was the application of eminent domain to coal mines, and the sale of electricity generated at the mines to communities outside the region to raise revenues. There was also interest in tax reform, and a rather elaborate scheme for a belt of new towns, lakes, and industrial areas stretching from West Virginia to Tennessee.

CAD envisioned a strategy of elite participation simultaneous with a grass-roots campaign. Notables included such people as former Pennsylvania governor Milton Shapp, and Mrs. Wilbur Cohen, wife of the secretary of health, education and welfare. Caudill made fund raising in Washington and New York his first priority. The second idea was to get a lot of grass-roots support, and to this end CAD planned an Appalachian People's Congress, and they "said they believed that thousands would attend."[38] Along with this, they proposed a popular campaign in Kentucky, Virginia, and West Virginia for legislation that would invest the public utility districts with the power of eminent domain to acquire coal properties. The reaction of the coal operators was opposition and ridicule. But Caudill, in a *New York Times* article, seemed committed to a populist strategy. He said:

> The Appalachian peoples congress this summer is where we will be made or broken . . . I suppose we will be denounced as Bolsheviks. But we are not against profits. It is just that these coal companies have taken everything out and left nothing behind. All we ask for is self-government and the right of economic self-determination.[39]

But by the middle of 1967, neither strategy seemed to be working, and CAD was dead. From the start Caudill and Ebersole had been unable to raise money. Whisnant quotes:

> "Not a dime has been contributed to our cause," Caudill wrote to Ebersole, "and it is now apparent . . . that none will be forthcoming . . . Contact after contact has lauded our goals . . . but like so many of the phonies who run modern America, they are unwilling to move . . . into active struggle for reform . . . I have just about exhausted myself in the effort."[40]

Meanwhile, the idea of a People's Congress, organization of which had been delegated to the Appalachian Volunteers, was abandoned, and any chance of generating local support for CAD was lost with it.

Peoples Appalachia. In the late 1960s a group of activists and academics constituted themselves in Morgantown, West Virginia, as the Peoples Appalachia Research Collective (PARC). There, for five years, they published a journal, *Peoples Appalachia*, which was devoted to reporting the activities of community and labor activists in the region and to helping in the formulation of a theoretical and policy basis on which community organizing could move ahead. While a range of positions was represented in articles that appeared in *Peoples Appalachia*, this range went far beyond the populism of CAD. One theme was opposition to existing federal programs in Appalachia, in which PARC was close to a number of Appalachian writers and journalists, including Caudill. One of these, which was reprinted in an edition of pieces on Appalachia and received national attention, was Robb Burlage's "Toward a Peoples ARC," which commented on the Appalachian Regional Commission's inability to address the question of absentee ownership of resources and criticized ARC's growth-center strategy, highway program, and apparent accommodation to strip mining, land development, and recreation interests.[41]

Second, PARC attempted to articulate the theoretical and practical possibility of linking the labor movement and community development. An issue of *Peoples Appalachia* devoted to the reform movement in the United Mine Workers, attested to the contribution a revitalized union might make to local communities: for example, health clinics, the contribution of union halls as community centers, and support of social services.[42] There were also theroetical pieces. The final issue of the journal, in 1974, discussed the contributions of Proudhon to a rationale for community organizing.[43] Finally, there was some effort to formulate a regional support system for local organizing.

This regionalism, which contrasted with ARC's approach, began by redefining the problem. They rejected the diagnosis that isolation was the difficulty, and pointed instead to the export of profits and control mechanisms that was impeding the development of an indigenous entrepreneurial class. Local community-development corporations were proposed as part of the answer, but the article also suggested the need for support by a regional authority that would represent them and provide some regional-government functions: pollution control, soil conservation, forestry, trustee for regional resources, and eventually, some business enterprise, and planning. The following principles were to guide planning:

1. The development of people out of conditions of exploitation, poverty, and oppression is more important than rapid increases in income per person.
2. Production must be geared to use, not profits.
3. There should be relative equality in the participation of the social product.
4. There should be worker control over production.
5. There should be community control over what is pro-

duced, the allocation of jobs and the incentive system.
6. Assurance of cultural pluralism, that is breaking down of the contradiction between countryside and city.

In addition, the article listed strategies that would "restrain the re-emergence of neocapitalist development":

1. Success is measured in terms of general social criteria rather than in terms of profits or rates of growth.
2. Trickle-down development strategies are rejected in favor of worst first or everyone growing together.
3. Technology is not imported but great reliance is placed on learning by doing (which includes the study of advanced technologies developed elsewhere).
4. Increasing reliance on moral incentives which implies continuous education.[44]

Peoples Appalachia ceased publication after its Summer 1974 issue, and PARC continued in a different form. It no longer was primarily a research organization. Some of its members moved away, while others entered the scene primarily interested in community organizing around issues. The demise of *Peoples Appalachia* has been explained in various ways. On the one hand, many felt that PARC was too theoretical. The journal, they point out, was never self-supporting, and the people they wanted to reach within Appalachia did not read it. It was pretty much confined to the intellectuals. At the same time, many other organizing activities, less well developed when PARC started, had gained momentum throughout the area by 1974. These included local organizing efforts by mine workers in the UMW, the development of the environmental movement around local strip-mining issues, and organizing around such problems as local revenue sharing and taxes.

The Growth of Local Organizing. While PARC was changing its interests, other national poor people's organizing movements were changing strategies. George Wiley, the guiding force behind the development of national welfare rights organizations, turned in 1973 to a broader strategy embodied in the Movement for Economic Justice, aimed at attracting a broader coalition across race and class lines. Wiley had some influence in Appalachia, and had been in contact with PARC.[45] Around 1973 some of the PARC people and others in Appalachia became interested in a broader-based movement, and sought to articulate a relationship between those interested in strip mining and tax reform and the more class-based issues they had focused on earlier.

Around Morgantown, many organizations were brought together by the Mountain Community Union (MCU), which included many former members of PARC, but was now expanded to include others. By 1977, MCU was a coalition of fifteen organizations operating mostly in Monongalia and Marion counties, with offices in Morgantown and Fairmont. Four committees had been established to coordinate activities: environmental, labor support, community support, and human rights. All the organizing issues were reported in a monthly paper, the *Mountain Journal*, which helped pull all these interests together. *Mountain Journal* was more local, less theoretical than *Peoples Appalachia*, but it covered much of the same organizing activity and had articles by some of the same people.

PARC also sought to bring together other organizations, hoping to spread the idea of community unions throughout Appalachia. In 1973 PARC took a major part in the annual conference of the Council of the Southern Mountains (CSM). It suspended publication of the journal while various members prepared working papers on "peoples' development." These covered such topics as coal taxes, land reform, strip-mine legislation, revenue sharing, and an "Appalachian people's responses to the energy crisis," which were then made available at the conference. The shift to these issues was a conscious effort to broaden the constituency for the basic ideas PARC had been formulating. Thus, the council adopted the following resolution:

> The CSM sees this next year as the Year of Mountains Community Union; we plan to emphasize the reorganizing

and expanding of the CSM board with representation from community unions in all areas of the mountains by the end of this year; the CSM board commits its leadership to this emphasis and calls for staff support toward this goal.[46]

The term, "community union," did not catch on outside of Morgantown, but, in general, the amount of community organizing going on seemed much greater during 1977 than a decade earlier. At the end of the 1960s, what organizing there was was built on a limited number of issues: welfare rights, antipoverty programs, the Black Lung Association, and the beginnings of the environmental movement. The Miners for Democracy movement within the UMW absorbed some of this energy for a time, but then disbanded with Arnold Miller's election in 1972. Strip-mining issues were fought at the state level, while many of the activists who had been employed in poverty programs were moving into relatively less exposed and less public positions. In 1977, organizing had a new vigor throughout Appalachia, and it seemed that much more of it was going on. In West Virginia, the environmental movement now had active organizations fighting strip mining in twenty counties. Save Our Cumberland Mountains (SOCM) was active in Tennessee, and was beginning to branch out from strip mining to more general community-development issues. The East Tennessee Research Corporation was producing analyses of TVA policies. Community Development Corporations seemed to be thriving. *Peoples Appalachia* reported twenty active cases in 1974.[47]

Local organizing in the mines continued after 1972.[48] The Miners for Democracy (MFD) campaign of 1972, which put Miller in office, was a close and harrowing affair. In 1969 a previous challenger to the UMW leadership, Jock Yablonski, had been murdered with his family, a crime for which UMW president Tony Boyle was later convicted of conspiracy. The challengers now endured constant threats of violence, and the MFD campaign was conducted, not primarily to organize the top-heavy UMW at the local level, but to do enough local campaigning to effect a change at the top. Miller made promises of local organizational improvements, but after the elections he disbanded the MFD. Nevertheless, mine organizing continued through the 1970s, mainly around the right-to-strike committees, which promulgated this as the main locally initiated issue in the 1977–78 contract dispute and strike. Moreover, during the 1977–78 strike, union activities spilled over into community activities, at least to some extent. Miners' support committees appeared in several places. One, in Beckley, West Virginia, was at particular pains to lay out the links between union organizing and community organizing:

> We believe that the UMWA health plan has fostered quality health care for the entire community, and we support the return of full health benefits to miners and pensioners. . . . Our support work so far has included petition drives, educational forums, and efforts to counter negative media coverage of the strike—such as frequent responses to television and newspaper editorials. Recently we organized a Miners Free Clinic for all activist and retired miners and their families. We also are involved in support and fund-raising for miners who are facing charges that have to do with alleged strike-related acts.[49]

There were miners support groups in many parts of Appalachia during the strike, but the strike's outcome left them without much to do. The structure that might have tied the union to the community was largely dismantled by the new contract: the union lost control of its health plan, and other provisions seemed likely to weaken the union. On the other hand, rank-and-file organizing, led by a new cadre of younger miners, seemed to be very vigorous. The result ultimately might be a more vigorous union at the local level with organizing capacity that might spill over into other community affairs.

The Appalachian Alliance. The hope of using the Council of the Southern Mountains as a regional support organization for community unions may have been premature in 1973, given the desire of most activists and organizers of that period to occupy themselves with projects that would provide tangible benefits that, in turn, would build clienteles. But by 1977 regionalism had developed again. One person in Morgantown said:

> In the 1960s, most activists in Appalachia came from a few movements: The Appalachian Volunteers and Welfare Rights. Then, they went off in several directions. Some went into the counterculture, in communes. Others went to work within the system in communities. Now, they are beginning to come together again.[50]

Another said:

> New people, not previously connected, are getting involved now. Some liberals: former Jay Rockefeller supporters who are disillusioned, an ex-mountain counterculture person publishing an activist newspaper, people politicized by strip-mining issues. The sectarian left has begun to develop some credibility among the miners.[51]

In 1977, the George Wiley strategy seemed to be developing. Whether consciously perpetrated by the organizers who hoped to engage the middle class in strip mining and tax structure issues, or because of the actual progress of strip mining and fiscal difficulties, a new middle-class constituency was beginning to join the poor. The initial impetus for the Appalachian Alliance apparently developed out of the frustrations of the Tug Valley Recovery Center, a group organized in 1977 to help deal with the effects of floods that had periodically devastated southern West Virginia. Members of this group soon felt a need to be in touch with other groups dealing with similar problems. The focus shifted from flood recovery to a variety of problems, all of which reflected themes that had repeated themselves: how to get action in the peoples' interest out of local officials, when most wealth and power was in the hands of large corporations, typically owned elsewhere; and how to get heard in Washington and in the state capitals. In the spring they called a meeting that involved some of the former PARC people, but also a much broader spectrum. One idea that emerged was to push for an energy policy, including public ownership of utilities and coal mines, with royalties going to support a community development bank—something like the CAD idea. This idea was particularly current in West Virginia, where State Senator Si Galperin was introducing a Model Energy Bill that would set up something like this. But there were many diverse interests represented in the alliance, and it did not seem like an opportune moment to push for priorities among policies. There did seem to be agreement on the need for a forum where relatively diverse interests could exchange views. and to create a voice for Appalachia that could speak to the region and the nation.

The alliance did become a rather active forum and voice for Appalachia. One member arranged a meeting with the White House domestic staff in June 1978, where some twenty Appalachian activists presented short discussions of the kinds of projects they were engaged in and the problems they were encountering with the federal agencies. One participant said later, the White House people were "amazed" at the reports. The problem of projecting Appalachia to centers of power in metropolitan America was a real one.

Later in the year, the alliance held more meetings and larger numbers of people began to attend: two hundred came to a meeting in August, seventy-five in January, despite bad weather. In 1978, one estimate was that about fifty organizations had joined the alliance, and that this represented about one hundred committee people. The organization had a ten-person steering committee, and was facing the question of what strategy it might then pursue, what issues it would focus on. It remained somewhat fluid and pragmatic, different in several respects from the regional groups like CAD and PARC that had preceded it. First, it had a broader base than either group, and seemed likely to persist. It had no budget, but it was not vulnerable because its constituent organizations had budgets. It did not have to depend on difficult fund-raising efforts, as had Caudill and Ebersole. One of its steering-committee members noted "I think it's better if we don't have a budget; having money would just screw us up"; and while the alliance might not have wanted to make this a principle, there seemed to be a desire to remain flexible. Another indication of this was the unwillingness to adopt a statement of objectives that would deter the group from remaining together. A pamphlet prepared in 1978 opened with this provision:

> Different members of the alliance have different ideas about what should be done. The short papers that follow are not intended as comprehensive statements of policy, but as reflections to the discussions that have been held since the first meeting of the Alliance in May 1977. . . . If there is a single unifying belief among them, it is that Appalachia has been a national sacrifice area long enough and that the people who live and work in Appalachia must provide the resources and the energy and the dedication to bring this long grim era to an end.[52]

There was even the thought that the alliance might not have to remain an organization that provides a comprehensive Appalachian policy perspective; that it might turn out to be more effective to organize around some of the more specific themes represented in the alliance. These included energy and coal, housing, tax reform, the abolition of strip mining, health care, and Appalachian migrants in metropolitan areas. But even if this happened, it seemed that the alliance would be strong enough to be reconstituted when necessary. The membership seemed strong in at least two respects. One is that their numbers had grown and their experience had increased. A statement was made in February 1978 about local mine organizing:

> The men have gone through a painful ten-year education. . . . During those years they learned . . . the grim details about black lung and how to use a strike to get legislative relief; they discovered the extent of their leaders corruption and how to unseat those leaders. They trained themselves to act forcefully in their own interests.[53]

This is related to the experience of the Appalachian community organizers. Beth Spence, one of the founders of the alliance mentioned the same decade:

> Ten years ago there were maybe two hundred people working in the mountains, and we thought we could work a

> revolution. Now we have had a decade working with specific groups. We have less rhetoric, more experience. We are more pragmatic and able to work together.[54]

One might ask, does pragmatism and an ability to hold together count for more than a unified policy position? The alliance program, as represented in the frankly less than comprehensive statements of the 1978 pamphlet, seemed less well composed than the programs PARC presented at times. But one sensed that the alliance people had at least a minimal position from which to build a program and a consensus. The idea that absentee corporate control and local dependency were the roots of Appalachia's problems seemed reasonably well established among them; it had been radical a decade earlier. And regarding the Appalachian Regional Commission, whose central failure in local eyes was its inability to confront absentee control, the alliance was willing to attack. "Putting ARC in charge of the interests of the people of the mountains," the pamphlet suggested, would be ". . . like putting Dracula in charge of the blood bank"[55] Ten years earlier, Caudill had ARC castigated only as being pitifully inadequate, while he tried in vain to get sufficient local support behind a locally controlled authority. It seemed in 1978 that more commitment and many more experienced people were available to push for something like what Caudill had proposed. The "Dracula" statement did not seem radical at all.

In one other respect, the alliance was strong. It had access to, if not great influence within, power centers and media in and outside of Appalachia. The White House meeting was one indication; another was the appearance of some of the alliance statements in the national press. *The Nation* made use of the pamphlet, for example, in a March 1978 editorial that provided one of the first balanced statements on the 1977–78 coal strike.

Local Government as Opposition?

In many places there was opposition to federal regional policy in Appalachia, and there were places where the opposition was able to unite and, as in the case of the Appalachian Alliance, to begin to lay out an opposition program. But in almost every place the opposition was scattered, and there was little formal authority for it to capture: no governorships, congressional or senatoral seats, or state offices. Nor was there very much effort to capture local political offices.

The viability of Appalachian local politics as an arena for opposition is problematic, an issue about which the core culture and the local opposition do not agree and hardly communicate. At a conference on regionalism, held in Morgantown in 1978, Donald Whitehead, a former federal co-chairman of ARC and an articulate and sympathetic outsider, helped demonstrate this. His position was that the failure of many local activists to seek elective office was itself part of the Appalachian problem.[56] His remarks, and the exchange it prompted from David Whisnant, an ARC critic in the audience, are worth some extended quotation:

> Whitehead: The first trip that I took into the Appalachian region after going with the commission was into East Kentucky . . . to meet ______. During the conversation with her she launched an attack on the local political structure . . . She really expressed outrage, and so I said to her, why don't you run for Congress here and change things? She said, "I'd never get elected." . . . I said, "why not?" She said, "The coal companies would send down a lot of money and oppose me." I said, "Well, why don't you tell your friends to take the money and vote for you anyway?" She said, "No, I couldn't do that, they wouldn't vote for me. They would think that I was getting uppity. They'd think I was getting above myself."
>
> Instantly I knew I was back in the environment . . . where people had a heritage and a tradition that placed such a high value on supposed independence and self-reliance that people had forgotten how to work in cooperation and conjunction with neighbors . . . It hit me very strongly that if I was going to do anything with the Appalachian assignment, I was going to have to do that assignment as intensely political . . . and about as far from Boston where the Boston Irish had introduced me to the kind of spontaneous and

enthusiastic political activity that I quite enjoyed—about as far from that as I could get.
Whisnant: Your conclusion was that when she chose not to run for office . . . she was an example of your independent Appalachian. . . . Well, in fact _____ spent three to four years in the late sixties in an intensely political organization with her neighbors. They formed the _____ County citizens association . . . The point . . . is that when her neighbors decided to become politically active, they did not necessarily conclude that running for office in that county or becoming active in the development district was the way to go. What they did was to get themselves together a local political organization, taking people from the hollows where they live. ARC has never understood that.
Whitehead: This is where we part company because the Appalachian Commision is devoted to the idea that the major change is through political structure . . . I am very well aware of activities . . . but *not* running for office—that's a big difference. It seems to me that the way to make a change is to gain political power and to be in a position to make decisions to create change and that's much different than simply being a part of a group that takes a position on a couple of issues. So this is just a basic difference of opinion of the best strategies to gain certain ends.

Whitehead and his questioners were far apart in their basic views of Appalachian politics and its potentials for change. He thought the electoral process was responsive to competition; the opposition thought the political system itself was stacked against them, and that unless something was done to alter that system they were better off working outside it, perhaps changing enough attitudes that, at a later time, they could exert more pressure on it.

One final possibility needs more examination: the LDD strategy *was* an effort to change the structure of local politics. Why is this not seen as a hope for the future by the Appalachian opposition? The predominant response is that the LDDs are invisible. "They don't do anything," or "They just seem irrelevant. I'd guess if you asked people, 99 percent would say they had never heard of the _____ Planning and Development Council."

Part of the problem for the LDDs is that they are identified with "planning," which has a bad name. One former PARC member said: "Frankly, the whole idea just turns me off." Partly, it is that planning is remote from real action, or has been in the past. During the 1960s the main support for planning was in HUD's "701" program, which gave funds to the states to support "comprehensive plans" at the county and local levels. These were physical plans and could be tied only to such instruments as zoning and urban renewal, which few Appalachian towns were in a position to enact. Moreover, since there was little local-level planning expertise, they were typically done by consultants from outside. These plans quickly gained a reputation as "rip-offs."

The other problem with planning, however, is that where it has been related to action, many people have seen the action as the wrong action. One case that received some publicity was the planning that would have moved residents out of rural hollows in Letcher County, Kentucky, so as to leave more land for coal mining, and that was opposed strongly as "communistic".[57] The growth-center bias, particularly in the regional agencies, is felt strongly by many Appalachians, who see it as both a culture and class bias. One person commented as follows:

> The growth-center ideology of many LDDs has made them hostile to service programs with an outreach component. Most LDD planners seem to wish in their heart-of-hearts that "these damn hillbillies would move down out of those hollers so we can help 'em."[58]

Despite this, the seeds of opposition to state and federal policies do exist in the LDDs. There are, to begin with, natural tensions between the LDDs and the state and federal agencies that fund and oversee them. LDD directors and boards like to be as independent as possible. Executive directors tend to present themselves as "running interference" for their boards against the higher-level bureaucracies. Moreover, the directors do not always take their constituencies as given. Some of them see themselves as attempting to "develop" them, and comments like "We're trying to bring West Virginia into the twentieth century" are typical. Most common is a modernization strategy. First, the LDD begins to tap grant sources and get projects for the county commissioners and mayors. Once the local officials begin to use these resources as political instruments, the LDD encourages them to hire administrators and planners to get their own grants and projects, while the LDD staff moves into a backup role.

Sometimes, the LDD goes beyond the elected official constituency, directly to the people. This is unlikely to be a dominant strategy, though there are some claims that some LDDs do this. But many LDDs have direct constituency-organizing components in which the committees set-up for "citizen participation" are used as leverage to get state or federal resources. In one agency, it was possible to maintain both programs of direct interest to the elected officials on the board and programs for the elderly, which involved direct organizing. Partly this was possible because of the availability of federal funds for programs that specify "advocacy" and "outreach" functions. This component of the LDD office is able to gain credits from its board of elected officials because it provides popular services directly. At the same time, other LDD-initiated programs are operated directly by the towns and counties, and the board can not easily give up the one without hurting the other.

Outreach and advocacy programs attract a kind of professional who, while not dominant in the LDDs, finds a haven there. These persons came into contact with some of the highly participatory organizing styles that developed and spread during the 1960s and later, and many of them found employment in the LDDs. There is no possibility that the LDDs could give them free rein, but at a minimum, they do provide a wage and often at least some scope to engage in constructive organizing work. One reason this can happen is the professionalism of some executive directors. One LDD staff member said:

> A few of us here are consumer oriented. Times are changing. The young staff people are much more consumer ori-

> ented. The director isn't, but he has hired some who are and he acts as a buffer for them; he is solid on professionalism, rigid about not hiring people for political reasons.[59]

But professionalism works in two ways in the LDDs. On the one hand, it confronts a traditional political system and attempts to build a new, popular constituency. As one LDD professional said:

> There has been a significant in-migration of a new kind of person. One county (in West Virginia) now has four food co-ops. The Eastern Panhandle has gotten a new in-migration of professional people, college graduates who don't want to stay in the cities. In one of the LDDs there is a University of Pennsylvania graduate for the director.[60]

The other side of professionalism is the drive to rationalize, which leads the LDD to get into direct service delivery and to establish professional managers in the counties and towns. This also challenges the local politicians, but mobilizes a business constituency rather than a popular one.

In Appalachia, the test of the amount of change the LDDs produce will be measured in the ultimate composition of the local elected officials and their constituencies. There is some change, though very little of it is reflected in elections. In Morgantown, a university town, one of the faculty said:

> A new type of politician is coming into power here. In Monongalia County, we used to be dominated by a rural, conservative machine under the sheriff. Now there is competition with the university-business faction. Now the new county judge, Larry Starcher, is building another machine with progressive candidates for county office.[61]

Certainly the LDDs do not produce these changes, but they reinforce them. In the region containing Morgantown, one county commissioner was said to be running for reelection almost wholly on the basis of what the LDD had accomplished. But these political themes are very minor in Appalachian local government. The examples cited here are exceptional, and the LDDs remain behind the scenes in almost all cases.

Planning. Was there opposition planning in Appalachia? Yes, in at least a rudimentary form, within the meaning I laid out in Chapter 1. There was progress toward an opposition theory or rationale for planning. There was progress toward a consensus on this rationale among diverse intellectuals and persons involved in organizing constituencies of the poor and some others. There was a great increase in the number of persons who knew this theory and rationale, who were capable of carrying out sophisticated analyses that would lead to specific policies and programs. There was a growing experience among organizers and administrators. Specialized opposition groups organizing around health or land or agricultural marketing seemed to have put together a critique, a program, and a plan for the future for their issues.

It is true that the Peoples Appalachia Research Collective and CAD were defunct by 1975, and the Appalachian Alliance was a loose confederation not given to planning in a formal sense. The earlier formulations of *Peoples Appalachia* were only a shadow compared to the published and titled *Economic Plan for Wales* achieved by Plaid Cymru. But rudimentary opposition formulations were composed, and they were widely disseminated among Appalachian activists who, by 1979, had a stronger and more organized doctrine and program than they had had previously.

Chapter 5

Territorial Opposition

In Chapter 1 I described Wales and Appalachia as "hegemony": low local capacity, high levels of penetration by metropolitan firms and government agencies. I hypothesized that this was an unstable situation and that territorial opposition (a transition toward separatism) would result.

What evidence of this is there in Wales and Appalachia? The case is clearer in Wales than in Appalachia, but in both places interests and organizations developed into a territorial opposition that included workers. The first part of this chapter establishes that territorial opposition occurred. The next section attempts to describe the conditions producing territorial opposition. At one level is an underlying condition true not only of peripheral areas like Wales and Appalachia, but of the modern state: a central government and external corporate apparatus, though closely attuned to and reinforcing vertical constituencies, are continually surprised by and at times unable to cope with emerging territorial groups. A second condition is the changing nature of the relations between central institutions and localities revealed in the course of events in Wales and Appalachia in the 1960s and 1970s. Next, territorial opposition is analyzed in light of the hypotheses suggested in Chapter 2, in order to more thoroughly explain the phenomenon. Finally, there is the question raised in Chapter 1 about political strategy. What is the best basis upon which to organize a political movement for redistribution of wealth and power: class or territory?

Evidence of Territorial Opposition

Territorial organizations, and coalitions of territorially based organizations, existed in both Wales and Appalachia. This was much stronger in Wales, where the political evidence was on the surface in the form of the activities of Plaid Cymru, including office holding both in local councils and in Parliament. In Wales, the characteristics of territorial defense suggested in Chapter 1 were all present. Community-level organizations, the attempt to forge links between territorial and working-class interests, and separatism were strong, and Plaid Cymru pulled them all into a coherent ideology. At the local level, Plaid Cymru contested elections in each municipality, as well as for each parliamentary seat, each compaign requiring a political party organization. Plaid Cymru, originally rooted in the universities and among clergymen and teachers, was not necessarily the spearhead for all local "territorial defense" issues. Struggles to save a village from inundation in a reservoir project, or to oppose new towns in Mid-Wales or Llantrisant, for example, were local issues that produced organizations like the Heads of the Valleys Standing Conference and were normally fought by ad hoc organizations with involvement of local government officials who were typically not Plaid Cymru members.

It is important to keep Plaid Cymru analytically distinct from Welsh nationalism. There were independent local organizing projects, and there were other Welsh organizations with their own separatist programs. The latter created a general context for Welsh nationalism, ranging from the Welsh League of Youth, with over forty thousand members over a period of decades, to relatively temporary lobbies and campaigns.[1]

As such organizations indicate, it was possible to mobilize voters on Welsh issues, and Plaid Cymru, at least through the 1960s, concentrated its attention on parliamentary, rather than local elections. But Plaid Cymru exploited this local base as issues accumulated, and by the mid 1970s there were reports of a new local strategy, signaled by Plaid Cymru control over the Merthyr Tydfil and Rhymney district councils after the 1976 municipal elections.[2] Merthyr was the first local council over which the party had gained a majority, an achievement that at the time seemed as valuable as would an additional parliamentary seat. In all, Plaid Cymru moved from a total of 46 municipal seats in 1973 to 109 in 1976.[3] In the following year it contested 236 seats in the county elections, three times its effort three years earlier, with modest improvement: from 22 to 37 seats captured.[4] Even after its defeats in 1979, it was possible to argue that it had the best local organization of any political party in Wales.[5]

Plaid Cymru also tried to engage working-class support and participation, with increasing success after 1966.[6] The established alliance between unions and the Labour Party, and the tendency of unions to ally with British national union organizations rather than cast their lot with Welsh nationalism were major obstacles. For a time the unions resisted nationalism, and encouraged by London, blocked the establishment of a Wales Trades Union Council (TUC). This position weakened in the 1960s, however, and in 1973 the Wales TUC emerged with a nationalist program and strong leadership. While the Wales TUC operated more as a force for change operating on the Labour Party than as a Plaid Cymru resource, it did not hurt Plaid Cymru. Union members defected to Plaid Cymru from Labour Party ranks in bringing Plaid Cymru the success it had in certain South Wales constituencies and localities.[7]

Development of a separatist ideology and program helped Plaid Cymru integrate community-defense and working-class interests. Until the 1960s, political disengagement from Britain was not a necessary part of Welsh nationalism, and the party was a political expression of a number of nationalist Welsh organizations which advocated such causes as bilingual road signs, the use of Welsh language in the schools, or the establishment of a Welsh Council or parliament, without taking the further step of advocating a break with Britain. Advocacy of political separation from Britain in the 1960s made it possible to clarify other concerns, as well as distinguish Plaid Cymru programs from those of the other parties. Phil Williams articulated the party's position with respect to the problem of the defense of community, linking community destruction to British regional policy, and the Plaid Cymru economic research group detailed the position in *An Economic Plan for Wales*.[8] The link to the interests of the working class was less explicit, though this was the purpose of gestures in the direction of worker self-management. Plaid Cymru claimed, however, that any program for Wales would perforce be in the interests of workers because of the concentration of working-class people in Wales. The turn toward an emphasis on economic policy in the 1960s, and the gains made in South Wales, tend to verify this claim. The charge that Welsh nationalism was largely a cultural phenomenon felt by "preachers and teachers" no longer had as much force. The electoral defeats of 1979, caused partly by scapegoating of nationalist positions during the campaign, attested to the continuing vulnerability of Plaid Cymru on this score. But the campaign probably pushed the nationalists into a more worker-oriented program than before, and after 1979 there were new efforts to move the party leftward.[9]

Territorial organization in Appalachia registered, in a weak fashion, all of the characteristics evident in Wales: community organization, working-class participation, and an overarching program stressing disengagement of Appalachian politics and economy from national control. The big difference was lack of a regional party organization and any realistic chance of winning state or local elections, except occasionally. But community organizing and struggles for community defense were widespread and growing. In contrast with the parliamentary and electoral strategy pursued by Plaid Cymru through the 1960s, Appalachian activists concentrated on local issues and avoided—due to relative weakness—electoral politics. The Appalachian Alliance was composed of fifty primary organizations, of which the overwhelming majority were locally rooted organizing groups. Their aggregate "size"—if there can be such an adjective in this case—was perhaps comparable to that of Plaid Cymru. There are no figures, but it seems a conservative guess that each of the fifty constituent organizations might have contained two to five leaders who put in large portions of their time, plus fifty to one hundred or more workers who could be called on temporarily on particular issues. This would suggest 100 to 250 very active people, plus 2,500 to 5,000 other members of grass-roots organizations in Appalachia, which compares to estimates of 2,500 or more of paid-up membership in Plaid Cymru during the early 1960s.[10]

Working-class participation in Appalachian local community organizing efforts is also hard to estimate. Most or all of the organizations involved in the Appalachian Alliance considered the poor as either a dominant or an important part of their clienteles. For many of these organizations, the interests of the poor and of the communities they lived in were all but coterminous, since the communities were poor. The link-up of community organizing with union organizing in the industrial work place remained weak, superficially paralleling the limited interaction between Plaid Cymru and the unions in Wales. In Appalachia, however, unlike the situation in Wales, no strong central organization existed to encourage contacts between community and union organizers, and each kind of activity found it difficult to move outside its own arena. This limitation was largely imposed by lack of resources rather than by principle or ideology. Community organization in Appalachia was not generally business-oriented or antiunion.

A policy of disengagement from national economic and political power gradually became widespread among Appalachian activitists. While not strictly comparable to separatism as a formal political objective, the underlying rationale was similar to that of Plaid Cymru and other devolutionists in Wales. The members of the Appalachian Alliance came to expect no benefits from simply increased attention from Washington or from national centers of economic power. This was a change from the situation in the 1960s, when the notion of Appalachia as a "colony" was just beginning to be broached by a few intellectuals, and the dominant reform proposal was for a TVA-like federal agency and for increased road access and economic links to major metropolitan areas. Growing economic and political sophistication regarding the real workings of the policies of the central government brought about the transition to widespread adoption of the disengagement position among community activists in Appalachia, paralleling—though less dramatic than—

Plaid Cymru's early movement toward separatism from nationalism. As in Wales, the rationale of disengagement provided an argument that supported community organizers and industrial workers. Both organizers and workers could see the problem as too much of the wrong kind of central bureaucracy: the United Mine Workers on the one hand, and federal and state bureaucracies on the other, were attacked as too concerned with accommodating the needs of large-scale corporate business to be useful to Appalachian communities. The policy of disengagement made some headway in Appalachia, although it found little political expression.

Underlying Conditions

This evidence presents a problem of explanation. Why did opposition occur in the form that it did? Why was it stronger in Wales? Why did it take a more coordinated, political form in Wales? Why, in both places, did the goals of opposition shift—from the demands for access that preoccupied some Appalachians and most Welsh prior to the establishment of ARC and the Welsh Office, to the more radical thrust toward disengagement and separatism that developed later?

Central Response. A first cut at explanation requires a review of certain underlying conditions that affected both places, in particular at the center. Central governments, in both the United States and Great Britain, had difficulty giving much prominence to territorial coalitions. The federal granting agencies, the Appalachian Regional Commission, the state governments, the British central ministries and the Welsh Office usually failed to give serious attention to groups not organized in the usual ways. Central governments implicitly defined political actors as those groups sufficiently organized and strategically situated for access to legislators and bureaucracies. Thus, in Appalachia, there was a sharp schism on the issue of Appalachian culture. Almost all public officials had the greatest difficulty accepting the alleged apolitical predispositions of Appalachians. It went beyond any suggestion of bias toward those in power. Bureaucrats and politicians did not see, they did not have the perceptual apparatus to take into account, the interests of those who did not mobilize politically in the accustomed ways. ARC accomplished a major organizational change in creating the LDDs, but this was aimed at a new constituency of elected officials, not the mass of people.

One of the byproducts of these political blinders was that groups organized territorially did not get noticed as easily, as regularly, as groups organized vertically. The UMW, the TUC, the BCOA all had offices in the capital, and transacted most of their business there. They were part of a system of regularly interacting interest groups, highly visible at the center. Territorial groups got shorter shrift. No one in London easily noticed Tŷ-Toronto Community Center in Aberfan or the planner for Merthyr Tydfil; and the activities of the Welsh Language Society, the Mid-Wales Industrial Association and even Plaid Cymru were regularly distorted. Appalachia was different, perhaps, but imperial nearsightedness existed in Washington, too: a member of the Tug Valley Recovery Center asked why a federally subsidized agency responsible for flood recovery had to be located two hours from the flooded area, and was told "because that's where there is a Holiday Inn."

National capitals were sometimes surprised by what happened in peripheral places. Thus much of the opposition in Wales took London by surprise—the opposition to the Llantrisant proposals, for example. More generally, the success of Plaid Cymru at various times surprised most people in London and in the government. Similarly, the White House staff was surprised by the revelations of the Appalachian Alliance at the "summit" in 1977. Perhaps the main example, however, was the rank-and-file resistance of coal strikers to successive settlements proposed by the BCOA and accepted by UMW headquarters and the White House. Neither the White House nor the UMW hierarchy had gauged local sentiment and organization. The most spectacular distortions were purveyed by the national press, which consistently stated the strike issues as they were interpreted in Washington, which in turn was sometimes the exact opposite of what was felt in the coal fields.

Washington and London saw the energies represented by these territorial groups, whether rank-and-file miners, organizers of the Appalachian Alliance, or Welsh decentralists of various sorts, as markets and as potential clients, but not as forces capable of changing the goals and structure of programs devised for more general consumption. Central agencies and institutions tried to defuse and absorb local activism: thus the attempts of the Labour Party to reflect the territorial interests in Wales, and of the UMW to get the loyalty of the rank-and-file miners in Appalachia. In the process both sought to civilize and to narrow local demands. Labour offered regional policy incentives and employment in Wales, while the UMW offered bargained wage increases. Broader local demands were compromised. This pattern was repeated for numerous central institutions and their local constituencies.

What external firms and governments did recognize, in fact, was the importance of local organization for the administration of policies made centrally. This motivated the creation of the Welsh Office and the administrative devolution that followed it, as well as the creation of the new local administration in the multicounty development districts in Appalachia. It would be wrong to say that there was no independence in these new agencies, for they found at least some local constituency. But they were certainly carefully organized, with a great deal of central control exerted as they developed; and for a time the main condition for their survival was their ability to be useful to the central government, not to the local constituency. The new agencies had to have some local constituency to be useful, but developing local support was not their most important goal.

Although the central governments of both countries were alike in their failure to recognize the potency of territorial issues, the threat of separatism was stronger in Wales than in Appalachia because of different cultural, political and economic forces. The most obvious contrast is Welsh cultural homogeneity, a Welsh language, and a Welsh national tradition. These elements were much less pronounced or absent in Appalachia. Economic and political organization were, however far more important differences. Centralized absentee control of economic activity was more pronounced in Wales, whereas widespread and concentrated absentee ownership was a more recent phenomenon in Appalachia. In Britain (and thus in Wales) all coal mines were controlled by the nationalized coal board, and all steel production was in the hands of the British Steel Corporation. There were few indigenous large-scale firms. Such centralized control made it relatively easier to organize labor in Wales. With one employer, there was one occasion for negotiation, and less reason to bargain separately with individual units.[11] A long history of successful labor organizing, in turn, made the transition to community organizing easier in Wales than in Appalachia. The parallel of community opposition and worker opposition, both versus the absentee employer, was clearer.

A second difference was the structure of government. The unitary structure of Great Britain provided fewer options for coopting local constituencies in Wales than the federal system provided in Appalachia. The Labour Party strategy for the Welsh after World War II presented a series of disillusionments: administrative decentralization that did not make much headway against the inherent centralization of the Civil Service, a Welsh Office that seemed more bureaucratic than Welsh, a Welsh Council that represented economic elites and was appointed, not elected, and a series of development schemes that seemed to threaten Welsh communities. When economic difficulties in Wales began to threaten the central government's economic policy, all of these agencies and programs had to shoulder the blame because of their identification with London. On top of this, the central government was blamed when major employers that were identified with it failed in Wales. In Appalachia, public responsibility was much more diffused, and the ARC, by putting more control in the hands of the states and the LDDs, kept local resentment more diffuse than it might have been.

A third difference was in the relative economic performance of the two places. In Wales, British Steel announced the closing of its Ebbw Vale works in 1978, amid a general background of economic inadequacy and Welsh decentralists and nationalists could make the argument that England was an economic albatross. Appalachia, in contrast, had a relative economic boom. The renewed demand for coal caused increases in employment in some places and the issue became the destruction that new production would cause, particularly in the case of strip mining, a less explosive issue than a mine closing, even though it would affect more people.

These differences underly the different ways territorial, decentralist programs were promoted, advocated, and handled politically in the two places. The programs themselves were similar, and they were formulated in response to economic conditions that were also similar in many ways. But in the United States, territorial politics was a matter mainly of mobilization, not, ordinarily, the capture of institutions, or of elective office. In Wales Plaid Cymru, with three parliamentary seats in 1974, found they, along with the Scots, could exert influence in Parliament for devolution and other Welsh interests. Moreover, election campaigns were a useful means of building organization and momentum.

Nothing similar happened in Appalachia. There are many dimensions to this nonpolitization. Most important, there was not the same labor organization in the coal fields of Appalachia as in those of South Wales. In Wales, there was a working-class machine, one with ideological roots quite different from the business-oriented, low-tax ideology that characterized the rural political machines in Appalachia. Plaid Cymru could attack a failed, centralist socialism, but was not itself subject to attack for being socialist, in contrast to the red-baiting that was a typical political tactic in Appalachia. Plaid Cymru could claim to be to the left of Labour, more radical, and get votes of a basically leftist, working-class constituency. In Appalachia, activists had to operate against local machines whose predilections were basically conservative. One scholar has characterized Appalachian labor as conservative on political issues, through radical on economic issues, and thus able to be mobilized by the right as well as by the left. In Appalachia workplace labor organizing was extended into community politics prior to World War I, but this was later effectively isolated and eliminated.[12] While there is a considerable literature on Appalachian organizing, there is very little on Appalachian politics. There were no campaigns where isssues got discussed from at least four different party perspectives, as there were in Wales. Analysis of attempts to organize people politically in Appalachia focused on the ways in which issues were kept off the public agenda, and even the processes of suppressing the motivation to get into politics.[13] In Britain, at least after 1966, Welsh nationalist issues were kept off the national agenda but locally they were hotly debated.

External Control and Uneven Development. The apparatus of uneven development and external control changed and evolved in Wales and Appalachia. Resources and personnel increased in the centers and in offices of central agencies in the regions, and the strategy for interacting with local governments and interest groups became more elaborate. In Wales, the dominant mechanism of external control was the growth of the Welsh Office and of official devolution, supported by an important coalition of interests in Wales as well as in Britain generally. These changes were significant. In 1964 there was no Welsh Office, only branches of central ministries in Cardiff or other locations in Wales; relatively few government decisions were made in Wales. Government attitudes toward Wales in the cabinet were characterized by impatience and condescension. "Quasigovernmental" bodies were few and ineffective.

After 1964, the Welsh Office grew in staffing and authority, and other agencies, tied closely to it, were created. The Welsh Development Agency took over the functions of the locally controlled Development Corporation for Wales, and the Welsh Economic Council began operations in a form dominated by the minister. Meanwhile the Welsh Office, hierarchically tied to the cabinet in London, realized increases in its resources and in its control over central government resources going to localities. As this happened, it developed a negotiating strategy with local governments and other groups, shifting the relationship from hierarchical, rule-based control over a few administratively defined issues, toward a much looser control more aptly described as negotiated compromise. The main evidence I found of this was a shift in the Welsh Office stance on county plans. The earlier practice had been to scrutinize every detail from the central ministry, and the Welsh Office initially carried over this attitude toward the new, and more broadly defined, structure plans. It was a somewhat domineering stance, but it did not last. The atmosphere created by the failures of Welsh Office planning and by the agressive stance of the reorganized South Wales counties as they proceeded with structure plans (they ridiculed *Wales: The Way Ahead* and branded a 1975 set of "Notes for Guidance" as "rubbish") led the Secretary of State, in 1978, to say that comprehensive views of planning in South Wales would now arise out of the structure plans of the counties.

In Appalachia there was a broadly similar development of local administration in its ability to resist central power. There, the main focus of attention was initially on the governors of the states concerned. While in Britain highly centralized government, gradually changed to a kind of delegated authority in the Welsh Office (along with the establishment of formal, elected governments in the new counties), in Appalachia the governors were already in place, and it was the local agencies (the LDDs) that had only delegated authority. Initially, the governors' offices had little state planning capacity, but the governors were able to use the Appalachia funds to create planning capacity. They tried to bring under their power, to a greater extent, the state functional agencies. They tried to coordinate the activities of federal agencies in their states. Finally, after a number of efforts (the pattern varied from state to state) they began to develop a constituency in the LDDs that would support them in their development efforts. As they did this, their control and planning functions developed, and those of ARC in Washington also developed.

ARC strategy for external control and for planning was different at the outset than was that of the British in Wales. It *began* as a negotiating, an overtly "antiplanning" strategy, and yet built itself into a situation where it took on many, if not all, of the functions of planning.

In both Wales and Appalachia, as the scale of central government involvement in localities increased, representation was redistributed to those bodies with larger administrative staffs: the LDDs in Appalachia, the new counties in Wales. Outside of government, this was paralleled by the increasing role of large-scale private and quasigovernmental bodies in the economy. This was accomplished through a continuing struggle best characterized as a process of "modernization," as it was self-consciously perceived by its advocates. Appalachian regional planners spoke of "bringing this county into the twentieth century," and those attempting to create new agencies in Wales had similar sentiments.

In Wales the new counties provide the most obvious example. Upon implementation of local government reorganization in 1974, they assumed the functions of local government on a bigger scale than previously had been possible either in the pre-reorganization counties or in the larger towns and cities. The multicounty LDDs were analagous instruments for modernization in Appalachia.

As these bodies gave the impression of being genuinely local in their development and representation of local constituencies, some might question whether it is appropriate to classify them as examples of "external control." Control shifted from bureaucratic control over a limited set of things to a bargaining relationship with a much larger realm and with larger flows of public funds. In consequence, the Welsh counties and the LDDs came to operate under a relatively loose rein, and had freedom to offer resources and participation to popular constituencies. They could hire persons whose after-hours work was local organizing. They could themselves organize constituencies, including locally elected officials. In the case of the LDDs, a typical practice was to "piggyback" quite specifically prescribed grant programs contracted by separate federal or state agencies, parts of each being used to support administrators who were free to work for the executive director on topics not covered by the original program. Executive directors conceived their roles as adversaries of and bargainers with central government agencies.[14]

But what was put under control of local constituencies as a result of the new administrative capacity was an administrative rather than a political service: structure planning and better access to the Welsh Office for obtaining subsidies in Wales; access to federal funds and more industrial development in Appalachia. While administrative capacity developed, financial pressure on localities was being increased by relatively remote forces: inflation and central government mandates in Britain; inflation, federal mandates, and state pressure in Appalachia. Local politicians became dependent on the larger agencies, simultaneously trying to symbolize strength and independence to their voters.

Explanation

The change in the manner of external control does not fully explain the course of opposition in Wales and Appalachia. A more fundamental explanation resorts to the hypotheses presented in Chapter 2. There is a difficulty with this: neither Wales nor Appalachia made the full transition from hegemony to separatism. Wales went further, but not nearly far enough to achieve economic and political autonomy. Appalachia moved even less. In both cases, however, movement was noticeable. What follows is an extrapolation from small changes, to put together a picture that would be more complete if the changes had been more extensive.

Centrality. Even the small changes are instructive. The change in central-local administrative relations initially increased centrality. The channels of access deepened through the elaboration of bureaucratic machinery and the increased flow of public resources. What is more interesting is that these channels, as facilities for access and representation, did not *widen* as much as they deepened. I mean this as follows: The new channels were largely technocratic, confined to a set of administrators, planners, and politicians devoted to modernization. They were deep in the sense that a great deal of money and technical resources could flow through them and that a great expansion of the number of administrative jobs was required to maintain them: in the state capitals and LDDs in Appalachia, and in the Welsh Office and new county governments in Wales. But perspectives and views of the world conveyed through these channels were narrow. Particularly at the center, the representative functions of the central ministries or federal agencies did not reflect the expanding capacities, the varieties of outlook, and the political interests that developed in the localities.

This observation suggests that we go back and look again at the way "centrality" was introduced in Chapters 1 and 2. There, it was defined in terms of access, representation and recognition, and entailed not only linking facilities in the periphery, but also a perception and organization at the center. We can now see that, in Wales and Appalachia, there was much more change in the former than in the latter. Access appeared to increase when the Appalachian Regional Commission and the Welsh Office were established. But the extent to which either move resulted in a real increase in representation and recognition is questionable. It is now more obvious what a change in centrality means. A change in centrality means not only a change in the position of the periphery, but reorganization at the center.

Some increases in centrality—in the sense of a reorganization at the center—did occur with the creation of the new agencies. With the creation of the Appalachian Regional Commission, a new presence and office existed in Washington, and new units were created in each state capital. There was a certain amount of change and response in the organization of the federal government. Appalachian appropriations were available to lever additional funds from the regular bureaucracies like the Department of Housing and Urban Development. When ARC began the public works programs and road construction, there was a sense within the region that Washington had begun to shift its priorities toward Appalachia. But there were strict limitations on the effects of such shifts. Since ARC avoided any major plan or goal-setting exercise, its operations came widely to be seen as a kind of pork barrel, an extension of business as usual in the capital.

It is possible to imagine some things might have achieved a greater increase in centrality: a real victory for the Miners for Democracy allowing Appalachian miners to bargain more effectively with the Bituminous Coal Operators Association and the White House, development of an indigenous industrial sector forcing adjustments in the national economy, or establishment of a TVA type regional agency able to exert effective control over an industry. Any of these developments would have meant a greater shift in attitudes and organization in Washington, and the local ramifications would have been varied and profound. The LDDs, for example, would have had more impact instead of being seen generally as "irrelevant" (despite their real contribution to administrative modernization). They would have taken on a more political dimension.

In Wales, the contrast between the apparent access offered by the creation of the Welsh Office and the actual impact on London was even greater. As in Appalachia, the changes wrought in the priorities given to the periphery were limited. In fact, the unitary system of government and the more hierarchical structure of public administration meant that the change at the center was *more* limited than in the United States. Welsh sentiment and opinion, while it formally had access through groups like the Welsh Economic Council, got little satisfaction from the government hierarchy. The events surrounding *Wales: The Way Ahead* were a dramatic example. A more thoroughgoing increase in centrality might have required alteration of Britain's unitary system. Short of that, if the Plaid Cymru MPs had become part of a coalition government, a greater central reorientation would have occurred. Perhaps a stronger Welsh Office, administratively, would have had some of this effect.

We now have a more precise view of "centrality" as a variable. The previous levels, what the Welsh Office provided, and what ARC provided, demonstrate three distinct gradations within the general "high" centrality category mentioned earlier: (1) the earlier situation where private sector operations intrude and provide minimal access and central recognition without government apparatus; (2) the Welsh case by 1970: a central agency office regulating local government interaction with the center; and (3) the Appalachian case by 1970: a regional agency providing decentralized local fund-raising opportunities. Wales and Appalachia also evidence further gradations in the "low" centrality category. In addition to the hypothetical isolation we mentioned in introducing the "hierarchy" category in Chapter 1, there is the relatively low centrality implied by the disengaged and separatist positions the Appalachians and Welsh tended toward in the 1970s: a kind of withdrawal from any policy role, the disinvolved protest that so frustrated Whitehead as head of ARC, and the more explicit separatism of the Welsh which resulted in a somewhat more conflictual response from the dominant British governments—say, in the 1979 referendum on devolution.

Local Capacity. The limited expansion of centrality in Wales and Appalachia contrasts with the very extensive development of local capacity, due in part to modernization of local administration made possible by the LDDs and the new Welsh counties. Some political developments also expanded local capacity: Plaid Cymru gained control over Merthyr Tydfil for three years, along with lesser local victories, and in Appalachia there were numerous small-scale successes where popularly controlled programs (like some community action programs) obtained some of the expanding flow of federal dollars.

The changes in local administration got some sustenance from other factors. The effect of cultural differentiation in Wales and Appalachia was, on the whole, to increase and reinforce local capacity. This is clearest in Wales, where Plaid Cymru, from a base devoted largely to cultural issues, developed local and national political organization dealing with economic policy issues relevant to a broad range of local and Welsh concerns. In Appalachia the case is not so clear because of the much more tenuous link between the concerns of the grass-roots organizations and official local governments and the

LDDs. Nevertheless culture strengthened these organizations, and it helped strengthen resistance to externally dominated development. One effect of culture, for example, was that it attracted the in-migration of young activists, some of whom staffed the new agencies.

The voluntary and protest sector also grew, often with loose ties to the new local administration. These non-governmental and unofficial developments in local capacity included grass-roots organizing and electoral work. Plaid Cymru and the Call to the Valleys contributed indirectly to the independence of Welsh local governments; they also supported the work of both the Heads of the Valleys Standing Conference and the Standing Conference on Regional Policy in South Wales, each evidence of increments of local capacity. Appalachia, however, lacked the complementary link between unofficial opposition and the LDDs or local governments. Peoples Appalachia Research Collective, the Appalachian Alliance, and other grass-roots and political initiatives had relatively little impact on the LDDs or local governments.

The fact that local capacity increased more in Wales than in Appalachia helps us define the variable. Just as the reduction in centrality went further—from disengagement to a conflictual kind of separate course for many Welsh people—the level of local organization developed further. The difference was in the voluntary and protest sector. The Appalachian protest sector was characterized at its best by the informal coordination of groups like the Appalachian Alliance. The Welsh also had a comparable protest sector, but it had an additional level of coordination and focus: the regional political organization signified by the MP's, regular party conferences and newspaper of Plaid Cymru, and a number of other formally organized regional bodies.

Interaction Effects and the Transition to Separatism. How does this description fit the model presented in Chapter 2? The sequence of events is best divided into two periods. The first culminated in the establishment of the regional agencies, the Welsh Office and the ARC, and ended, not exactly with their creation, but perhaps with the relatively general perception of what they mean, as their operations in each case became routinized toward the end of the 1960s. The second period, roughly the 1970s, saw the move towards separatism. It is possible to show how the interaction of centrality and local capacity occurred in each period. In general terms, this sequence can be displayed on a diagram such as was introduced in Chapters 1 and 2.

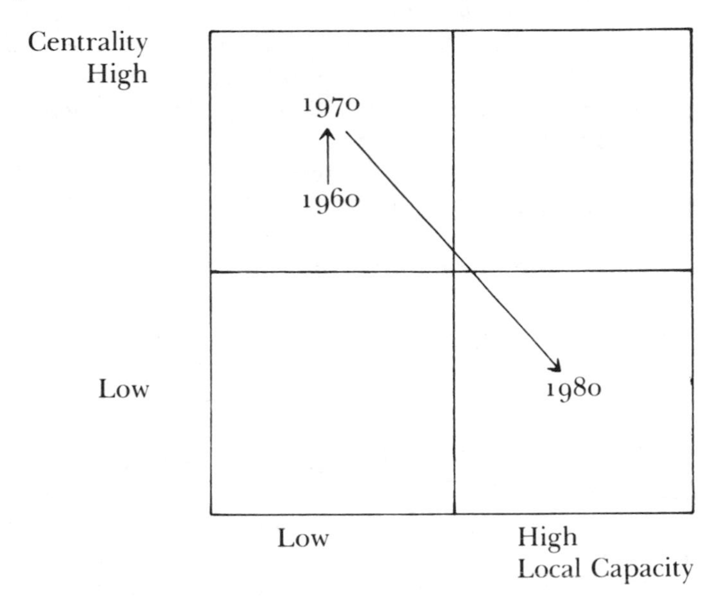

During the first period there occurred the apparent and limited increases in centrality just described. In Wales, after years of agitation for some kind of special institutional recognition in London including demands for a Welsh Parliament, the Labour Party created the Welsh Office in 1964—in effect, a branch office of the civil service, though headed by a junior minister. In Appalachia, after agitation for a TVA-like agency, Congress created the Appalachian Regional Commission as a kind of partnership between the governors and a federal co-chairman, but with limited mandate. By the end of the 1960s it was apparent that neither agency was going to make a tremendous difference in the way central governments did business in the periphery. Everyone agreed they made *some* difference, but earlier expectations had been disappointed and the general feeling was that by creating minimal regional agencies, central governments had avoided doing anything fundamental. In Wales the disappointment may have been sharpest, as the discrepancy was greater between what was hoped for and what the Welsh got.

After the new agencies were created, local capacity increased, solidarity grew, and centrality was reduced. It is hard to be precise about the sequence, but the following review is possible:

1. Local capacity increased in both places. Development of a modern economic and public administration sector, side by side with a voluntary and protest oriented sector of new organizations, were mutually reinforcing. In Wales, modernization came from the creation of the new counties with larger scale administrative staffs, a development that was general to Great Britain with local government reorganization in 1974. In Appalachia the LDDs, authorized in 1965 but not really functioning until the 1970s, played a similar role. The protest and voluntary sector was most strongly symbolized by the Plaid Cymru in Wales, and by the grassroots organizations in Appalachia. Their relationship to the modern sector was complementary, if occasionally conflictual. Both were fed by the in-migration of young professionals and counter-culture people. The modern sector provided at least some jobs and the protest sector helped legitimize a somewhat more independent course for the modern sector.

The growth of local capacity was more pronounced in Wales. There was a greater collective presence, more coordination. A Welsh Counties committee was created in 1974, the Plaid Cymru was a coordinated body, and such sub-regional moves as the Call to the Valleys and the Heads of the Valleys Standing Conference coordinated local protests. Coordination in Appalachia was much more sporadic.

2. Solidarity increased in both places, around the themes I described for a separatist opposition in Chapter 1: defense of community, disengagement from central authority, incorporation of working people. In Wales solidarity coincided with Plaid

Cymru's incorporation of the "modernist" elements that produced *An Economic Plan for Wales* in 1969, but these ideas spread far beyond Plaid Cymru. In Appalachia, similar themes spread after 1965, but they were community oriented for the most part. By 1978 the Appalachian Alliance was able to dramatize a collective perception of the whole region as "a colony," but this was nothing like the almost tangible sense of Wales as a separate state.

3. Centrality decreased after the initial gains associated with the creation of the new agencies. For the Welsh, this was particularly true. The modest beginning for the Welsh Office was quickly overshadowed by other events: the disillusion when the Welsh Economic Council turned out to be an appointed, advisory body, and when in 1967 its advice was ignored in the production of *Wales: The Way Ahead*; and the quick gains made by Plaid Cymru after Gwynfor Evans' parliamentary election in 1966. These events brought a withdrawal of commitment of the Welsh from the British state, combined with persistent civil service attitudes which treated Wales as if it were any other province. The in-migration of younger people and the new popularity of Welsh language classes were other indicators of withdrawal from Britain. Later on, even the new county administrators, who might have been expected to be most likely allies of central government bureaucracies, exhibited extreme impatience and some antagonism towards the Welsh Office, partly because they felt it blocked their way to Whitehall, and in some respects they became more independent than their English counterparts. The Plaid Cymru, meanwhile, thought of the build-up of administrative machinery in Cardiff in terms of a set of resources that they would slowly get control of, rather than as a means of access to the central government. Rather than think of Whitehall as a government they would increasingly influence, Plaid Cymru sought to get the machinery of Welsh government away from it. To that extent, centrality decreased in Wales.

Something similar happened in Appalachia, though there was no political event comparable to a parliamentary victory, and there was less coordination and a more fragmentary response.

But it is certainly true that many Appalachians stopped trying to influence federal policy after 1965 and adopted relatively autarkic goals.

What this account has provided is a crude separation in time periods, (the 1970s contrasted with the 1960s), evidence of differing increases in centrality in the first period (higher in Appalachia, lower in Wales), and differing changes in centrality, local capacity, and solidarity in the second time period. The analysis is very general; a more satisfactory analysis would separate the sequences more specifically, perhaps by providing a

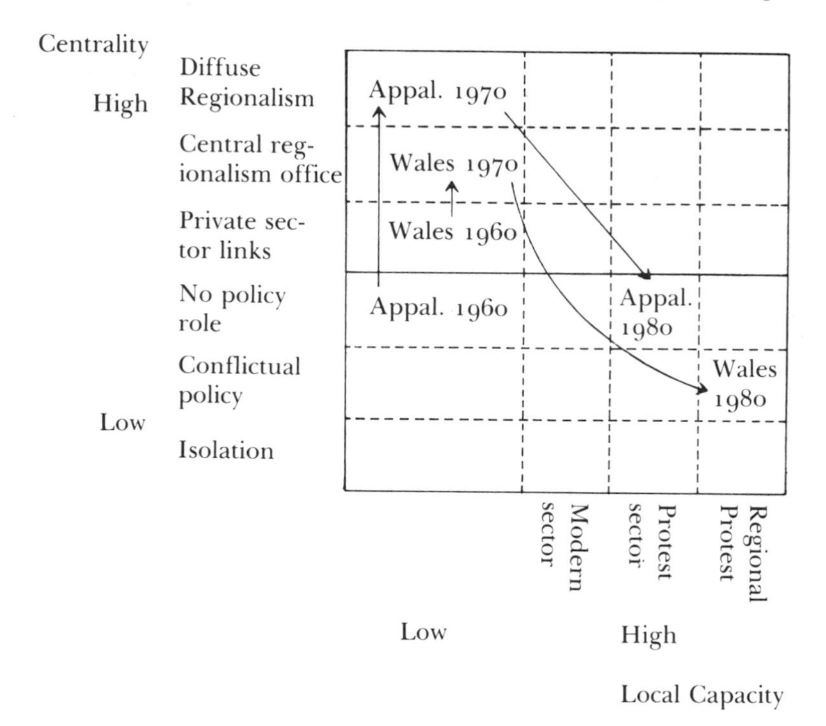

more complete list of steps on each axis, with the timing when each attribute appeared. But a more complete though still hypothetical diagram can now be drawn. The diagram is hypothetical because it describes only what might have happened in Wales and Appalachia had separatism moved further and been reflected more thoroughly in official agencies. As it was, only the opposition positions are represented by the heads of the diagonally pointing arrows. The modal positions, if expressed at all, would be less extreme.

Choice of Strategy

This account has described the dynamics of an opposition movement as the transition from hegemony toward separatism. But what does it tell an organizer who, committed to egalitarian goals, must choose between a territorial and a workplace strategy? Will a territorial strategy, such as the one followed by the activists in Wales and Appalachia, be egalitarian? What theoretical reason is there to think it should be?

Under the conditions of hegemony, community and territorial strategies worked in an egalitarian direction. The first point to bear in mind is the fact of worker participation in these movements, particularly after the middle or end of the 1960s. Both the revitalization of Plaid Cymru after 1966 and the Appalachian opposition of the 1970s were not only separatist, but in contrast to earlier territorial movements, sought working-class involvement. The reasons are inherent in the conditions of hegemony and the transition toward separatism. Because of the weakness of local business classes, it was natural for the organizers to turn to workers for support. Moreover, the development of external control and, in its somewhat differenty way, centrality opened arenas for community organizing that were not available to traditional industrial (union) strategies: as external ownership proliferated, it became a community target on issues like strip-mining, as external government bureaucracies proliferated they became community targets on issues like new town and reservoir development in Wales, flood recovery in Appalachia.

Under conditions of well-developed separatism or polyarchy, the consequences of territorial organization might be quite different. There, community organizing or broad regional or national movements might encounter support from strong business elements, which might for their own sound business reasons desire a separate or more independent economy, and seek to coopt any labor movement using territorial identifications and goals to deflect class equality goals. More subtly, such business forces might support government or voluntary sector programs aimed at community organizing as a means of purchasing labor peace even temporarily.

Chapter 6
Planning

Most studies of planning that have observed planners in action have noted the discrepancy between the rationalist thinking of planners and the somewhat different logic of politics. Planners appear as technical, apolitical, and idealistic. They organize and order different goals and try to conceptualize the means to these goals. Their bosses and clients, in contrast, bargain, trade off, and shift their priorities among goals. Mayors, legislative bodies, and special interests either do not set goals or change them frequently. Much of the literature on planners at work is preoccupied with the tension between these positions.[1] It is not a trivial problem. In its application to public problems, the rationalism, the means-ends thinking of planners, is impelled by the increasing interdependencies of any modern economic system. Bargaining between interest groups is also basic, and so the dilemma results. For the system to work, it is as if planners must be rational and politics must at times contradict that rationality.

In Wales and Appalachia planners seemed to be aware of the problem. They saw that "politics" would not provide a stable set of goals. Official planners at all levels in Appalachia perceived the power of elected officials and avoided making elaborate statements of goals, instead taking an incrementalist or indicative line. Welsh Office planners, after the publication of *Wales: The Way Ahead* in 1967, avoided any further policy statements and contented themselves with the modest role of providing statistics. In both cases they were adapting to their political constraints as they saw them. They backed off from the idea of planning as "intendedly rational."[2] I will describe this adaptation below. But adaptive though it was, official planning in Wales and Appalachia produced reaction that the planners themselves did not anticipate: opposition planning that became the basis for organizing new territorial coalitions. Thus there was a dual conflict of official and opposition planning, external and locally rooted clienteles. Official planners might have been successful in their avoidance of grand policy statements and their retreat from rationalism, if all significant groups had been willing to play their game, that is, engage in a pluralist bargaining system. But many significant groups either refused to participate or participated as opposition.

In this chapter I review the dual conflicts in Wales and Appalachia. I then suggest how these conflicts followed naturally from hegemony and incipient separatism. Next I suggest ways that official planning and opposition planning might be better conceived under conditions of transition from hegemony to separatism. Finally, I return to the dilemmas I began with: maintaining public rationality under a political system devoted to bargaining; and increasing participation under hegemony or separatism.

Dualism: Official Planning and Opposition

In their professional role, planners try to be rational. They try to take into account all goals and viewpoints they are aware of, and they try to become aware of all possible courses of action. They try to use methods that connect goals to courses of action, and they communicate these courses of action, together with their rationale, to some clients. They may be attacked, but they have faith that these procedures are worth following regardlessly. In addition, they have defenses against attack. They can find clients who will support them against attack and allow them to continue planning.

The first observation about official planning in Wales and Appalachia is that not all of these conditions were met. Most important, there was no sufficiently broad local clientele to support the kinds of policies the planners were trying to pursue. There were two sets of clienteles, with little communication between the two. One was that group of administrators and business interests who, with external backing, pursued a kind of economic development policy under the auspices of the Welsh Office or the Appalachian Regional Commission. The other was the diffuse and largely unorganized amalgam of community and labor and some business interests who on occasion could be aroused to resist these external policies. Even when not organized, however, they posed a formidable obstacle to the first group. They refused to participate in economic development. They were united, at their least organized, by a common culture undergirded by a perception of economic interest separate from that of full participants in the central economy. On occasion, these perceptions could be mobilized as opposition by the programs of the Appalachian Alliance, or the full-blown party politics of Plaid Cymru.

The adaptation of official planners to this fragmentation of clientele is best illustrated in Wales by the conditions surrounding the production of *Wales: The Way Ahead*, and the subsequent Welsh Office stance regarding planning. By all accounts, *Wales: The Way Ahead* was produced in difficult circumstances. The ballyhoo from George Brown and DEA raised expectations. The secrecy restrictions on the Welsh Office planners prevented them from linking up with Welsh expertise. The hierarchical relationship of the Welsh Office planners to the cabinet constrained them from meeting the standards that local experts expected of them, most importantly on the issue of the employment gap, and their own apparent lack of expertise left them open to additional attack. probably the most important constraint was the hierarchical one. The Welsh Office was sold by the Labour Party as providing the access to central decision making that part of the Welsh clientele had been demanding. It was not supposed to provide any independent authority, and while its minister was to represent Welsh interests in the cabinet, he was also subject to cabinet discipline, and he had to share responsibility for cabinet policy once it was set. Thus Welsh Office planning had to be an extension of cabinet planning. When the plan was finally produced by an expert from another ministry who was brought in at the last minute, the procedure was not a serious attempt to meet existing expectations. Even if there had been adequate expertise and time, it seems unlikely that *Wales: The Way Ahead* would have been thought of a serious document, because of the other constraints.

Why did the Welsh Office allow the plan to be released in that form? They do not say, but probably the reason was to have something in the public record as a line of defense against the charge that they were not planning. They could use it as a lightning rod, let it take abuse, defend it, and go on with their other business. At a minimum, *Wales: The Way Ahead* could confuse at least some of the opposition, muddy up the waters, and serve as a focus of discussion while the real work went on on other topics. The real work of Welsh Office economists was to keep abreast of the economic indicators and give advice on projects that might be proposed. As this work went on, one could argue that a kind of shadowy, informal plan developed and evolved. But it was not out on view like the public report. There was no public debate about it, and no reason to subject it to really searching analysis. One does not know how much impact Welsh Office analysts had on Welsh Office development projects in the period after *Wales: The Way Ahead*. The projects did tend to go awry, and in at least one instance, the Llantrisant proposal, observers said the quality of Welsh Office analysis was so bad compared to that of the opposition that they simply could not fight. Whether this was due to the quality of analytical staff, or to the staff's failure to penetrate to decision makers at the ministerial level, is hard to say.

Method. To really understand Welsh Office planning it would be necessary to understand the methods they used and the thought processes they went through to come up with their recommendations. Every plan, every recommendation moves from some premise to a conclusion. *Wales: The Way Ahead* seemed to start from the premise of a continuation of trends in the structure of the Welsh economy, and, at least implicitly, a continuation of British regional policy subsidies. The plan did not ask what might happen if either of these changed. The outcome of these projections was the disputed 1971 job gap of 15,000. This in turn was proposed to be dealt with by increases in regional policy subsidy programmed by the Government, so that there would be no job gap by 1971. The rest of the plan's proposals traced out the implications of this sort of employment figure for the total population and the services and public works it would require.

After the plan was published in 1967, it appeared the job figures would have to be revised, and the Welsh Office planners may have keyed most of their analysis to the problem of providing jobs. The South Wales proposals certainly would be a reflection of such a premise. There was, apparently, no general strategy analysis, one that related the total jobs problem to particular government actions. The Welsh Office instead retreated to ad hoc analyses on a project-by-project basis.

ARC planners had different constraints, but in broad outline the outcome was similar: ARC decided at the outset to put projects ahead of planning. Partly its structure dictated this. The Welsh Office was in a hierarchical relationship not only to its superiors in the cabinet but, at least formally, to local governments in Wales. It was expected to produce a plan. ARC was the delegatee of several governors, and it was expected to deliver projects. There was no DEA saying there would be a plan for each region of the United States. The climate was much more experimental in ARC. In the early stages, when the Litton report proposing growth centers appeared, the ARC federal co-chairman was able to pretend to take it seriously, then leave the growth-center issue to the states. In Wales this could have been more difficult.

If there was an ARC plan, it was an informal one that existed in the minds of the governors and their staffs, and that the ARC staff simply tried to keep somewhat in touch with. There was the ARC Code, and the annual budget that the commission adopted. There were no explicit growth targets for the region as a whole or, in most cases, for individual states. Each state simply was out for what it could get in employment and in projects. Thus ARC started out somewhat the way the Welsh Office ended up.

Both Welsh Office and ARC planners failed to deal explicitly with the issues raised by the opposition: the structure of ownership of industry and land being the most important of these, the maintenance of communities and limitations on migration being others. These are conceptual issues related to the initial premises of their plans and analyses. Instead of raising these issues explicitly, the official planners allowed them to be settled implicitly through their procedures and methods, and through their understanding of the needs of their clientele. Part of the failure to address fundamental issues raised by the opposition may have been due to a distaste for comprehensive strategy analyses as opposed to ad hoc project work, but this itself is in part a methodological position. An examination of Welsh and Appalachian official plans and statements shows that procedures and clientele were the determining factors.

The reason the procedures are important is that they lock the analysts attention on some phenomena at the expense of others. The planners who worked on *Wales: The Way Ahead* in 1965–67 have not commented on this, but it is an important question whether they examined the issue of migration policy that Plaid Cymru later raised, before doing their analyses. They probably gave it brief consideration at most, then accepted the premise that any job generation in Wales would have to come from the private sector and nationalized industries, together with the stimuli afforded by regional policy. The detailed planning then would serve not to bring up the issue, but to reinforce its resolution. Further, this acceptance of premises would then tend to be transmitted to other planners in different jurisdictions: in functional bureaucracies and at the local level. For if the central planners do not debate the premises of plans, there is not too much reason to expect that other planners, who lack the formal mandate or the overview information of a central office, will do so.

The clients of planners may reinforce all this. The clients of the Welsh Office planners were apparently the cabinet and central ministries in London, the Welsh Economic Council, possibly some imagined set of publics, and perhaps some informal contacts. The Welsh Office kept the plan hidden from the Welsh Economic Council until just before its unveiling, so its clientele was not even as wide as this. Thus there was little possibility that the Welsh Office planners would be influenced to change or question its premises through clientele contact. More likely, the opposite was true. Probably, these selective contacts that the planners were allowed reinforced the premises that appeared in *Wales: The Way Ahead.*

Opposition planners, on the other hand, were not constrained in this way. Their constraints were of resources and technical information, but they were in a good position to review and question the premises of *Wales: The Way Ahead,* as well as the positions of other interest groups and parties.

Similar points can be made about official planning in Appalachia, with the difference being that there was no one plan or consistent position taken by a central agency like the Welsh Office. In this case, the state planning agencies took the central position, with ARC providing a stimulus and the LDDs providing inputs in the form of their own plans.

Opposition Planning. In Wales, at least, an opposition appeared that challenged the premises of the Welsh Office planners and put these in the form of a plan document—Plaid Cymru's *An Economic Plan for Wales,* which they prepared as written evidence to submit to the Commission on the Constitution, and also as a demonstration of their ability to provide an economic policy should Wales become independent. The Plaid Cymru plan was different from the Welsh Office analyses. Its concepts and its premises were different. Its clientele was different. Its methods were for the most part the same.

The premises of the Plaid Cymru plan were what most dramatically set it apart from the Welsh Office. Plaid Cymru set a target for Welsh population and employment, and asked what economic policies would be needed to reach it, rather than accept present trends and British regional policy. This in itself opened up many avenues for analysis that were not open to the official planners: the determination not to lose population through net out-migration, and the determination to control migration within Wales at a level that would save communities. Not that all these lines were analyzed in the plan, but the premises of the plan opened up these kinds of analyses for later development.

The clientele of the Plaid Cymru plan was of course different from that of official planning. It was, firstly, Welsh. It had no obligations to the cabinet or DEA. It was, moreover, an effort by the modernizer wing of the party to produce a document that would satisfy both the cultural, community interests of the Plaid Cymru traditionalists, and the economic and business concerns in South Wales. It was produced by the Plaid Cymru Research Group, exclusively modernists, but written as a broader party document. But this group was active in party affairs and so was in close contact with a broad constituency. Thus it contrasted with the relative isolation of the official planners, who not only had a narrower constituency in Wales but also largely an imagined constituency that they got in touch with only at the disastrous April 1967 meeting of the Welsh Economic Council. These constraints did not affect the Plaid Cymru planners.

Were the methods employed by the Plaid Cymru planners different from those of the official planners? At first glance they do not appear to have been. As in *Wales: The Way Ahead*, they projected demand and they estimated the requirements of different localities (i.e., the demand) for infrastructure such as roads and housing. The premise on which they based their original projection was different, and their derived estimates of the amount of roads and houses that should be built were lower. But the methods did not seem radically different, and this imagery of sound methodology probably helped impress people with the soundness of the Plaid Cymru position.

In a fundamental sense, though, the premises of the Plaid Cymru plan might have affected methodology as much as it affected their prescribed actions and policies, and this is worth exploring. As Lord Crowther noticed, the plan took a supply orientation.[3] Most official plans take a demand orientation and the kinds of data and analyses that are made public related to the demand side. They start from a projection of population or incomes (sometimes some other indicator of demand, such as the number of poor people needing social services), and then apply factors or multipliers to predict the scale of public or privately supplied construction and services that will be required. Thus, *Wales: The Way Ahead* started from a projection of the numbers of jobs there would be in Wales in 1971, and then worked out the demands for housing, roads, and other capital construction and services. The important methodological issues involved in this are, first, what projection one starts from and how one arrives at it; second, what factors are used in moving from demand to an estimate of needed construction or services. To say that official planning took a demand orientation means that it took demand (e.g., the number of jobs that would exist, and the population that would reside in Wales) as a given, or as a result of natural, uncontrollable forces, rather than as a matter for policy debate. (This was true in the case of *Wales: The Way Ahead* even though the estimate itself depended on some policies, in particular the regional policies in effect at the time, plus the proposed regional employment premium. The major point here is that the policies were not the objects of debate or proposal, they were simply assumed to hold.) The same logic can apply to the multipliers used in projecting facilities and services from demand. If past ratios of, say, housing to population size are used as multipliers, then the implicit assumption is that these ratios are given, not the objects of policy. Thus, a planner might study the past performance of the housing industry and find that, say, one thousand units of public housing and five thousand units of private housing had been produced, on the average, per year per 100,000 population. A simple projection of these trends, or of additional ratios based on past experience only, assumes the present structure of public and private investment decision making remains the same and is not subject to policy. This sort of thinking is common among planners. It starts from demand and ends with a project supply in a way that does not question the structure of relationships that produce supply in response to demand.

Thus the methods used in planning divert the attention of planners—and those who use the plans—away from some aspects of the world they deal with, and toward others.

What does not get looked at in this kind of planning is the structure of supply, of production. To look at supply would entail looking at how the various inputs of productive processes—labor, capital, land, and organization—are organized. This kind of analysis, if it is done at all, usually is not done by central planners. Usually it is left to private entrepreneurs or to the specialized public agencies that provide public construction or services, partly because it is just too difficult for central planners to get the knowledge necessary to understand production. Often they can acquire this knowledge only at the expense of the overview knowledge possible from the more general, demand-oriented perspective. What they lose by taking the demand perspective, on the other hand, is the capacity to be critical of the production organization stipulated by the private sector and the specialized public agencies that take responsibility for production.

The Plaid Cymru plan, by taking a supply perspective in some of its basic premises, raised the possibility that the planners might, given enough resources, make some basic shifts in methodology as well. What they actually achieved in this respect was modest. They did propose a higher level of infrastructure spending than did the Welsh Office, and in doing so assumed a higher level of investment per person: that is, they altered some of the multipliers. Not in the plan, but in some of its later pronouncements and reports, the party also made comments about production organization: in advocating a transfer of the nationalized industries to Welsh control closer to the workers and communities. Plaid Cymru planners, however, did not seem to have any sophisticated method for examining the structure of production.

Agenda Setting. The premises of the plans controlled what the planners thought about. The plans, however, also were rationalizations in other people's minds and thus influenced what politicians and the public thought. They influenced the agenda of public debate.

Wales: The Way Ahead was used this way even before it appeared. The fact that the Welsh Office was doing a plan was used in response to questions about Labour regional policy during 1965 and 1966. This heightened expectations, but it also reinforced the premise that the Welsh Office, as an arm of the cabinet, could legitimately perform the regional planning function. Once the plan came out, the Welsh Office used it to promote the premises of its planning and regional policy, as much as to justify particular projects. The projects, as critics pointed out, generally failed to materialize.

The fact that ARC did no plan, but instead led with projects first, did not diminish its impact as an agenda setter. The rationalizations for ARC's activities were as important, if not stronger, than those justifying the Welsh Office's activities. The growth-center debate after the Litton report, for example, occupied a great deal of attention among the constituency of ARC. The highway projects, also, could be seen as agenda-setting devices. They occasioned many maps and studies of their potential impacts, and years later people were still discussing them as features that structured the other aspects of the ARC program. For example they imprinted the theme of access as a solution to Appalachia's problems and later made possible the new thrust to tourism and second homes. In addition, by stressing the access theme, they may have even influenced the push toward a concentration of services in the larger places.

Opposition plans and analyses were also used to influence agendas. Plaid Cymru and the various opposition groups in Appalachia did not control budgets and they could not claim a need for plans to coordinate or rationalize projects. Plaid Cymru said that the main reason for its plan was to show how a responsible Welsh government could develop the economic potential of Wales. It was thus a demonstration, but it focused on the general results of changing the premises of planning, rather than on specific projects. This was true on such issues as the agricultural policy to encourage amalgamation of farms, the effort to specify a distribution of employment so that most communities would not be hurt, and the fundamental decision not to accept emigration. There was also, implicitly, the idea of trading off scale economies for jobs. While the Plaid Cymru planners were willing to accept the necessity of scale economies up to a point—for example they accepted the inevitability of closing some steel works and some concentration in farming—they were careful in each case to limit the concentration in argument. They would accept some concentration, but not too much. Some of the premises of Welsh Office planning and official regional policy were challenged by other opposition groups. MWIDA, in promoting factories in Mid-Wales, rejected the notion of free emigration and depopulation. Certainly the Heads of the Valleys Standing Conference was trading off Welsh gains in industrial concentration, which might have been obtained by promoting development in Llantrisant and other coastal locations, in favor of preservation of the valley communities. In all of these cases, projects were secondary to the analyses, brought in as examples or demonstrations of what might be feasibly done if the premises of official planning were changed. One could argue that this is in the nature of protest: not having the capability of building projects, one must plan to oppose projects. But this would be a narrow view of what happened in Wales. Challenging the basic agenda of the Welsh Office may have been negative, but it certainly was comprehensive in nature. The result was to allow basic debate, not a purely negative exercise.

The opposition in Appalachia was similarly basic in nature, a challenge to the agenda of ARC as much as it was a project-by-project opposition.

The agenda-setting effects of the plans were accentuated by the existence of polarized constituencies in Wales and Appalachia. Official planners knew that in some way or another they were not in a "normal" situation, and this led them to try to create at least the trappings of normality in the form of a set of premises that would allow them to get on with their work. This was all the more necessary since they were continually faced with inquiries about what they were doing. They had to present some sort of public face. It might have been less necessary in a less polarized situation. The opposition, in contrast, was led to challenge the official agenda because it needed premises in order to get on with its work. In fact, the challenge to the official agenda was in large part the work of the opposition.

Planning and Hegemony

These characteristics—the separation of official planning from any general local clientele, the effect on agenda-setting, and the development of opposition planning—are particularly important in the type of area described in Chapter 1 as hegemony. As we defined it, hegemony is a situation characterized by external domination through an alliance of central and local elites and by relatively undeveloped independent local political and administrative structure. We later elaborated this as "high centrality" and "low capacity." The relatively high centrality, expressed as an understanding between central and local elites, makes an externally oriented modernization strategy attractive for official planners. Yet local capacity and the local, stigmatized culture makes it impossible for official planners to develop a local clientele outside of a rather narrow elite, and thus planning becomes "dualistic."

However, the stability of hegemony is precarious. In Wales and Appalachia, the potential for opposition always existed within the local culture. This led official planners to use agenda setting to keep opposition from forming. They kept major projects out of the formal planning process to avoid alerting and mobilizing a potential opposition. Yet opposition, perceiving the external domination inherent in hegemony, tried to organize. While the political gains were not sufficient to upset external control, opposition did create a move toward separatism (minor in Appalachia, significant in Wales). Through opposition planning, it created a tracing of what an alternative situation might look like. Official planners, seeing this, became all the more oriented to agenda control, all the more dualistic.

We can examine the impact of hegemony on planning in more detail by looking at what high centrality, low local capacity, and the insider-outsider cultural schism meant to the planners. High centrality meant, to begin with, the development of an understanding between central and local elites on the desirability of modernization. In Britain George Brown's economic development programs tried to engage the cooperation of local business elites in regional economic development programs. In Wales, despite some popular protest that the Welsh Economic Council was only appointed and advisory, many businessmen and professionals participated with enthusiasm at the outset based on their understanding of what Brown and the Labour government had in mind for Wales. Though this relationship between local elites and central government eroded somewhat, particularly during the debacle associated with the production of *Wales: The Way Ahead*, a core of local support for Welsh Office and government regional policy persisted, to the point that at least some observers thought a "regionalist consensus" persisted through the 1970s, forming a context within which a particular type of official planning took place. In Appalachia planning likewise got underway in the 1960s, motivated by a consensus among the governors and some local officials on the desirability of "development" based initially on highway access, using the Appalachia Regional Commission as the major instrument. As I indicated in Chapter 5, centrality developed further than in Wales.

Low local capacity, compounded by the indigenous culture, constituted a problem for planners who hoped to implement modernization. There was relatively little in the way of private-sector entrepreneurs or of local administration and planning in either Wales or Appalachia. There was nowhere near enough to form an active constituency for the kind of modernization the central planners had in mind.

In these circumstances official regional planning, which might have been used to coordinate the implementation of modernization policies like the new towns or land development schemes related to the Appalachian highways, was instead used for selling the official policy, and for selling to national as well as to local clienteles. It is hard to prove this, but it is the best explanation of some of the things that actually happened. Why did *Wales: the Way Ahead* come out with the apparently fabricated 15,000-job gap, despite the protests of the Welsh Economic

Council? The minister acceded to cabinet orders to stand firm with the superficially plausible picture that had been previously constructed, relating the analysis to existing regional policy. Changing the job estimate would have destroyed the picture and required many additional changes, possibly of the general policy itself. Such a result would have been tantamount to a threat to the control structure implied in the policy, that is, the structure of external domination. Contrast this with what would have happened in a region without external domination. In the English North West, regional planning was much more in the control of regional industrialists, who would never have stood for a plan that would embarrass them the way *Wales: The Way Ahead* embarrassed the Welsh Economic Council and the Welsh Office.[4] But in Wales no regional industrial elite could have had that much control, due to the dependent situation of Welsh business and ministerial control over planning there.

A similar analysis can be made for some of ARC's actions, though in this case the mechanism of domination was different. ARC was insulated from direct external economic domination for the most part, because corporate interests exerted control in the statehouses and Congress, only indirectly on ARC—an agency that was essentially independent of these bodies. While the Welsh Office was hierarchically dependent on the most important sources of British state power, ARC stood formally equal to the comparable agencies in the United States. But it had to play politics with them. It tried to find ways to promote "development" in Appalachia without directly confronting, say, the coal companies. Planners, working in this kind of environment, constructed rationales to justify these gaps in approach. There is no one view, but an amalgam might contain the following: (1) doing some good is better than doing nothing; (2) ultimate responsibility for defining the problem in Appalachia rests with the state and local governments, which ARC is prodding to the utmost in its efforts at modernization; (3) Appalachia's most basic problem is its political quiescence at the grass roots, which leaves ARC and its state and local government constituencies with little choice but to pay a certain amount of attention to the most highly organized interests; and (4) the role of business in meeting both local and national interests (e.g., for coal production) is in any event a legitimate one. The elaboration of these thoughts in ARC reports and in reports by state planners and local planners, constituted an agenda for action. The formulation of projects consistent with these ideas did the same thing.

Faced with the relatively strong links available from central ministries and agencies, and the lack of local enthusiasm for modernization, the official regional planners (that is, those in the Welsh Office, in ARC, and in some state planning offices) had difficult choices as to constituency. One choice *not* taken would have been to abandon modernization, and instead accept the goal of preserving the indigenous culture. This was difficult, not only because it would have had little economic backing locally, but also because of heavy competition from central government sources, which offered rewards for the alternative, modernization policy. A second alternative, more characteristic perhaps of Wales than Appalachia, was to accept the modernization strategy while temporizing with local opposition: the use of planning to control agendas, continual promises of projects attracting the attention of those anxious for growth. A third choice, not implemented in either Wales or Appalachia until the 1970s, was to create local capacity by importing and training personnel to be installed in new regional or subregional agencies. These included the new counties and devolved administration in Wales, the LDDs in Appalachia.

The second strategy, that of simply allying with whatever local support for modernization existed, while it seemed effective in the short run, alienated local people and opened the way for mobilization of defensive opposition organizing. Thus, in Appalachia, strip mining, urban renewal, and centrally controlled flood recovery efforts, and the major new town proposals in Wales were poles around which opposition could, and did, develop and organize. Official planning, in these circumstances, became a target for opposition, and the actions of agencies like the Welsh Office and ARC repeatedly helped rally opposition. It is true that both the Welsh Office and ARC adopted trappings of an indigenous group. But, particularly in Wales, these were nothing compared to the symbolic position of the opposition. The hiring of Welsh speakers at the Welsh Office did little to cancel out the image of bureaucracy and hierarchical control by Whitehall. ARC suffered similar problems, though less severe. its attempts at cultural development, for example, were derided by Appalachian folklorists, who could not countenance an ARC effort in this direction because of where ARC was "coming from"—a development orientation, in contrast with indigenous interest in preservation.[5]

The third strategy, on the other hand, defused local opposition in some ways, while fueling it in others. It provided jobs for some activists, and because it had administrative capacity, it could broker the interests of local people versus the central government. But it also fed opposition, because the administrative machinery it represented seemed to be out there for the taking, if local groups could devise ways to take them over. Thus Plaid Cymru felt, during the 1970s that the tide of events would eventually turn over the Welsh Office and the devolved administration in Wales to the Welsh; in Appalachia the new agencies and programs offered at least some citizen access so that a voice could be established in them.

Differences in Planning: Hegemony vs. Hierarchy and Polyarchy

The pressures and influences on planners are different in cases other than hegemony, and planners behave differently. In two other cases, which we called "hierarchy" and "polyarchy," there is a kind of stability. Hierarchy is characterized by low levels of local political and administrative development, but also remoteness from central policy control. In the terms we used, both local capacity and centrality are low. There is little written about planning in these circumstances.[6] What exists suggests that planning under hierarchy proceeds as a purely technical excercise. Business-dominated boards set goals, and planners devise detailed plans.

Polyarchy, on the other hand, is extensively documented. A

study of northeastern Pennsylvania, the area around Wilkes-Barre and Scranton, found a multiplicity of governments, agencies, and interest groups, who were able to use their congressmen to extract economic development subsidies from federal agencies.[7] In this situation the most effective local planning was a kind of indicative, market-research style, oriented to coalition-building. The regional planning agency played down regional policy proposals and mostly tried to put local governments and businesses in contact with each other and with sources of funds. A similar situation existed in North West England, where local business was competitive with central authorities and London business centers. An economic planning council involved both business and local government representatives in a series of projects that ended with more access to central ministries, in the form of an important decentralization of government offices in Manchester. Numerous other accounts of planning under conditions of polyarchy exist: This is the dominant form of the literature. Most studies of metropolitan planning and metropolitan government integration describe polyarchy, and these include reports on Minneapolis-St. Paul, New York, Los Angeles.[8] Meyerson and Banfield reported on public housing in Chicago, Altshuler on local planning in Minneapolis-St. Paul, and other studies dealt with urban renewal: Dahl for New Haven, Kaplan for Newark.[9] These studies described the difficulty of applying any kind of technical or comprehensive solutions in a nonhierarchical political environment. The politics was in each case polyarchy: there was no extreme external economic or political domination, and politics was governed by rules that all parties agreed upon, or at least acceded to. When these authors found planning to "work," they found highly entrepreneurial, coalition-building planning initiatives, complementary to the initiatives of political leaders, combined with responsiveness to the most important political interests. But high local capacity was subsumed in all these studies and seems reasonable for most of them. Nothing like the issues that divided the Welsh from the British, or the Appalachian activists from the economic developers existed in most of these cases. The major exceptions are the cases where race was the fundamental issue. In these cases—for example, the Meyerson and Banfield study—it was possible to treat the conflict as between other groups—white neighborhood representatives, in this case—who themselves were alike in their desire to keep blacks out.

Planning in the Transition to Separatism

The transition to separatism presents a different set of constraints and opportunities for planning.[10] In Chapter 5 I argued that in hegemonic places like Wales and Appalachia, a movement toward separatism offered the best possibility for the emergence of popular coalitions. In fact, what one actually sees in Wales and Appalachia is some pressure—in part successful—for disengagement from central control of policy. That is what Plaid Cymru campaigned for in Wales, and was the position the Appalachian Alliance came to. This, together with increases in local capacity, would constitute a shift toward the separatism case. Even a partial shift, however unlikely the prospects of any "pure" separatism, is still the most likely change in prospect for hegemonic regions, more likely than a shift to polyarchy or hierarchy, and worth examining for the possibilities it holds out for rationalism—the elaboration of goals and courses of action in planning for an area—and the footholds it affords for new participation.

In the transition to separatism, planning would be different from what it is under hierarchy, polyarchy, or hegemony. It would be different because the conditions defining the case are different: the high centrality of elites committed to modernization would be gone, though there might be a great deal of external trade and communication. But the externally rooted core culture would still be in place: in Wales, the Anglo-Welsh, in Appalachia the outsider culture. Living alongside that culture would remain the indigenous territorial group. No longer dominated from outside, it would be part of a territorial political coalition strong enough to win elections at least part of the time. This change in situation would radically alter the doctrine, clientele, and methods of planning. The doctrine could no longer be the technical one possible in the hierarchical situation, nor could planners play the indicative role, adapting to the possibilities of coalition building, offered under polyarchy. The first role was possible under hierarchy because of relative homogeneity. The second role was possible because, though there was no broad agreement on goals, there was agreement on the rules of the game: coalitions could be formed and a framework of data and research would be seen as useful on all sides. Under hegemony, external domination made it possible to act out the first two roles to the satisfaction of at least the central ministries and agencies, though local response might seem inadequate. But under separatism, none of these roles would suffice. With external dominance gone, external support for planners would probably vanish or be entirely ineffective. With cultural schisms now marked and open, local quiescence would diminish, and planners who adopted the technical or indicative roles would be attacked from within and, in addition, would lose outside support.

Doctrine. One can predict, however, from the experience of opposition planners and activists in Wales and Appalachia and ask what might be possible for them if the external domination now present were dissipated. The cultural schisms would still be there; the question now for the opposition planners would be how to make the transition from critic to contributor to a new government or a new set of independent institutions. My conclusion is that these planners would avoid the problems of the official planners by avoiding the modernizer view: its theory, techniques, and implied support coalition. They should avoid the indicative or incrementalist approach. They should adopt instead a point of view and doctrine that fills the gaps in rationality and participation that will accompany the withdrawal of centrally linked institutions, as happens in the transition toward separatism.

Planning under such a doctrine might conceive its mission as developing the full potential of each culture, each community, and orienting its methods to paying much more attention to monitoring their status and development. It would not have to reject the concerns of indicative planning, but the added community/culture dimension would open up new areas of research and analysis and would make possible new programs. For example, planners not only might research the relationships between industrial structure and incomes but also relate both to community structure and income distribution. To the indicative mode of planning, which tends to look only at the first two of these, such efforts would add both a research and a policy dimension.

This view would have advantages to planners in separatism situations. It offers an explanation and mandates a concern for two kinds of discontents, and thus can be attractive for two kinds of support groups. First, it could be attractive to those particularly concerned with income inequality, including those historically organized in unions along class and occupational lines: coal miners and welfare rights organizations in Appalachia, the TUC in Wales. Second, it would attract those concerned with lack of access to control over the most important political decisions, which includes some of the former, but also environmentalist and other territorially organized groups. In general, it offers support to territorial coalitions. The modernization view, with the indicative planning it implies, says, in effect, "trust elites, since they have the interests of universal participation at heart." Apart from making information available, indicative planning does nothing to ensure the use of that information or the participation in the system by interests not already mobilized. An alternative model, in contrast, would imply a different viewpoint: "watch elites, and watch particularly how they deal with peripheral groups." It would direct attention to characteristics of the periphery, and its connections to the center. In addition to its concern with center-periphery relationships, an alternative model would deal with the whole system, not just some particular interests or aspects. It would draw attention to peripheral groups, but also monitor core elites.

Agenda Strategy. Would there be a clientele, a coalition in support of this kind of planning in the separatism situation? First, what is the evidence that this kind of planning is useful to a territorial coalition under any circumstances? We can give a tentative answer for the hegemony case in Wales and Appalachia because in these places opposition planning was politically useful. *An Economic Plan for Wales* was useful to Plaid Cymru. It countered the common argument against Welsh nationalism: that it was a movement of "teachers and preachers," concerned mainly with the language and the preservation of Welsh customs. The plan answered Nairn's comment that the Welsh needed to balance their cultural interests with more materialism. In fact, it was in most ways not a very radical document at all. It did not, for example, make any mention of economic democracy or worker self-management, a theme that Plaid Cymru has mentioned since; its main aim was to show that its economists could plan "responsibly." The preparation of the plan in 1969 in time to present it to the Commission on the Constitution was, in addition, an occasion for the Plaid Cymru Research Group to organize and work out its positions. This activity generally was an encouragement to the modernist wing of the party. Certainly the plan was of symbolic importance. When the party gave evidence to the commission, it spent as much time on the plan as on the language, an allocation that would not have been possible earlier. The research group was also prominent in the party later on. It had an impact on its election manifestos, and prepared an extensive commentary on the Common Market referendum.

It is probably true also that *An Economic Plan for Wales*, in challenging the premises of Welsh Office and British policy, had an impact outside the party itself, for example on local government planners. Local planners need to relate their concerns to larger premises, and planners in Wales found the Welsh Office to be a vacuum in this respect. The Plaid Cymru plan was a temptation and stimulus to them, an encouragement to think independently of the Welsh Office, despite the enormous importance of official legitimacy the Welsh Office had. No local planner could afford to ignore the Welsh Office, since the government, not Plaid Cymru, was the source of funds for almost all their projects. But the more independently they thought, the more pressure they would place on Welsh Office planners to justify their actions and premises and either look foolish or question government policies.

Some of the Appalachian opposition also benefited from analyses that were similar in theme to those used in the Plaid Cymru plan. The difference was that the analyses either had less formal standing, as in the case of some of the PARC pieces, or they were of relatively narrower scope, as in the case of the coal impact study and the various short, fragmentary journalistic reports. Nevertheless, the existence of written analysis helped form the beginnings of a territorial coalition. Weak though the coalition was, it otherwise would have been weaker. Interviews with activists in Appalachia consistently unearthed references to other activists and to writers, most typically investigative journalists, who had produced parts of the analysis I am comparing to the Plaid Cymru plan. There were dozens of such analyst/writers in Appalachia, who knew each other, read each other's work and, when possible, joined in projects and enterprises to affect the course of events in Appalachia. The Appalachian Alliance was the primary example of a joint enterprise, but there were many others. The big difference is that there is no political party like Plaid Cymru, nor the structural conditions to make one possible. But the emergence of an analysis of events in Appalachia, clearly different from that advanced officially in Washington and the state houses, does resemble Plaid Cymru's planning and economic analyses.

Avoid Misplaced Pragmatism. I am suggesting the usefulness of the kind of analyses employed by Plaid Cymru and the Appalachian activists to support and strengthen territorial organization, despite the tendency of some activists to denigrate the notion of "planning." Pragmatism came easily to organizers, and elaborate analyses tended to try their patience. The "projects-first" approach employed by ARC would appeal to the activists in Appalachia, if only they had control of the projects. They would be just as antitheoretical as ARC. In fact, if it was true that ARC operated from an unwritten set of planning ideas, flexible and always changing, the opposition was equally flexible. Thus the Appalachian Alliance said they had no single position, but a collection of similar positions. As long as ARC did not have to state a single plan, there was no pressure on the alliance to do so, in contrast to the Plaid Cymru Research Group, which was in a position to show the kind of plan a "responsible Welsh government" could produce.

To argue that plans helped organization, in either the Welsh or the Appalachian context, is to argue that ideology is important for organization. Ideology is a set of ideas about what causes what, a structure of thought, which governments use to justify policies and which oppositions use to counter them. Party platforms reflect ideologies, and every political movement relies on them. Not to rely on ideologies is to abandon ground on the most basic structural issues, both economic and political. For the Plaid Cymru to have had no ideology, or to have stayed with the relatively narrow culture/language issue, would have been to leave the economic issues to Labour and the Liberals. For the opposition in Appalachia to have limited their arguments to the essentially defensive platform of the community organizers, without developing a more farreaching argument about dependency, land ownership, and the corporate energy giants, would have been to abandon ground to those who argue that community preservation stands in the way of the nation's energy and other production needs. In this sense at least, planning was important to territorial organization.

The Role of Official Planners. In the transitional situation described above, official planners need not constitute last-ditch resistance to the opposition. In the transitional case, their economic underpinnings from the center might be reduced so that in any event it would be to their advantage to cultivate the opposition. If they chose this route, there might be some actions they could take complementary to the opposition. They could provide employment and representation and various kinds of resources and services. They could provide a middle ground between local business and community and labor segments of the oppostion. As the opposition acquires political control, they could allow themselves to be taken over intact. Opposition planning would then make the transition to official planning. A ruling territorial coalition that based its support on the preservation of communities and cultural diversity would have a need for the kind of planning I described. Communities do not survive automatically. They depend on the perpetuation of sources of support and the maintenance of structure. Policies to support communities will have to be based on knowledge of the conditions of preservation, which planners could provide.

Shifts in Planning Method. Thus, in the transition to separatism it is possible for substantial staff resources to be devoted to planning under an alternative to the modernization doctrine. I suggested that such an alternative doctrine would direct attention as follows:

1. It would stress the importance of groups and communities as participants in politics and the economy. This implies a program that monitors participation and seeks its causes, rather than assumes it.
2. It would direct attention to central control systems and the role of elite response to group and community participation.
3. It would seek a conceptualization of the whole system rather than an ad hoc, project-by-project approach.

What planning methodology would implement this doctrine? It may be worth mentioning, in passing, that this doctrine is congruent with the theory presented in Chapter 2, but that is not my main purpose. Numerous existing methodologies seem generally relevant to this doctrine; their codification into a "planning methodology" is beyond my scope here, except to say that the methodology will differ in several respects from that subsumed under the modernization model described earlier. Methods for studying and monitoring the distribution of economic and demographic characteristics over population groups and communities seem relevant, though they only meet a few of the above criteria. Methods for dealing with cultural differences, including community case studies and survey research, would have increased importance. There are numerous possibilities for using and developing the concepts and measurement tools of social science, given the kind of clientele demand projected here.

Some of the possibilities can be illustrated if we imagine how they might be applied to the cases of Wales and Appalachia. For example what if the Plaid Cymru Research Group were constituted as a Welsh National Planning Office: what might it do? It would no doubt be interested in many things, but one of its interests might be that of community studies, consistent with the goal of preserving communities. Recent work in this area has moved from case studies to more systematic theoretical work that employs indicators, not only of demographic and economic transactions, but the structure of communities, the formal and informal rules governing interactions within them and with the larger nation.[11] Information about structure, if obtained along with the other data that are normally collected by planners, promises to increase our understanding of the dynamics of community growth and decline. It enables us to view communities as production units. To look at their structure is to look at them as units that combine land, labor, capital, and organization in various ways, some of which lead to survival, others to decline. Planners able to analyze these phenomena would be in a position to suggest policies consistent with the goal of preserving communities. Planners who have only a demand orientation are too often in the position of simply counting people or houses in communities, and are at a loss in dealing with basic structural decline.

The case of "growth centers" provides an example of how planners might use indicators of structure. Both Welsh and Appalachian activists have questioned whether induced external investments and populations seriously threaten existing community structure and local culture. This problem has an important structural dimension, what we called community "local capacity" in previous chapters, defined in terms of information: the number of different information types processed in a place.[12] But capacity can be readily thought of as the ability to handle the new institutions and populations entailed in the creation of a growth center. A large part, though not all, of the growth-center problems the Welsh experienced in the case of Newtown, or the Appalachians in the Kentucky River District, was the result of policies that did not account for capacity, and therefore were inundating towns with new people and problems, in excess of local ability to cope with them. (The converse problem may also be true, though unnoticed, in other places that have the capacity to handle more growth than they are getting.)

An indicator of differentiation can be constructed by observing sample attributes of a set of places. Since they are "structural" attributes, this is not simply a matter of counting. But it is possible to devise measurements whereby particular attributes are established as symbolizing levels of a variable such as differentiation.[13] Such indicators would greatly aid central planners who wish to preserve communities. As in other planning methods, no sophisticated theory is required if the indicators are relevant to an obvious problem, as for example, the assumed persistence of past population trends or past population ratios of city to region is considered relevant to predictions of population. Similarly, if structural indicators capture information that is relevant to the context in which planners make policy, they can be utilized quickly and simply. In the growth-centers problem described earlier, it becomes important to be able to predict when towns are ready for a new institution and to be able to distinguish the situation of readiness from that in which the new institution would constitute a destructive invasion by the metropolitan core population.

It is likely that much structural analysis will prove to be exceedingly simple. Its first applications will represent nothing more than an expression of the kind of sensitivity many observers have developed toward community development processes through case studies, applied to a large number of cases through scaling techniques.[14] More complex procedures are always possible, but a theoretical focus on structure can help maintain a sense of limits on data proliferation, and a rootedness of data in real cases.

Implications for Planning Administration. Planning technology affects the organization of planning activities, and the adoption of the methods described above produces an organization different from that adapted to the methods associated with the official agencies I described. This difference can be demonstrated on several points. First, structural data are best gotten from key informants, as few as two or three for each community or organization. This is possible because structural information, by definition, exists collectively in the minds of most community members. From a strictly technical point of view the advantage of this is efficiency in getting information, compared with massive surveys of attitudes or census taking. There are also fewer problems of breaches of privacy. But for the organization of planning, the chief effect is that the analyst has to establish a different quality of communicative relationship with key informants than does the survey researcher or the census taker. Rather than seeking individual responses or information about relatively tangible things, structural analysis seeks symbolic information that ties the key informant to the community or organization. To do this, the analyst must attempt to replicate, in his or her own mind, the way informants think about their community or organization. The result is a sensitivity not characteristic of survey research or a census. Consequently the analysts in the planning unit that makes such use of key informants will tend in many respects to become representatives of the community, and the problem of being too distant from these populations, significant in planning agencies operating under the modernization model, will be alleviated. Second, many planning agencies have action units, with community organizers or other workers operating within or in close contact with the groups in their service areas. A problem that tends to arise in these cases is that the organizers and the research staff divide themselves into separate units. Researchers (and planners) may have such important functions as program evaluation and the generation of data to inform the overall directions that policy should take and yet be frustrated by the impatience community organizers have for them. Part of the problem is in the kinds of information the researchers use and need. Structural information is apt to be both closer to what seems important to organizers and of high relevance to major policy issues. "Capacity to solve problems," for example, is both a continuing concern of organizers and an important issue for high-level policy makers. The problem of assessing the incidence of concepts like these could potentially bring planners and field organizers together, for example by means of a range of contacts varying from occasional seminars to exchanges of personnel.

Finally, perhaps the most profound effect of planners' use of structural information would be to set up an explicit relationship between the theoretical, conceptual bases of their plans or policy analyses, and the real thoughts and feelings of their clientele. For a long time, planners have thought that the latent casual beliefs of clients might be explicated and incorporated by planners in public policy. Geddes suggested this in 1904, Davidoff and Reiner argued something similar in the 1960s.[15] It is *not* simply a belief that theories come from the bottom; it is, more importantly, a conviction that planners can influence the way theories are explicated and used.

Wider Applications

Thus far this study has described planning and the coalitions that support it in areas characterized by hegemony or moving into separatism. The last few pages have provided a description of what planning could be if hegemony moved toward separatism, assuming opposing factions could be controlled by a governing coalition and that a major share of power was placed in the hands of groups like Plaid Cymru or some of the Appalachian opposition groups. These assumptions make the argument easier, for they presuppose a resolution of some of the most difficult political problems that confront anyone trying to institute the kind of planning I have described. But now that I have described this kind of planning, it seems important to ask next whether it might find a role in the other cases of my typology: hierarchy and polyarchy.

Finding a role for it would be very difficult. The problem

with the polyarchy and hierarchy cases is that they tend to be dominated by business coalitions, and such coalitions have proved very resistant to this kind of planning. A decade or more ago one might have been more optimistic. Shonfield, in *Modern Capitalism*, described a situation where planning appeared to have become a necessity to preserve the stability of Western economies and to ensure growth.[16] Galbraith made similar statements in *The New Industrial State*.[17] It seemed to some that the goals of planning might be widened, under this umbrella of legitimacy and necessity, to include objectives other than economic growth, such as environmental conservation and broadened political participation. What happened instead was that, while many other objectives did appear, important centers of business and state power became more conservative, rather than more liberal. Hayward and Watson, in a review of planning a decade after Shonfield's, observed that:

> After planners had momentarily succeeded in flirting with a "less partial view of man"—in more concrete terms, favouring a greater stress on social schemes—they were now brought back to the reality of the needs of the economy, to the recognition that these were still largely determined by the behavior of private investors and industrialists.[18]

The general retreat in the last decade, from what seemed to be the promise of planning, could be seen in the operational difficulties faced by "liberal" local and regional planners. The great liberalizing idea among planners in the 1960s was "advocacy planning," a term first advanced by Paul Davidoff, but soon adopted not only in urban ghettos in the United States, but in rural areas, in other countries, and in other professions.[19] The idea was that professionals, who had access to technical skills, information, and professional and social status, as well as friends in high places, could put themselves to use working for disadvantaged groups and thereby increase the power of the latter. The planners who helped the Heads of the Valleys Standing Conference in the opposition to Llantrisant development were in this sense operating as advocate planners. The difficulty with mere advocacy was that many disadvantaged groups were not sufficiently organized to exploit the skills of planners. They needed organizers, not planners. Planners in these circumstances might do as much harm as good. Second, advocacy might gain access and some concessions, but it did not change the rules of the game in any fundamental way. Central institutions and central planners still operated the same way and even, in some cases, supported advocacy professionals. The quid pro quo seemed to be that however much the advocacy gained in individual cases, the essential system must survive.

Lisa Peattie described a case in Boston that I think illustrates these points. Planners worked for groups in Cambridge who opposed the construction of an expressway in their neighborhood. In their analyses, they transformed the issues from a particular problem for their clients, to a more general one of race and class.

> The controversy soon developed a new form. The construction of a road is a classic instance of the social principle that at times some persons must be inconvenienced or disadvantaged in order to execute a project which benefits many people. Urban Planning Aid, in taking up the issue of the Inner Belt, could hardly make a case simply in terms of the interests of the people in Cambridge whose homes were being taken. It found itself escalating the issue into one of the procedures and criteria used in planning the highway and others like it . . .
>
> In defining the issue in these terms, UPA did not lack supporters, especially from the academic community. But who was now its client? . . . Urban Planning Aid now had neither a clearly defined client nor a clearly defined opponent; it was speaking for institutional restructuring, and its apposite model now appeared not so much that of the lawyer defending an indigent client as that of the radical political action group.[20]

The problem is how to build support for a "radical political action group," which is what planners must have to be effective in such situations. In Boston, support of this sort would be difficult to obtain. Low-income groups that might have an interest in common with those in Cambridge were scattered and not well organized. Groups that were better organized had more reason to support the beltway than to oppose it. This is generally the case with polyarchy, which encourages groups to deal for incremental gains, but not to press more fundamental issues.

This difficulty led some liberal planners to pursue a different strategy, which I will call the "guerrilla" strategy. The idea was to work within government bureaucracies to force change. To some, this seemed a better alternative than advocacy alone:

> With the growing fashion of advocacy and the current disdain for establishment organizations, talented graduate planners seem to rush to the offices of consultant firms or stay in universities to teach and do advocacy work, while the positions of importance in city government . . . are sadly bereft of talent and leadership . . . For all the limitations of the old line bureaucracies, it is *within* their organizational operations and budgetary limitations that urban institutions are changed.[21]

The hiring of liberal or even "radical" planners, some with experience in nongovernment advocacy work, became quite common in some larger cities in America, and many of these jobs were formally defined as "advocacy"-like positions. Model Cities agencies, for example, were supposed to represent the residents of their neighborhoods.[22] Moreover, in some cities the city planning commissions themselves took a decidedly liberal posture as spokespersons for antibusiness or at least pro-poverty group positions. The Cleveland City Planning Department, perhaps the best example of this in a large city, proclaimed the objective of redistribution to "those who benefit least."[23]

But after a few years of experience with these efforts, few planners felt they had made much headway in forcing basic changes either within the system or outside it. A study of advocacy planners within major city agencies found them largely frustrated, rather than fulfilled.[24] It seemed that the more planners learned about the workings of power, the fewer possibilities they saw for achieving redistribution. Conservative and liberal planners agreed that both the advocacy and the guerrilla strategies failed to create a new system of central planning. Conservatives argued that the dissident planners had developed a tool for stopping programs conceived on behalf of a more diverse clientele, but had not produced an alternative capable of winning general support. This elicited agreement from all sides.

An extensive literature on polyarchy suggests why these attempts by planners to achieve institutional change were doomed. This book has not been a study of polyarchy, however, but of planning under hegemony. Still, I can think of two ways that planners in areas they consider polyarchical can use the evidence I have reported here, and can perhaps adapt their planning practice. Planners in polyarchical systems have not correctly perceived the official planning there; it is in fact more similar to what I described for hegemony. Thus, these planners could adopt in a limited way the model I described above as appropriate for the transition to separatism. The second possibility in polyarchy would be for planners to improve their ability to diagnose the transition or incipient transition to other cases. I will deal with each of these points below.

Planning within Polyarchy. Polyarchy in its pure form as described by its theorists, resists planning. At least, it resists any central planning. Like the market economy, it encourages planning by its segments, but discourages planning at the center. The difference is that participants in the market are business firms and entrepreneurs, but participants in polyarchy also include interest groups, government agencies, and politicans. Planners enter this system largely as adjuncts to the operations and plans of the more segmental participants. There is an elaborate rationale for this, which I will not review here.[25] The promise of indicative planning did not change this.

The chief inadequacy in the theory of polyarchy had been in its treatment of the rules of entry into the system. As far as I have been able to see, entry and access have in fact been handled by means that are far from polyarchical. Attempts at basic change in the constitution of polyarchical systems seem to be thwarted by severe restraints on participation.[26]

It also seem true that entry is regulated by the control of the agenda of politics. In Wales and Appalachia I found political agendas were influenced by plans, but it seems that this function of planning is at least possible in polyarchical systems as well. The difference may be that agenda setting is the major real role for planning under hegemony but, under polyarchy, agenda setting would have a subordinate role. This would be true because under polyarchy, the functions of indicative planning, such as reducing the uncertainty of private decisions, would still be performed. The factors constraining indicative planning under hegemony would not exist under polyarchy. But as a secondary role, planners in polyarchical systems acquire a good deal of prestige and often find themselves advising the most important political leaders.[27]

Planners themselves have not widely recognized this role, though, and there has been little effort to be systematic and professional about the knowledge involved. It is a very common and human situation. The way you become an advisor is not particularly related to becoming qualified to give advice. This problem is not unique to planners. Economists generally are trained technically, not politically, yet they give political advice. The rationale here, as in planning, is that technical training is needed to get a job; the opportunity to give political advice is rather remote for those in training, while the technical need is immediate. Yet there may be ways around this that would brighten the prospects for a more conscious strategy and that might employ elements of the kind of planning I describe above. First, planners could try to get support for more explicit policies and procedures governing entry into the political and planning processes. Building on a tradition of professional support for civil rights and minority employment, they could argue to their political superiors that keeping significant groups out of the system, or denying them public funds, is destabilizing. They could also argue that providing access and funds to groups not able to use them is a source of rigidity, that it maintains interest groups and public agencies whose only purpose is to perpetuate themselves. They could argue that decisions on such questions are not only issues for legislatures and courts, but should also be within the jurisdiction of planners. The kinds of techniques I described earlier would be appropriate for this argument. The most obvious applications, within the context of polyarchy, would be neighborhoods and neighborhood groups within metropolitan areas.

In the case of polyarchy, the territorial context for planning methodology might become less important than, or only of equal importance to, the industrial context. If community surveys can be advocated as complementary to community organizing, then industrial research is equally complementary to workplace organizing. One of the significant failures of planners has been their inability to make sufficient contact with labor movements.

The Limits of Polyarchy. The ideology of polyarchy has developed far beyond its practical applicability. It might in a sense be called an overdeveloped theory, whose power in the minds of its adherents has far outstripped their abilities to be critical of its applications and restrictions. It is clear, for example, that some of the ideology of polarchy was applied in Wales and Appalachia, cases that we have identified as hegemony bordering on separatism. We also know that the ideology of polyarchy is commonly applied in communities and regions that are better characterized as hierarchies: some suburban towns, for example. There are two phenomena at work in this "overdevelopment." One is the extension of an ideology from a place where it once seemed true and applicable, to another place where it was never true, but where people from the original place have now established control. This seems to be what happened when "modernizers" moved into Wales or Appalachia, perhaps bringing liberal values and views of the world with them. Another phenomenon is the situation that once was polyarchical, but because of new circumstances—for example, the immigration of blacks into central cities—is polyarchical no longer. In either case what may be happening is the intensification of ideology by a dominant elite that is stimulated by the challenge of a new contact with a different subculture. This is not necessarily a creative process or one involving extensive contact. Business elites, living in the suburbs and out of contact with inner city blacks, most likely do not have a very complete acquaintance with those they are reacting to.

The misapplication of the ideology of polyarchy may offer an opportunity to planners who wish to plan for social objectives not possible within that ideology. Thus, if they can isolate situations in which supposedly polyarchical system is unable to deliver rewards to its participants, they can call into question the ideology and propose an alternative one. To my mind, opposition groups (or planners in the "guerrilla" role) might adopt the following policies in encouraging a move out of the polyarchy case.

First, opposition groups ought to consider, within their resources, a move away from advocacy planning and research on a case-by-case basis to what I have described as opposition planning: a thorough regional program based on an opposition ideology. The purpose would be to combat and challenge the official agenda. In the United States this is made difficult partly by a prevailing pragmatism that rejects plans that lack an achievable end. But pragmatism concedes the agenda-setting function, as well as the legitimacy of the overall regional planning machinery. Thus, locals oppose development-minded regional elites point by point, but offer no overarching challenge.

There is something to be said for pragmatism. Cloward and Piven recently argued that poor peoples' movements ought to avoid becoming organized, that they achieved more in the way of tangible benefits by remaining unorganized and, thus, more potentially disruptive.[28] The same logic might be turned against the idea of opposition planning. My argument, though, is that, to succeed in the long run, any opposition ultimately must confront official planning in a fundamental way, and connect specific with more general issues.

Second, opposition groups should adopt, as either a temporary or a permanent strategy, the goal of widening the opposition, linking the poor, the working class, and elements of the middle class in a territorially based coalition. Thus, as happened in parts of the Appalachian coal fields, workplace organizing can be consciously linked to community organizing.

Notes

Chapter 1

1. Wales includes the counties of Clwyd, Dyfed, Gwent, Gwynedd, Mid Glamorgan, Powys, South Glamorgan, and West Glamorgan, which in 1971 contained a total population of 2,723,596 or 5.1 percent of the population of the United Kingdom. Appalachia includes all of West Virginia and parts of twelve other states, with a population of 18,217,100 in 1970, 9 percent of the U.S. total. Central Appalachia, comprised of parts of West Virginia, Kentucky, Virginia, and Tennessee, in 1970 had a population of 1,744,900 a useful size for comparison to Wales. Population and income for these three areas are shown below.

	Wales*			Central Appalachia†			Appalachia†		
	1961	1971	1976	1960	1970	1975	1960	1970	1975
Populations (millions)	2.6	2.7	2.8	1.9	1.7	1.9	17.7	18.2	19.0
Population as % of U.K. or U.S.	5.2	5.1	5.0	1.1	0.8	0.9	9.9	9.0	8.9
Personal Income per Capita		£633	£1441	$1447‡	$2342	$3544§	$2178‡	$3203	$4498§
Personal Income per Capita as % of U.K. or U.S.		90.8	93.4	52‡	59	65§	78‡	81	83§

* *Welsh Economic Trends*, no. 6, 1979 (London: HMSO, 1979), tables 8, 9.

† *Appalachia: A Journal of the Appalachian Regional Commission*, Vol. 10, no. 2 (Oct.–Nov. 1976), pp. 48–51.

‡ 1965.

§ 1974.

2. The idea of "peripheral sectionalism" to describe this situation, was elaborated by Michael Hechter in "The Persistence of Regionalism in the British Isles, 1885–1966," *American Journal of Sociology*, vol. 79 (Sept. 1973), pp. 319–42.
3. For a summary of this position, see Seymour M. Lipset and Stein Rokkan, *Party Systems and Voter Alignments* (New York: Free Press, 1967).
4. The term "equality" is used in various ways; as used here it means equality of opportunity to participate in the economy and politics.
5. A review of the "national question" is provided in Eric Hobsbawm, "Some Reflections on 'The Break-up of Britain,'" *New Left Review*, no. 105 (Sept.–Oct. 1977), pp. 3–23; other works have also addressed this issue; see Ralph Miliband, *Marxism and Politics* (London: Oxford University Press, 1977).
6. This formulation roughly follows Hechter, "The Persistence of Regionalism."
7. The most general formulation of this position in relation to planning is Friederich Hayek, *The Road to Serfdom* (Chicago: University of Chicago Press, 1944). But the position was also applied to *regional* inequalities. Thus theorists of interregional trade began to consider economic development as the result of trade in those commodities or services that give a poor region an absolute advantage in the market (see Douglass C. North, "Location Theory and Regional Economic Growth," *Journal of Political Economy*, vol. 63 [June 1966] pp. 243–58). The analogous position in political sociology stresses the importance of communications among population segments and the development of diverse and complex relationships marked by bargaining rather than extremist conflict (see Seymour Martin Lipset, *Political Man* [New York: Doubleday, 1960]); and it generally permeates the work of the exponents of the "marble cake" federalism model (see Morton Grodzins, *The American System: A New View of Government in the United States* [Chicago: Rand McNally, 1966]).
8. On the growth-center and regional doctrine generally, see John Friedmann and Clyde Weaver, *Territory and Function: The Evolution of Regional Planning Doctrine* (London: Edward Arnold, 1978); on multistate regionalism in the United States, the main references would include Philip Selznick, *TVA and the Grass Roots* (Berkeley, Calif.: University of California Press, 1949), and Martha Derthick, *Between State and Nation* (Washington, D.C.: The Brookings Institution, 1974); on U.S. multicounty regionalism the main references

are: James Sundquist and David Davis, *Making Federalism Work* (Washington, D.C.: The Brookings Institution, 1969); John Fischer, *Vital Signs, U.S.A.* (New York: Harper and Row, 1975); and a series of publications by the U.S. Advisory Commission on Intergovernmental Relations, particularly, *Substate Regionalism and the Federal System*, vol. 1, no. A-43, *Regional Decision-making: New Strategies for Substate Districts* (Washington, D.C.: USGPO, 1973), and vol. 2, no. A-41, *Regional Governance: Promise and Performance* (Washington, D.C.: USGPO, 1972); perhaps the best summary of work on U.S. regionalism is from the U.S. Office of Management and Budget: William Brussat, "The Administrative Aspects of Regionalism within the United States of America" (Paper presented at the Sixteenth Triennial Congress of the International Institute of Administrative Sciences, Mexico City, 1974); on administrative regionalism in Britain, see J. P. Mackintosh, *The Devolution of Power* (London: Chatto and Windus, 1968); for Britain and Europe more generally, see Jeremy Alden and Robert Morgan, *Regional Planning: A Comprehensive View* (New York: Leonard Hill Books, 1974), ch. 5, and Jack Hayward and Michael Watson, eds., *Planning, Politics, and Public Policy: The British, French, and Italian Experience* New York: Cambridge University Press, 1975).

9. Hechter, *The Persistence of Regionalism*; in the literature on community politics there is additional argument for the proposition that connections to central metropolis result in a "modernization" of local politics; John Walton, in a review of community power studies, found interdependence to be an important predictor of competitive power structures (John Walton, "The Vertical Axis of Community Organization and the Structure of Power," *Social Science Quarterly*, vol. 48 [Dec. 1968], pp. 353–68); in a later paper, he suggested that a propensity for community-organization politics and riot politics—as opposed to a consensual, service-delivery approach to urban services—occurs in similar types of urban localities—larger, with prior experience in federal programs and the civil rights movement—and is subject to similar extralocal influences—federal welfare policies as well as absentee-owned corporations, which dilute local consensus (John Walton, "The Structural Bases of Political Change in Urban Communities" [Paper presented to the American Sociological Society, New York, August 1973]).

10. See, for example, Alfred Shonfield, *Modern Capitalism: The Changing Balance of Public and Private Power* (London: Oxford University Press, 1965).

11. Convergence in regional policy has been a theme in comparative works. See James Sundquist, *Dispersing Population: What America Can Learn from Europe* (Washington, D.C.: The Brookings Institution, 1975), and Lloyd Rodwin, *Nations and Cities* (Boston: Houghton Mifflin, 1970).
12. Michael Watson, "A Comparative Evaluation of Planning Practice in the Liberal Democratic State," in Hayward and Watson, eds., *Planning, Politics, and Public Policy,* pp. 445–83.
13. Tom Nairn, *The Break-up of Britain* (Atlantic Highlands, N.J.: Humanities Press, 1977) is an exception, which I touch on below.
14. On this point generally, see Friedmann and Weaver, *Territory and Function*; on Geddes and Mumford, see Roy Lubove, *Community Planning in the 1920's* (Pittsburgh: University of Pittsburgh Press, 1963); on Odum, see Harvey A. Kantor, "Howard W. Odum: The Implications of Folk, Planning, and Regionalism," *American Journal of Sociology*, vol. 79 (Sept. 1973), pp. 278–95; on Arthur Morgan, see Selznick, *TVA*.
15. Kantor, "Howard W. Odum."
16. Selznick, *TVA*.
17. The interpretation of the New Deal period as bifurcated into an early phase that emphasized planning, and a second New Deal devoted more to regulating business to maintain competition, is a common one (see Merle Fainsod et al., *Government and the American Economy* [New York: W. W. Norton, 1959]; another more recent interpretation is Otis L. Graham, *Toward a Planned Society* [New York: Oxford University Press, 1976], ch. 1); the inference that the regionalists suffered a fate similar to planning generally under the second New Deal is generally plausible, though I have not seen an explicit, detailed treatment of this; perhaps Friedmann and Weaver come closest (Friedmann and Weaver, *Territory and Function*); Graham notes the emergence of "piecemeal planning," that is, planning oriented to industrial sectors, as a main theme during the late 1930s, while the National Resources Planning Board, which was the main institution that sanctioned regionalism (apart from TVA), was going into eclipse (Graham, *Toward a Planned Society*, p. 66).
18. I have adopted these methodological principles:

    1. In comparative research and analysis the method is to examine cases drawn from different places, and to look for similarities and contrasts. Any similarities found under such conditions are probably important. Any set of "causes" found in common are probably more general than specific to any individual case.

If a theory emerges, it will be relatively general.

2. This research is exploratory. Some researchers would not present hypotheses prior to reporting the cases, but the hypotheses are presented in this chapter and the next for two reasons. First, they reflect the concepts I brought to my interviews. Second, they introduce the theoretical elaboration I will provide in subsequent chapters, elaborations stimulated by the research and by later reflection on other works.
3. My method of analysis is to seek a causal structure that includes both a phenomenon to be explained (a dependent variable) and a set of explanations (independent variables) that, in optimal circumstances, could be considered causes. Much of the analysis does not reach such an explicit level. Rather than "variables," there are descriptions of situations, and instead of "causes," many explanations are merely associated conditions. Nevertheless, causal structure of variables is what I am after, and this goal underlies the analysis.
4. In addition to seeking variables and causal relationships, I wish to distinguish between material and nonmaterial (ideational) phenomena. Thus, I distinguish between an unemployment rate and a program for reducing unemployment. I do not exclude either type of phenomena from consideration as either explanation or object of concern, in fact I consider both as necessary. But they are different. One result of this is the separate treatment of planning that follows. I see planning as a way of affecting how people think about material things, without always or primarily directly altering them. The result is an analysis that treats the relation of underlying conditions to the development of opposition politics separately, and only then describes and hypothesizes about planning.

19. *Journal of Contemporary History*, vol. 6, no. 1 (1971), is a special issue on contemporary nationalisms.
20. The literature is voluminous; on neighborhood groups I have referred particularly to Milton Kotler, *Neighborhood Government* (Indianapolis: Bobbs Merrill, 1969), and David Morris and Karl Hess, *Neighborhood Power: The New Localism* (Boston: Beacon Press, 1975).
21. Quote (as recorded a few hours later) from an interview with Dr. Phil Williams in Aberystwyth, Wales, June 2, 1975.
22. Jonathan E. Maslow, "Third Party Phoenix: The Liberty Union of Vermont," *The Nation*, vol. 221, (October 18, 1975), pp. 366–69;

on Puerto Rico, the main reference is Gordon K. Lewis, *Puerto Rico: Freedom and Power in the Caribbean* (New York: Monthly Review Press, 1963).

23. One recent account is that of C. W. Gonick, "Is Canada Falling Apart?" *The Nation*, vol. 224 (Jan. 8, 1977), pp. 13–17.
24. Anna Gutierez Johnson and William F. Whyte, "The Mondragon System of Worker Production Cooperatives," *Industrial and Labour Relations Review*, vol. 31, no. 1 (Oct. 1977), pp. 18–30.
25. My original source for the concepts of centrality, local capacity, and solidarity is Frank W. Young, "A Proposal for Cooperative Cross-Cultural Research on Intervillage Systems," *Human Organization*, vol. 25 (Spring 1966), pp. 46–50; an application of these ideas to regional development is contained in Pierre Clavel, Harold R. Capener, and Barclay G. Jones, *Alternative Organizational Models for District Development* (Ithaca, N.Y.: Cornell University Agricultural Experiment Station, 1969).
26. Major case studies and analyses include: for New York, Wallace S. Sayre and Herbert Kaufman, *Governing New York City* (New York: Russell Sage Foundation, 1960); for Chicago, Edward C. Banfield, *Political Influence* (New York: Macmillan, 1961); for New Haven, Robert A. Dahl, *Who Governs?* (New Haven: Yale University Press, 1961); on bargaining and the rules of conflict, abstracted from the experience of large metropolitan areas, see Charles E. Lindblom, *The Intelligence of Democracy* (New York: Macmillan, 1965); on bargaining among governments, see Vincent Ostrom, Charles M. Tiebout, and Robert Warren, "The Organization of Government in Metropolitan Areas: A Theoretical Inquiry," *American Political Science Review*, vol. 55 (Dec. 1961), pp. 831–42.
27. For a similar definition of planning, see Martin Meyerson and Edward Banfield, *Politics, Planning, and the Public Interest* (Glencoe, Ill.: The Free Press, 1955); a more recent review that reflects the range of thinking among planners in the 1970s is Robert Bolan, "Emerging Views of Planning," *Journal of the American Institute of Planners*, vol. 33 (July 1967), pp. 233–45.
28. Plaid Cymru Research Group, *An Economic Plan for Wales* (Cardiff: Plaid Cymru Research Group, 1970; rpt. 1976).
29. The classic statement on planning versus the market is Hayek, *The Road to Serfdom*; a more general comparison, including the role of interest groups and bargaining, is Robert A. Dahl and Charles E. Lindblom, *Politics, Economics, and Welfare* (New York: Harper and Brothers, 1953).
30. On planning institutions at the local level, the study that most

systematically relates planning to alternative political patterns is Francine Rabinowitz, *City Politics and Planning* (New York: Atherton Press, 1969).

31. Meyerson and Banfield, *Politics, Planning and the Public Interest*, and Alan Altshuler, *The City Planning Process* (Ithaca, N.Y.: Cornell University Press, 1965), are outstanding examples; these generalizations have been extended to regional development in Dennis Rondinelli, *Urban and Regional Development Planning* (Ithaca, N.Y.: Cornell University Press, 1975).
32. Dahl and Lindblom, *Politics, Economics, and Welfare*.
33. John Hackett and Anne-Marie Hackett, *Economic Planning in France* (Cambridge, Mass.: Harvard University Press, 1963).
34. Shonfield, *Modern Capitalism*, is perhaps the best formulation of the practice and rationale of this kind of planning.
35. On urban planning, one of the best summaries and interpretations is John Dyckman, "Introduction to Readings in Planning Theory," an unpublished paper; on European urban planning, see Patrick Geddes, *Cities in Evolution* (London: Ernest Benn, 1915); national planning did not get much attention outside the Soviet Union until later, becoming incorporated into social democratic programs in the 1930s (see C. A. R. Crosland, *The Future of Socialism* [New York: Schocken Books, 1963], ch. 20); the best comprehensive description of the development of regional policy and planning doctrine is Friedmann and Weaver, *Territory and Function*; see also, for Britain, Maurice Wright and Stephen Young, "Regional Sector: U.K.," in Hayward and Watson, eds., *Planning, Politics, and Public Policy*, pp. 237–68; J. D. McCallum, "U.K. Regional Policy, 1964–72," in Gordon Cameron and Lowden Wingo, eds., *Cities, Regions, and Public Policy* (Edinburgh: Oliver and Boyd, 1973), pp. 271–98.
36. Martin Meyerson, "Building the Middle-Range Bridge for Comprehensive Planning," *Journal of the American Institute of Planners*, vol. 22 (Spring 1956), pp. 58–64.
37. See James O'Connor, *The Fiscal Crisis of the State* (New York: St. Martin's Press, 1973), and Watson, "A Comparative Evaluation of Planning Practice," pp. 445–83.
38. This suggests that plans have a particular effect on what students of community power structures call the "second face of power"—influence on the agenda for decision; plans have a different kind of effect once agendas have been set (see Peter Bachrach and Morton S. Baratz, "The Two Faces of Power," *American Political Science Review*, vol. 56 [Dec. 1962], pp. 947–52.
39. For one view, see Alan Kravitz, "Mandarinism and Planning," in

Thad L. Beyle and George T. Lathrop, eds., *Planning and Politics: Uneasy Partnership* (New York: Odyssey Press, 1970), pp. 240–68; for another, see Aaron Wildavsky, "If Planning Is Everything, Maybe It's Nothing," *Policy Sciences*, vol. 4 (1973), pp. 127–53.

40. Dyckman, "Introduction to Readings."
41. On the institutional structure for planning, the main positions were stated in Robert Walker, *The Planning Function in Urban Government* (Chicago: University of Chicago Press, 1941), and in a rejoinder by John Howard, "In Defense of Planning Commissions," *Journal of the American Institute of Planners*, vol. 17 (Spring 1951), pp. 89–94; on the role of analysis, see Britton Harris, "Plan or Projection: An Examination of the Use of Models in Planning," *Journal of the American Institute of Planners*, vol. 26 (Nov. 1960), pp. 265–72, and Paul Davidoff and Thomas Reiner, "A Choice Theory of Planning," *Journal of the American Institute of Planners*, vol. 28 (May 1962), pp. 103–15; on the comprehensive versus incrementalist approaches, see Richard Bolan, "Emerging Views of Planning," *Journal of the American Institute of Planners*, vol. 33 (July 1967), pp. 233–45, and Albert O. Hirschman and Charles E. Lindblom, "Economic Development, Research and Development, Policy Making: Some Converging Views," *Behavioral Science*, vol. 7 (1962), pp. 211–22.
42. See Ira Katznelson, "The Crisis of the Capitalist City: New Perspectives on Urban Politics," in Willis Hawley, et al., *Theoretical Perspectives on Urbun Politics* (Englewood Cliffs, N.J.: Prentice Hall, 1976), pp. 214–29.
43. This point was made in O'Connor, *Fiscal Crisis of the State.*
44. Harris, "Plan or Projection."
45. Davidoff and Reiner, "A Choice Theory of Planning."
46. Herbert Simon, *Administrative Behavior* (New York: Macmillan, 1957). An interesting comment, applied to public administration rather than planning, but with some parallels, is Alan Altshuler, ed., *The Politics of the Federal Bureacuracy* (New York: Dodd Mead and Company, 1971), ch. 3.
47. Kenneth Arrow, *Social Choice and Individual Values*, 2d ed., (New Haven: Yale University Press, 1963).
48. John Dyckman, "Planning and Decision Theory," *Journal of the American Institute of Planners*, vol. 27 (Nov. 1961), pp. 335–45.
49. Altshuler, *City Planning Process.*
50. John Friedmann, *Retracking America: A Theory of Transactive Planning* Garden City, N.Y.: Anchor Press, 1973).

Chapter 2

1. Loss of the sense of community was perhaps the best-known idea advanced by sociologists at the beginning of this century; in the post–World War II period, the work of Toennies, Weber, and Durkheim influenced social scientists, who attached great importance to this idea; an important statement of the 1960s was Roland Warren, *The Community in America* (Chicago: Rand McNally, 1963); see also John Friedmann and Clyde Weaver, *Territory and Function: The Evolution of Regional Planning Doctrine* (London: Edward Arnold, 1978).
2. Seymour M. Lipset and Stein Rokkan, *Party Systems and Voter Alignments* (New York: Free Press, 1967), Chap. 1.
3. V. O. Key, *Southern Politics in State and Nation* (New York: Alfred A. Knopf, 1949).
4. Seymour M. Lipset, *Political Man* (New York: Doubleday, 1960), p. 322.
5. James Sundquist, *Dynamics of the Party System* (Washington, D.C.: The Brookings Institution, 1973).
6. Robert A. Dahl and Chales E. Lindblom, *Politics, Economics, and Welfare* (New York: Harper and Brothers, 1953), suggested the end of "isms"; Daniel Bell entitled a book *The End of Ideology* (New York: Free Press, 1960); David Braybrooke and Charles E. Lindblom later argued for the efficacy of nonideological politics in *A Strategy of Decision* (New York: Free Press, 1963), as did Edward Banfield in *The Unheavenly City* (Boston: Little, Brown and Company, 1970).
7. The functionalist, diffusion perspective on modernization has so characterized social theory and practice in the West that it is difficult to specify one particular source. I would cite Neil Smelser, *Social Change in the Industrial Revolution* (Chicago: University of Chicago Press, 1959), as the best example; Michael Hechter provides a comprehensive review of the modernization-diffusion argument in *Internal Colonialism* (Berkeley, Calif.: University of California Press, 1975).
8. Morton Grodzins, *The American System: A New View of Government in the United States* (Chicago: Rand McNally, 1966).
9. James Madison, *The Federalist*, no. 10, in Edward Meade Earle, ed., *The Federalist Papers*, Modern Library (New York: Random House, n.d.), pp. 57ff; see also James MacGregor Burns, *The Deadlock of Democracy* (Englewood Cliffs, N.J.: Prentice-Hall, 1963).

10. Jeffery Williamson, "Regional Inequality and the Process of National Development: A Description of the Patterns," *Economic Development and Cultural Change*, vol. 13, Part II (July 1965), pp. 3–84; for an argument disputing this position, see William W. Goldsmith, "The War on Development," *Monthly Review*, vol. 28 (March 1977), pp. 50–57.
11. The advantages of central sponsorship were cited widely during the period of the Office of Economic Opportunity in the late 1960s and were repeated by liberals during the Nixon administration, which tried to institute changes in the federal system by means of revenue-sharing proposals (see Joseph T. Sneed and Steven A. Waldhorn, eds., *Restructuring the Federal System* [New York: Crane, Russak, 1975], pp. 35–60).
12. Philip Selznick, *TVA and the Grass Roots* (Berkeley, Calif.: University of California Press, 1949).
13. Samuel Beer, "The Modernization of American Federalism," *Publius*, vol. 3 (1973), pp. 49–95.
14. For this and other comments on Marxist political theory, I have relied on Ralph Miliband, *Marxism and Politics* (London: Oxford University Press, 1977).
15. Miliband, *Marxism and Politics.*
16. See, for example, Braybrooke and Lindblom, *A Strategy of Decision*, and John Kenneth Galbraith's *American Capitalism* (Cambridge: Houghton Mifflin, 1952), which proposed the doctrine of countervailing power among conflicting interests and implied the legitimacy of government intervention to foster a balance.
17. Miliband, *Marxism and Politics.*
18. Robert Michels, *Political Parties* (Glencoe, Ill.: The Free Press, 1949).
19. Miliband, *Marxism and Politics.*
20. Rosa Luxemburg was one important Marxist who made this interpretation (see Horace B. Davis, ed., *The National Question: Selected Writings by Rosa Luxemburg* [New York: Monthly Review Press, 1976], pp. 65ff).
21. See Davis, ed., *The National Question*, "Introduction," and a more extended review, Horace B. Davis, *Toward a Marxist Theory of Nationalism* (New York: Monthly Review Press, 1978).
22. Davis, ed., *The National Question*, p. 9.
23. Eric Hobsbawm, "Some Reflections on 'The Break-up of Britain,'" *New Left Review*, no. 105 (Sept.–Oct. 1977), pp. 3–23.
24. Tom Nairn, *The Break-up of Britain* (Atlantic Highlands, N.J.: Humanities Press, 1977).
25. Editorial Collective, "Uneven Regional Development: An Intro-

duction to This Issue," *Review of Radical Political Economics*, vol. 10 (1978), pp. 1–12.

26. Ann Markusen, "Class, Rent, and Sectoral Conflict: Uneven Development in Western U.S. Boomtowns," *Review of Radical Political Economics*, vol. 10 (1978), pp. 117–29; see also Ann Markusen, "Regionalism and the Capitalist State: Theoretical and Political Issues," in Pierre Clavel, John Forester, and William W. Goldsmith, eds., *Urban and Regional Planning in an Age of Austerity* (Elmsford, N.Y.: Pergamon Press, 1980).
27. Santiago Carrillo, *Eurocommunism and the State* (Westport, Conn.: Lawrence Hill, 1978); Manuel Castells, *The Urban Question: A Marxist Perspective* (Cambridge, Mass.: The MIT Press, 1977); and Manuel Castells, "The Service Economy and Postindustrial Society: A Sociological Critique," *International Journal of Health Services*, vol. 6 (1976), pp. 595–607.
28. See Hechter, *Internal Colonialism*; on Appalachia, the most comprehensive collection is Helen Matthews Lewis, Linda Johnson, and Donald Askins, eds., *Colonialism in Modern America: The Appalachian Case* (Boone, N.C.: The Appalachian Consortium Press, 1978); on the urban ghetto, see William W. Goldsmith, "The Ghetto as a Resource for Black America," *Journal of the American Institute of Planners*, vol. 40 (Jan. 1974), pp. 17–30.
29. On the boundaries issue, one critique that makes this point is David Walls, "Internal Colony or Internal Periphery? A Critique of Curent Models and an Alternative Formulation," in Lewis, Johnson, and Askins, eds., *Colonialism in Modern America*; the best criticism I have seen from the second standpoint is John Lovering, "The Theory of the 'Internal Colony' and the Political Economy of Wales," *Review of Radical Political Economics*, vol. 10 (Fall 1978), pp. 55–67, but this, like the Marxist literature in general, resorts to the traditional prescription of a widespread, spatially nonspecific, working-class movement.
30. James O'Connor, *The Fiscal Crisis of the State* (New York: St. Martin's Press, 1973), passim.
31. Edith Penrose, *The Theory of the Growth of the Firm* (New York: John Wiley, 1959).
32. Frank W. Young, "A Proposal for Cooperative Cross-Cultural Research on Intervillage Systems," *Human Organization*, vol. 25 (Spring 1966), pp. 46–50.
33. One summary is to be found in Frank W. Young, *A Rural Development Inventory* (Honolulu: East-West Center, 1976).
34. The specific hypotheses are provided by Young, "A Proposal for

Cooperative Cross-Cultural Research on Intervillage Systems," p. 46. They are worth quoting exactly:

> I. Under conditions of high solidarity in the intervillage system, the differentiation of the component communities varies directly with their relative centrality in the system.
>
> IIa. Under conditions of lower intervillage system solidarity, the greater the discrepancy between a community's differentiation (high) and its relative centrality, (low) the greater will be its solidarity.
>
> IIb. Under conditions of lower intervillage system solidarity, the greater the discrepancy between a community's differentiation (low) and its relative centrality (high), the lower will be its solidarity.
>
> III. Under conditions of lower intervillage system solidarity, the greater the solidarity of a community, the more likely it is to increase its relative centrality.
>
> IV. If the solidarity of the intervillage system is increasing, an increase in a community's relative centrality will lead to an increase in its differentiation relative to other communities, after which the condition of hypotheses I will apply.

35. Young, "A Proposal for Cooperative Cross-Cultural Research on Intervillage Systems," p. 48.
36. Galbraith, Bell, Shonfield, Heilbroner, and others have noted this development as a shift in economic relationships (see John Kenneth Galbraith, *The New Industrial State* [Boston: Houghton Mifflin, 1967], Daniel Bell, *The Coming of Post-Industrial Society* [New York: Basic Books, 1973], Andrew Shonfield, *Modern Capitalism* [New York: Oxford University Press, 1965], and Robert L. Heilbroner, *Between Capitalism and Socialism* [New York: Random House, 1970]); others have noted shifts in the political coalitions involved, particularly in studies of urban politics and particular service sectors (see Stephen Elkin, "Cities without Power: The Transformation of American Urban Regimes," in Douglas Ashford, ed., *The Politics of Urban Resources: A Cross-National Comparison* [New York: Methuen, 1980], pp. 265–93; David Gordon, "Capitalist Development and the History of American Cities," in William K. Tabb and Larry Sawers, eds., *Marxism and the Metropolis* [New York: Oxford University Press, 1978], pp. 25–63; Ira Katznelson, "The Crisis of the Capitalist City: New Perspectives in Urban Politics," in Willis Hawley et al., *Theoretical Perspectives on Urban Politics* [Englewood Cliffs,

N.J.: Prentice-Hall, 1976], pp. 214–29; and John Mollenkopf, "The Postwar Politics of Urban Development," in Tabb and Sawers, eds., *Marxism and the Metropolis*, pp. 117–52).

37. This formulation of technocratic control draws on several sources: Galbraith, *New Industrial State*, O'Connor, *Fiscal Crisis of the State*, Beer, "Modernization of American Federalism," and Arthur Stinchcombe, "Social Structure and Organizations," in James March, ed., *Handbook of Organizations* (Chicago: Rand McNally, 1965), pp. 142–93.

38. One early formulation of this theme is Kenneth Kenniston, *Youth and Dissent* (New York: Harcourt, Brace Jovanovich, 1971), pp. 303 and passim.

39. See O'Connor, *Fiscal Crisis of the State*, also his "The Democratic Movement in the United States," *Kapitalistate*, vol. 7 (1979), pp. 15–26, and Louanne Kennedy and Robb Burlage, "Repressive versus Reconstructive Forces in Austerity Planning Domains: The Case of Health," in Clavel, Forester, and Goldsmith, eds., *Urban and Regional Planning* pp. 117–39.

40. Harvey Molotch, "The City as a Growth Machine: Toward a Political Economy of Place," *American Journal of Sociology*, vol. 82 (Sept. 1976), pp. 309–32.

41. Grant McConnell, "The Environmental Movement: Ambiguities and Meanings," *Natural Resources Journal*, vol. 11 (July 1971), pp. 427–35; Kenniston, *Youth and Dissent*, pp. 303–17.

42. Nairn's main idea was that national movements, rather than being autonomous forces or "ideas whose time has come," are local responses to uneven development; Nairn's viewpoint anticipates the model I presented above, but requires a reformulation that accounts for the dynamics of local response.

43. Tarrow, *Between Center and Periphery*, p. 37.

44. Selznick, *TVA*.

45. Tarrow, *Between Center and Periphery*.

46. Quinton Hoare and Goeffrey Nowell Smith, eds. and trans., *Selections from the Prison Notebooks of Antonio Gramsci* (New York: International Publishers, 1971), p. 94.

47. For a summary, see Castells, "The Service Economy."

48. Herman Turk, "The Occurrence of New Interorganizational Events in Urban Communities: An Application of Norminal Theory and Specification to Social Systems Analysis" (Paper presented at the 1971 meeting of the American Sociological Society); and Herman Turk, "Interorganizational Networks in Urban Society: Initial

Perspectives and Comparative Research," *American Sociological Review*, vol. 35 (1970), pp. 1–19.
49. Molotch, "The City as a Growth Machine."

Chapter 3

1. For Welsh historical background cited here and below, I have had recourse most generally to Sir Reginald Coupland, *Welsh and Scottish Nationalism* (London: Collins, 1954).
2. In addition to sources that I cite, this chapter is based on interviews with thirty-five persons, conducted in 1975, 1976 and 1979, including persons in these positions: universities (8), business or industrial development (5), Welsh Office civil servants (5), local government (5), unions (2), political party staff (2), other (8); also included in this total were five present or past members of the Welsh Council or its predecessor, the Welsh Economic Council. Assistance in arranging the interviews was provided by Mr. Jeremy Alden of the University of Wales Institute of Science and Technology, Professor Harold Carter of the University of Wales, Aberystwyth, by Mr. Aalwin Jones of the Welsh Office and Ms. Teresa Rees.
3. Evidence of the persistence of Welsh national identity is easily found in literary and historical works (see Ned Thomas, *The Welsh Extremist: A Culture in Crisis* [London: Gollancz, 1971]; and Peter Stead, "Welshness and Welsh Nationalism," *New Community*, vol. 1 [Autumn 1972], pp. 393–99); the major historical treatment is Coupland, *Welsh and Scottish Nationalism*. The Royal Commission on the Constitution (the Kilbrandon Commission) attempted to get more systematic survey research findings on the matter, and found substantial differences on a number of dimensions, between Welsh and English respondents (see Royal Commission on the Constitution, Vol. 1, *Report*. London: HMSO, Cmnd. 5460, 1973), pp. 114–16; see also Raymond R. Corrado, "Welsh Nationalism: An Historical Perspective and Empirical Evaluation" [Paper presented at the 1973 Annual Meeting of the American Political Science Association, New Orleans]).
4. Coupland, *Welsh and Scottish Nationalism*, p. 231.
5. See Kenneth O. Morgan, *Wales in British Politics, 1868–1922* (Cardiff: University of Wales Press, 1970), p. 306.
6. Morgan, *Wales in British Politics*, p. 55.
7. Walter E. Minchinton, "The Evolution of the Regional Economy," in Gerald Manners, ed., *South Wales in the Sixties: Studies in Industrial*

Geography (Oxford, England: Pergamon Press, 1964), p. 18; and Coupland, *Welsh and Scottish Nationalism,* p. 212.

8. Coupland, *Welsh and Scottish Nationalism,* p. 337.
9. Coupland, *Welsh and Scottish Nationalism.*
10. See Robert Griffiths, "The Other Aneurin Bevan," *Planet,* no. 41 (Jan. 1978), pp. 26–28.
11. Coupland, *Welsh and Scottish Nationalism,* p. 369.
12. On British regional policy, see Gavin McCrone, *Regional Policy in Britain* (London: Allen and Unwin, 1969); Lloyd Rodwin, *Nations and Cities* (Boston: Houghton Mifflin, 1970); J. D. McCallum, "U.K. Regional Policy, 1964–72," in Gordon Cameron and Lowdon Wingo, eds., *Cities, Regions, and Public Policy* (Edinburgh: Oliver and Boyd, 1973), pp. 271–98.
13. *Report of the Royal Commission on the Distribution of the Industrial Population* (London: HMSO, Cmnd. 6153, 1940). This is known as the Barlow Report after the Commission's chairman, Sir Montague Barlow.
14. James Sundquist, *Dispersing Population: What America Can Learn from Europe* (Washington, D.C.: The Brookings Institution, 1975), ch. 1.
15. The design and establishment of DEA are recorded in several places (see G. A. Brown, Baron George-Brown, *In My Way* [London: Gollancz, 1971]).
16. McCallum, "U.K. Regional Policy," p. 279.
17. On these councils there are several general accounts and case studies. See J. P. Mackintosh, *The Devolution of Power* (London: Chatto and Windus, 1968), Maurice Wright and Stephen Young, "Regional Sector: U.K.," in Jack Hayward and Michael Watson, *Planning, Politics, and Public Policy: The British, French, and Italian Experience* (New York: Cambridge University Press, 1975), McCallum, "U.K. Regional Policy," and Brian Smith, *Advising Ministers* (London: Routledge and Kegan Paul, 1969); other general treatments include Jesse Burkhead, "Federalism in a Unitary State: Regional Economic Planning in England," *Publius,* vol. 4 (Summer 1974) pp. 39–61, and David V. Donnison, "The Economics and Politics of the Regions," *Political Quarterly,* vol. 45 (April-June 1974), pp. 179–89; additional case studies include C. Painter, "The Repercussions of Administrative Innovation: The West Midlands Economic Planning Council," *Public Administration,* vol. 50 (Winter 1972), pp. 467–84; and a series of papers—Gethin Williams, "Economic Planning Machinery in Wales, 1965–68," R. V. Clements, "Economic Planning Machinery in the South-West, 1965–69," and Catherine Storer and Alan Townsend, "The Northern Eco-

nomic Planning Council"—in Regional Studies Association, Occasional Papers, Series A, "Regional Planning Organization," mimeographed (London: Regional Studies Association, 1971).

18. Sundquist, *Dispersing Population.*
19. Banks, for example, asserted: "Some form of regional government is certain to be devised for the 1970's" (J. C. Banks, *Federal Britain?* [London: George Harrap, 1971], p. 150).
20. These complaints are reviewed in the report of the Royal Commission on the Constitution (see Royal Commission on the Constitution, *Report*, Ch. 9; see also *People and Planning: Report of the Committee on Public Participation in Planning* (London, HMSO, 1969), called the Skeffington Report after the committee's chairman, A. M. Skeffington, M.P.
21. Royal Commission on Local Government in England, *Report* (London: HMSO, Cmnd. 4040, 1969) (Lord Redcliffe-Maud Report).
22. Royal Commission on the Constitution, *Report*, pp. iii-iv.
23. For Britain generally, many have noted a tendency toward centralization; a recent example is John Osmond, *Creative Conflict* (London: Routledge and Kegan Paul, 1977), ch. 1.
24. There is little record of what Brown intended for the regional councils; former council members I interviewed expressed retrospective curiosity about Brown's real intentions, and I tried to pursue the theme of supply management down to the regional level but with little success; apparently some of the council members were interested in the regional supply relationships, but got no encouragement in this direction from Whitehall; subsequently, in a brief interview with Brown, I learned that he had no intention of involving the councils in economic planning, but wanted them to concentrate on the implications of the national plan for physical planning in their regions: "Too political," he said, "I wanted them to stick to planning, and let me take care of the politics"; on the other hand, when members of the newly formed councils met with Brown at their initial meetings, Brown reportedly told them they had a loose mandate: They were to inform him what their role would be.
25. Jeremy Bray, "The Politics of Regional Planning: The Prospects and Problems of Decentralizing Government" (Paper prepared for the Conference on Regional Planning before and after Crowther, Regional Studies Association, Northern Branch, Oct. 20, 1970), p. 14.
26. Royal Commission on the Constitution, p. 40.
27. Ibid.

28. Geraint Talfan Davies, "The Welsh Office and the Council," in William John Morgan, ed., *The Welsh Dilemma: Some Enigmas of Nationalism in Wales* (Llandybie, Carmarthenshire: Christopher Davies, 1973), p. 94; see also Royal Commission on the Constitution, *Report* p. 41. Banks, *Federal Britain?* p. 155.
29. See Stead, "Welshness."
30. Wright and Young, "Regional Sector."
31. Royal Commission on the Constitution, *Report*, pp. 109–11.
32. See E. Rowlands, "The Politics of Regional Administration: The Establishment of the Welsh Office," *Public Administration*, vol. 50 (Autumn 1972), pp. 333–51.
33. Davies, "Welsh Office and the Council."
34. Royal Commission on the Constitution, *Report*, p. 41.
35. Rowlands, "Politics of Regional Administration."
36. On the establishment of the Welsh Economic Council and its relationships with the Welsh Office, I was able to rely on the account of Gethin Williams: (Williams, "Economic Planning Machinery in Wales, 1965–68"), in addition to my interviews.
37. Williams, "Economic Planning Machinery in Wales, 1965–68."
38. *Wales: The Way Ahead.* (Cardiff: HMSO, Cmnd. 3334, 1967).
39. Ibid., pp. 33–34.
40. Edward Nevin et al., *The Structure of the Welsh Economy* (Aberystwyth: University of Wales Press, 1966).
41. Williams, "Economic Planning Machinery in Wales, 1965–68," p. 31.
42. Ibid., p. 49.
43. Ibid.
44. Ibid.
45. At least two persons formerly on the Welsh Economic Council used essentially this language to describe their frustration with the 1964–68 council.
46. Brinley Thomas, quoted in Williams, "Economic Planning Machinery in Wales, 1965–68," p. 45.
47. Interview, Sir Melwyn Rosser, Cardiff, June 11, 1975.
48. The devolution proposals are summarized in Anthony H. Birch, *Political Integration and Disintegration in the British Isles* (London: George Allen and Unwin, 1977), ch. 9.
49. Progress in county "structure plans" is summarized in Teresa L. Rees, "Structure Plans: Progress report on West Glamorgan, Mid. Glamorgan and Gwent," in Paul H, Ballard and Erastus Jones, eds., *The Valleys Call* (Ferndale, Rhondda: Ron Jones Publications, 1975), pp. 402–13.

50. For a general background account, see D. P. Garbett-Edwards, "The Development of Mid-Wales—A New Phase," *Town and Country Planning*, vol. 35 (1967), pp. 349–52.
51. Arthur Beacham, *Survey of Industries in Welsh Country Towns* (Oxford, England: Oxford University Press, 1951).
52. Great Britain. Committee on Depopulation in Mid-Wales, *Depopulation in Mid-Wales* (London: HMSO, 1964).
53. The original consultant report is Economic Associates, Ltd., *A New Town in Mid-Wales: A Report to the Secretary of State of Wales* (London: HMSO, n.d.).
54. Pertinent documents include *Draft Llantrisant New Town Designation Order 197* (Cardiff: Welsh Office, 1971), and testimony presented at the Public Local Inquiry; some of this is summarized in J. Arwel Edwards and Wyn Thomas, eds., *Llantrisant New Town: The Case Against* (Heads of the Valleys Authorities Standing Conference, March 1974).
55. Edwards and Thomas, *Llantrisant New Town*, pp. 10–30.
56. The activities are summarized in Paul H. Ballard and Erastus Jones, eds., *The Valleys Call.*
57. See Osmond, *Creative Conflict*, p. 76; local planners I interviewed, frustrated with the Welsh Office, had simply decided, at least for the time being, to go ahead on their own.
58. Alan Butt Philip, *The Welsh Question: Nationalism in Welsh Politics, 1945–1970* (Cardiff: University of Wales Press, 1975), ch. 5 (figures drawn from p. 99).
59. *Op. cit.*, pp. 111–12.
60. On the period up to 1970, see Philip, *The Welsh Question*; my figures are taken from p. 113; on local electoral activities since then I have relied on news reports, from which it is apparent that Plaid Cymru has continued, overall, to gain; in the 1976 local elections it moved overall from a total of 46 to 109 seats, including the majority in Merthyr and a plurality in Caerphilly (*London Times*, May 8, 1976); a year later, in the county elections, Plaid Cymru increased its holdings from 22 to 37 seats overall in Welsh Counties, though these were still only a small minority of the total of 578 seats (*London Times*, April 21, 1977, May 7, 1977).
61. Phillip M. Rawkins, "Welsh Nationalism and the Crisis of the British State" (Paper presented at the Glendon Conference on Minority Nationalism, York University, Toronto, 1977).
62. Philip, *The Welsh Question*, p. 184
63. Phillip M. Rawkins, "Rich Welsh or Poor British?" (Paper presented

at the 1974 Annual Meetings of the American Political Science Association).

64. Ibid., p. 39.
65. Ibid., p. 11.
66. Philip, *The Welsh Question*, pp. 178–83.
67. Plaid Cymru Research Group, *An Economic Plan for Wales* (Cardiff: Plaid Cymru Research Group, 1970; rpt., 1976).
68. Royal Commission on the Constitution, *Minutes of Evidence*, V. Wales (London: HMSO, 1972), p. 113.
69. Quote from interview with Phil Williams, Aberystwyth, June 2, 1975, and from subsequent letter to me.
70. Plaid Cymru Research Group, *Economic Plan*, p. 43.
71. Ibid., pp. 88–92.
72. Ibid., p. 107.
73. Royal Commission on the Constitution, *Minutes of Evidence*, pp. 124–26.
74. Plaid Cymru Research Group, *Economic Plan*, ch. 9.
75. For some additional perspective on Plaid Cymru economics, see Osmond, *Creative Conflict.*
76. *Power for Wales: Plaid Cymru Election Manifesto* (1974; no place, publisher or date given).
77. Philip, *The Welsh Question*, p. 119.
78. Cited in Rawkins, "Welsh Nationalism and the Crisis of the British State," p. 44; quote excerpted from Emrys Roberts, Letter to the Editor, *Tribune* (London), April 28, 1972.
79. The idea of a "regionalist consensus" is elaborated in Gareth Rees and John Lambert, "Urban Development in a Peripheral Region: Some Issues from South Wales" (Paper prepared for the Center for Environmental Studies Conference on Urban Change and Conflict, University of Nottingham. Jan. 5–8, 1979).
80. By 1978, John Morris, the Secretary of State for Wales, was saying that Welsh Office regional planning would come out of the structure plans; rather than provide a regional policy for the county plans to fit into, he appointed an examiner to review the four South Wales county plans; he said: "My preference in the field of economic planning is not the imposition of a grandiose all-Wales plan from on high, but rather to approach the needs of Wales area by area and to collate the proposals drawn from the experience of those nearest to the problem. This is what democracy is about" (Press notice, Welsh Office, Feb. 16, 1978).
81. Andrew Shonfield, *Modern Capitalism: The Changing Balance of Public and Private Power* (London: Oxford University Press, 1965).

Chapter 4

1. The official jurisdiction of the Appalachian Regional Commission is fixed by the Appalachian Regional Development Act of 1965, Pub. L. No. 89–4, 79 Stat. 5 (1965). Two studies contain extensive descriptions of the background of the legislation and region: Monroe Newman, *The Political Economy* of Appalachia (Lexington, Mass.: Lexington Books, 1972), and Donald N. Rothblatt, *Regional Planning: The Appalachian Experience* (Lexington, Mass.: Heath Lexington Books, 1971); I have also made use of an untitled, unpublished paper by Cathy Esser, Department of Government, Cornell University, 1976.

   Other sources for this chapter, in addition to work cited here and below, are formal interviews I conducted in 1977 and 1978 with some thirty persons—officials at the commission, state officials in West Virginia, local and regional agency people, and local activists and others in West Virginia and Tennessee—and my previous research, parts of which I have reported elsewhere, most comprehensively in Pierre Clavel, "The Politics of Planning: The Case of Non-Metropolitan Regions," in Thad L. Beyle and George T. Lathrop, eds., *Planning and Politics* (New York: Odyssey Press, 1970) pp. 190-212.
2. Figures from *Appalachia: A Journal of the Appalachian Regional Commission*, vol. 10 (Oct.-Nov. 1976), pp. 45–55.
3. Other indicators of "conscious regionalism," in addition to the organizing efforts described in this chapter, are the burgeoning, and increasingly political, outpouring of published journalism, serious literature, and academic work, of which the following collections represent only the tip of the iceberg: David Walls and John Stephenson, eds., *Appalachia in the Sixties* (Lexington, Ky.: University of Kentucky Press, 1972), and Helen Mathews Lewis, Linda Johnson, and Donald Askins, eds., *Colonialism in Modern America: The Appalachian Case* (Boone, N.C.: The Appalachian Consortium Press, 1978).
4. Norval Glenn and J. L. Simmons, "Are Regional Cultural Differences Diminishing?" *Public Opinion Quarterly*, vol. 31 (1967), pp. 176–93.
5. Tom D. Miller, "Who Owns West Virginia?" *Huntington* (W.Va.) *Herald Advertiser and Herald Dispatch*, Dec. 11–15 1974; see also John Gaventa, "Property Taxation of Coal in Central Appalachia: A Report for the Senate Subcommittee on Intergovernmental Relations from Save Our Cumberland Mountains, Inc." No place, publisher or date given.

6. Richard M. Simon, "The Labor Process and Uneven Development in the Appalachian Coalfields" (Paper presented before the Conference Group on Political Economy of Advanced Industrial Societies, New York, Sept. 2, 1978).
7. This assertion is, I believe, so widely circulated and current that a particular note seems unnecessary; (see Harry W. Caudill, *Night Comes to the Cumberlands* (Boston: Little, Brown and Company, 1963), for elaboration, and David Whisnant, *Modernizing the Mountaineer: People, Power, and Planning in Appalachia* (Boone, N.C.: Appalacian Consortium Press, 1980) as well as numerous other works cited below); it is worth noting, however, that many detailed and careful works—for example, Rothblatt, *Regional Planning*, and Newman, *Political Economy of Appalachia*—make no particular mention of the domination of Appalachian politics by absentee or local business.
8. This view was expressed in Charles McKinley's important work on regional planning, *Uncle Sam in the Pacific Northwest* (Berkeley, Calif.: University of California Press, 1942); more recently Martha Derthick repeated this theme in *Between State and Nation* (Washington, D.C.: The Brookings Institution, 1974), pp. 42–5.
9. Philip Selznick, *TVA and the Grass Roots* (Berkeley, Calif.: University of California Press, 1949).
10. Representation requirements in agencies receiving federal funds were controversial and the subject of much journalistic and scholarly attention throughout the 1960s; the reaction in Appalachia was at times extreme. Caudill suggests this extreme reaction in his postmortem on the 1960s, *The Watches of the Night* (Boston: Little, Brown and Company, 1976); and I encountered it in interviews in the region.
11. On this general point, see Kermit C. Parsons and Pierre Clavel, *National Growth Policy: An Institutional Perspective* (Washington: National Science Foundation, 1977).
12. Estimate made by Tom Anton during a seminar paper presentation, Cornell University, 1977. See Thomas J. Anton, "Federal Assistance Programs: The Politics of System Transformation," in Douglas E. Ashford, ed., *National Resources and Urban Policy* (New York: Methuen, 1980), p. 17.
13. This point is made for social programs generally in Peter Marris and Martin Rein, *Dilemmas of Social Reform: Poverty and Community Action in the United States* (New York: Atherton Press, 1967).
14. For an argument pertinent to this point, see James Sundquist, *Making Federalism Work* (Washington, D.C.: The Brookings Institution, 1969).

15. Caudill, *The Watches of the Night.*
16. President's Appalachian Regional Commission, *Appalachia* (Washington, D.C.: USGPO, 1964). See also the accounts in Newman, *Political Economy of Appalachia*, and Rothblatt, *Regional Planning.*
17. Janet Patton, "The State Development Planning Process: Implementation of the Appalachian Regional Development Act of 1965 in West Virginia" (Ph.D. diss., University of California, Berkeley, 1970), p. 38.
18. Ibid., p. 162.
19. Ibid., p. 167.
20. According to ARC planners, the documents that most resembled a "plan" to guide them in project selection and other decisions were, until 1978 at least, the program as reflected in legislation, and the ARC "Code," a handbook on procedures, circulated in the agency and to state and local officials; in 1978 ARC was mandated to begin a more formal planning process (interview with James Pickford, Feb. 1978).
21. See Newman, *Political Economy of Appalachia.*
22. Gerald Ter Horst, "No More Pork Barrel: The Appalachian Approach," *The Reporter*, vol. 32 (March 11, 1965), pp. 27–29.
23. Newman, *Political Economy of Appalachia*; the following comments on ARC activities are based on the works cited, together with my own impressions from conversations, extending over several years, with ARC staff members, staff members of local development districts, and persons in charge of local programs that receive ARC support.
24. Ralph R. Widner, staff memorandum, Feb. 21, 1966, pp. 1–2, quoted in Patton, "State Development Planning Process," p. 83.
25. Deborah Baker, "Mingo County, West Virginia: Social and Economic Impacts of Coal Production," in Lee Balliet, et al., "A Pleasing Tho' Dreadful Sight: Social and Economic Impacts of Coal Production in the Eastern Coalfields," photocopy (Washington, D.C.: Office of Technology Assessment, 1978), appendix E-3, p. 14.
26. Interview with Donald Whitehead, May 11, 1978.
27. Interview, Charleston, W.Va., May 2, 1978.
28. Ken Rainey, "An Assessment of Development Planning in Appalachia" (ARC Staff Discussion Paper, unpublished, 1971).
29. Interview, John D. Anthony, Fairmont, W.Va., April 24, 1978.
30. On TVA, the classic study is Selznick, *TVA*; on OEO in Appalachia, two case studies are Richard A. Couto, *Poverty, Politics, and Health Care: An Appalachian Experience* (New York: Praeger, 1975), and

Huey Perry, *They'll Cut off Your Project: A Mingo County Chronicle* (New York: Praeger, 1972).

31. An often-cited example is Jack Weller, *Yesterday's People: Life in Contemporary Appalachia* (Lexington: University of Kentucky Press, 1965); for a counter-argument, see Helen Lewis, "Fatalism or the Coal Industry?" *Mountain Life and Work*, vol. 46 (Dec. 1979), pp. 4–15.
32. Caudill, *Watches of the Night*, pp. 49–50.
33. See Perry, *They'll Cut off Your Project.*
34. See Couto, *Poverty, Politics, and Health Care.*
35. Marie Cirillo, "Model Valley: Five Years and Still Running," Peoples Development Working Papers, Regional Economic Development Commission (Clintwood, Va.: Council of the Southern Mountains, no date given).

    Community development organizations are seldom constituted as formal parts of governments and often do not appear in rosters of organizations, so comprehensive surveys or enumerations are next to impossible; moreover, these organizations may go out of existence, only to reappear under other names, so that even the evidence provided in published accounts tends to be out of date; the accounts I have been able to find are the following: Judith Stitzel, "Student Action for Appalachian Progress," *Appalachian Review*, vol. 3, no. 1 (Summer 1969), pp. 24–30; and Thomas E. Woodall and Beryl B. Maurer, "A Case Study in Community," in Max E. Glenn, ed., *Appalachia in Transition* (St. Louis: Bethany Press, 1970) pp. 93–108; on local organizations, see Sidney Bell, "The Athens Peoples' Congress," Chester Workman, "Raleigh County People's Community Action," and Brenda Neeley, "Pipestem Community Action," all in *Appalachian South*, vol. 2, no. 2 (Fall-Winter 1967), pp. 27–30; also Marie Cirillo, "Clairfield, Model Valley," and Ann Leibig, "A Community Development Corporation: Appalachia, Virginia," both in *Peoples Appalachia*, vol. 3, no. 2 (Summer 1974), pp. 36–49; the same issue reported on the emergence of some twenty community unions located in Tennessee, Virginia, West Virginia, and Kentucky (p. 35).
36. On regional organizations, see particularly two articles by David Whisnant: "Power to the People," *Peoples Appalachia*, vol. 3, no. 1 (Spring 1973), pp. 16–22, and "Controversy in God's Grand Division: The Council of the Southern Mountains," *Appalachian Journal*, vol. 2, no. 1 (Autumn 1974), pp. 7–45. These also appear, revised, as chs. 8 and 1, respectively, of *Modernizing the Mountaineer.* See also Loyal Jones, "Problems in Revisionism: More Controversy

in 'God's Grand Division,'" *Appalachian Journal*, vol. 2, no. 3 (Spring 1975), pp. 171–80.

37. For a concise summary of the development of CAD, see Whisnant, "Power to the People,"; the 1965–67 issues of *Appalachian South* also track closely the emergence and formation of CAD (see Harry W. Caudill, "Poverty and Affluence in Appalachia," *Appalachian South*, vol. 1, no. 2 [Fall-Winter 1965], pp. 33–6, Harry W. Caudill, "An 'Operation Bootstrap' for Eastern Kentucky," *Appalachian South*, vol. 1, no. 3 [Spring-Summer, 1966], "Congress for Appalachian Development," *Appalachian South*, vol. 1, no. 3 [Fall-Winter 1966], p. 42, and the Summer 1967 issue of *Appalachian South*, vol. 2, no. 1 [Summer 1967], pp. 6–26, which features CAD, describing its organization, goals and "code of ethics," in articles by Caudill, Ebersole, and others).
38. Ben Franklin, "Public Role of Coal Resources Proposed in Three Appalachian States," *New York Times*, March 26, 1967, p. 71.
39. Ibid.
40. Whisnant, "Power to the People," p. 20.
41. Robb Burlage, "Toward a Peoples ARC," *Peoples' Appalachia*, vol. 1. (Aug.–Sept. 1970), pp. 14–30; reprinted in Walls and Stephenson, eds., *Appalachia in the Sixties*, pp. 246–58.
42. Robb Burlage and Roger Lesser, "Vital Trade Unionism: An Interview with Meyer Bernstein," in *Peoples Appalachia*, vol. 2 (Winter 1972–73), p. 18.
43. Bill Taft, "A Libertarian Proposal," in *Peoples Appalachia*, vol. 3 (Summer 1974), pp. 3–14.
44. Richard Simon and Roger Lesser, "A Radical Development Strategy for the Mountains: A Working Community Commonwealth," in *Peoples Appalachia*, vol. 3, no. 1 (Spring 1973), pp. 9–15.
45. Nick Kotz and Mary Lynn Kotz, *A Passion for Equality: George Wiley and the Movement* (New York: W. W. Norton, 1977), p. 302.
46. *Peoples Appalachia*, vol. 3 (Summer 1974), p. 39.
47. Ibid.
48. On local mine organizing, the following sources were useful: *Peoples Appalachia*, vol. 2 (Winter 1972–73), and Mike Yarrow, "What the Miners Really Want," *The Nation*, vol. 225 (March 4, 1978), pp. 230–35.
49. Mimeographed statement, Miners' Support Committee, Beckley, W.Va., n.d.
50. Interview, Jon Hunter, Morgantown, W.Va., July 12, 1977.
51. Interview, Rick Diehl, Morgantown, W.Va., July 13, 1977.

52. Appalachian Alliance, *Appalachia 1978: A Protest from the Colony* (no publication data given).
53. Yarrow, "What the Miners Really Want," p, 231
54. Interview, Williamson, W.Va., February 18, 1978.
55. Appalachian Alliance, *Appalachia 1978.*
56. The panel was part of the Symposium on Regional Research in the Humanities, West Virginia University, Morgantown, W.Va., May 10–12, 1978; the audience participant was David Whisnant.
57. This case is described in David Whisnant, "Revolt! Against Planners in the Kentucky River Area Development District," *Southern Exposure*, vol. 2 (Summer 1974), pp. 84–102. A later version is Whisnant, *Modernizing the Mountaineer*, Ch. 9.
58. Personal communication from John Davis, 1980.
59. Interview, Morgantown, W.Va., May 9, 1978
60. Ibid.
61. Interview, Morgantown, W. Va., April 25, 1978.

Chapter 5

1. Alan Butt Philip, *The Welsh Question: Nationalism in Welsh Politics, 1945–1970* (Cardiff: University of Wales Press, 1975), chs. 9, 10.
2. *Washington Post*, Nov. 14, 1977, p. F-1.
3. *Times* (London), May 9, 1976.
4. *Times* (London), April 21, 1977.
5. Phil Williams, "So Do We Deserve It?" *Welsh Nation*, vol. 51, no. 8 (Sept. 1979), pp. 3, 8. Williams argues: "We've built up the best political organization in Wales. It may be inadequate, but it's far more efficient and effective than any other political organization in Wales" (p. 3).
6. See Philip, *The Welsh Question*, p. 158; he reports that some local-level Plaid Cymru office holders are working class, while the parliamentary candidates have been mostly university professors; see also Rawkins, "Rich Welsh or Poor British?" (Paper presented at the Glendon Conference on Minority Nationalism, York University, Toronto, 1977),
7. John Osmond, *Creative Conflict* (London: Routledge and Kegan Paul, 1977), pp. 115–22.
8. See Chapter 3 above.
9. For a rather sanguine view of nationalist prospects after the

election, see John Osmond, "Mr. Morris and the Elephant," *Planet*, no. 48 (May 1979), pp. 2–8.

10. On Wales, see Philip, *The Welsh Question*, p. 170; of course, the total population of Wales (2.7 million) is not comparable to that of Appalachia.
11. This point was made to me in an interview in July 1977 by John Gaventa, who had studied coal miners in both Wales and Appalachia.
12. Fred Barkey, interview, May 1978; see Barkey, "The West Virginia Socialist Party, 1898–1920: A Study in Working-Class Radicalism" (Ph.D. diss., University of Pittsburgh, 1971).
13. See Richard A. Couto, *Poverty, Politics, and Health Care: An Appalachian Experience* (New York: Praeger, 1975), Huey Perry, *They'll Cut off Your Project: A Mingo County Chronicle* (New York: Praeger, 1977), and John Gaventa and Richard A. Couto, "Appalachia and the Third Face of Power" (Paper delivered at the 1976 Annual Meeting of the American Political Science Association, Chicago, Sept. 2–5, 1976).
14. The style varies; an executive director in East Tennessee picked up the phone when I called him for an interview and, before finding out who I was, said: "Are you a fed? I ain't talking to no feds. I'll see you if you ain't a fed"; in Pennsylvania, on the other hand, a director said he would rather deal with officials from Washington than those in Harrisburg (the state capital), because they were further away and thus less intrusive.

Chapter 6

1. I am referring here to the literature on the "politics of planning," some main early examples include Herman Somers, *Presidential Agency* (Cambridge, Mass.: Havard University Press, 1950); Martin Meyerson and Edward Banfield, *Politics, Planning, and the Public Interest* (Glencoe, Ill.: The Free Press, 1955); and Alan Altshuler, *The City Planning Process* (Ithaca, N.Y.: Cornell University Press, 1965).
2. This term was first used, as far as I know, by Herbert Simon to describe administrative behavior, and I extend the idea to planning (see Herbert Simon, *Administrative Behavior* [New York: Macmillan Co., 1957]).
3. Royal Commission on the Constitution, vol. 1, *Report* (London: HMSO, Cmnd. 5460, 1973), p. 121.

4. Something of the flavor of this in the North West is conveyed in Maurice Wright and Stephen Young, "Regional Sector: U.K.," in Jack Hayward and Michael Watson, eds., *Planning, Politics, and Public Policy: The British, French, and Italian Experience* (New York: Cambridge University Press, 1975) I also got this from interviews with former members of the Northwest Economic Planning Council in 1974, reported in Pierre Clavel, "Regionalism in North West England, 1964–1974" (Paper presented to the Western Societies Program, Cornell University, 1975).
5. This was reported by David Whisnant in a conference at the Symposium on Regional Research in the Humanities, West Virginia University, Morgantown, W.Va., May 10–12, 1978.
6. Perhaps the clearest example is provided in Francine Rabinowitz, *City Planning Politics* (New York: Atherton Press, 1969).
7. Dennis Rondinelli, *Urban and Regional Development Planning: Policy and Administration* (Ithaca, N.Y.: Cornell University Press, 1975).
8. Stanley Baldinger, *Planning and Governing the Metropolis: The Twin Cities Experience* (New York: Praeger, 1971); Wallace S. Sayre and Herbert Kaufman, *Governing New York City* (New York: W. W. Norton, 1965); Robert Warren, *Government in Metropolitan Regions: A Reappraisal of Fractionated Political Organization* (Davis, Calif.: Institute of Governmental Affairs, University of California, Davis, 1966).
9. Altshuler, *City Planning Process*; Meyerson and Banfield, *Politics, Planning, and the Public Interest*; Robert A. Dahl, *Who Governs?: Democracy and Power in an American City* (New Haven: Yale University Press, 1961); Harold Kaplan, *Urban Renewal Politics: Slum Clearance in Newark* (New York: Columbia University Press, 1963).
10. Rather than attempt a treatment of a pure case of separatism, this section focuses on the transition from hegemony to separatism; the data on Wales and Appalachia are clearly on transitional cases at most; there probably is no pure case, even the most extreme examples, Third World nations freeing themselves from colonial domination, do so only with strong outside backing, and with the voluntary withdrawal of the dominating power.
11. A more detailed elaboration of these ideas is contained in Pierre Clavel, Harold R. Capener, and Barclay G. Jones, *Alternative Organization Models for District Development* (Ithaca, N.Y.: Department of Rural Sociology, Cornell University Agricultural Experiment Station, 1969); many of the concepts had been developed by Frank W. Young and Ruth Young (see Frank W. Young and Ruth Young, *Comparative Studies of Community Growth* [Morgantown, W.Va.:

West Virginia University Bookstore, 1973]). Also see Pierre Clavel, "Structural Indicators: A Methodology for Social Planning," multilithed, Working Papers in Planning, Department of City and Regional Planning, Cornell University, No. 2, January 1979.

12. The phrasing is loosely based on Young's. See Frank W. Young," A Proposal for Cooperative Cross-Cultural Research on Intervillage Systems," *Human Organization*, vol. 25 (Spring 1966), pp. 46–50.
13. See, particularly, Frank W. Young and Ruth Young, *Comparative Studies of Community Growth*; also Pluma Kluess and Pierre Clavel, "An Operational Index of System Response Capacity," mimeographed, Cornell University Agricultural Experiment Station, 1969.
14. This scale was based on a more extensive survey, summarized for Appalachian counties in several states, contained in Pluma Kluess and Pierre Clavel, "An Operational Index of System Response Capacity" (Ithaca, N.Y.: Department of Rural Sociology, Cornell Agricultural Experiment Station, 1969; available from U.S. Department of Commerce, National Technical Information Service).
15. Patrick Geddes, "Civics: As Applied Sociology," Parts I and II, *Sociological Papers*, vols. 1 and 2 (London: Macmillan and Co., 1905, 1906); and Paul Davidoff and Thomas Reiner, "A Choice Theory of Planning," *Journal of the American Institute of Planners*, vol. 28 (May 1962), pp. 103–15.
16. Andrew Shonfield, *Modern Capitalism: The Changing Balance of Public and Private Power* (London: Oxford University Press, 1965).
17. John Kenneth Galbraith, *The New Industrial State* (Boston: Houghton Mifflin, 1967).
18. Hayward and Watson, *Planning, Politics, and Public Policy*, p. 449.
19. Paul Davidoff, "Advocacy and Pluralism in Planning," *Journal of the American Institute of Planners*, vol. 31 (Nov. 1965), pp. 331–38.
20. Lisa Peattie, "Reflections on Advocacy Planning," *Journal of the American Institute of Planners*, vol. 34 (March 1968), p. 86.
21. Langley C. Keyes and Edward Teitcher, "Limitations of Advocacy Planning: A View from the Establishment," *Journal of the American Institute of Planners*, vol. 36 (July 1970), p. 225.
22. Representation tended to involve a struggle, however; for one case study, see Judith May, "Two Model Cities: Negotiations in Oakland," in Ira Katznelson, ed., *The Politics and Society Reader* (New York: McKay, 1974); for the situation of neighborhood-level planners within big-city planning agencies, see Martin L. Needleman and Carolyn Emerson Needleman, *Guerillas in the Bureaucracy: The Community Planning Experiment in the United States* (New York: Wiley, 1974).

3. Norman Krumholz, Janice Cogger, and John Linner, "The Cleveland Policy Planning Report," *Journal of the American Institute of Planners*, vol. 41 (Sept. 1975), pp. 298–304.
24. Needleman and Needleman, *Guerillas in the Bureaucracy.*
25. Most exhaustive, perhaps, is David Braybooke and Charles E. Lindblom, *A Strategy of Decision* (New York: Free Press, 1963).
26. Theodore Lowi, "The Public Philosophy: Interest Group Liberalism," *American Political Science Review*, vol. 61 (March 1967), pp. 5–24; and William A. Gamson, "Unstable Representation in American Society," *American Behavioral Scientist*, vol. 12 (Nov.–Dec. 1968), pp. 15–21. Douglas F. Ashford, "Reorganizing British Local Government as a Policy Problem" (Paper presented to a seminar of the Western Societies Program, Cornell University, 1976).
27. See Altshuler, *City Planning Process*, ch. 5, on proposals for planner generalist roles; see also Robert Daland and John A. Parker, "Roles of the Planner in Urban Development," in F. Stuart Chapin, Jr., and Shirley Weiss, eds., *Urban Growth Dynamics* (New York: Wiley, 1962), pp. 188–205.
28. Frances Fox Piven and Richard A. Cloward, *Poor People's Movements: Why They Succeed, How They Fail* (New York: Pantheon Books, 1977); see also a critique by Eric J. Hobsbawm, "Should the Poor Organize?" *New York Review of Books*, vol. 25 (March 23, 1978), pp. 44–48.

Index

ACORN, 23
ARC. *See* Appalachian Regional Commission
Agenda setting, 186–89
Altshuler, Alan, 37, 194
Appalachia: description, 4–5, 16, 213; economic performance, 161–62; federal agencies in, 121; local programs in, 133–35, 141; official planning in, 25, 28, 30, 31, 59, 124–32, 179–83; opposition planning in, 27, 28, 59, 132, 135–52; region, 116–18, 135; regionalism in, 5–6, 117–18, 135, 142–43; regional planning, 6, 123, 124–32; regional policy, neglect in, 121; regional politics in, 5–6; selection of, for study, 4; territorial opposition in, 156–58, 175, 179, 199; territorial organization in, 154, 156–58, 162, 169, 170, 172; variable centrality in, 168. *See also* Appalachian Regional Commission; Local development districts; Opposition organizations in Appalachia; Tennessee Valley Authority
Appalachian Alliance, 152, 157; activity of, 144, 170, 173; composition, 156, 199; emergence of, 143; program, 145–47, 179, 200
Appalachian People's Congress, 136
Appalachian Regional Commission (ARC): aims, 122–23; creation of, 122–23, 124, 167, 171; effects of, 125–32, 159, 161; as example of U.S. regional policy, 5, 117–18, 191; lack of program, 124, 181, 183, 187, 199–200; and local politics, 127–29; opposition to, 132–33, 137–38, 146–47, 158, 187–88, 192; regional planning under, 60, 124–32, 164–65, 179, 181–83, 187, 190, 191–92, 234
Appalachian Regional Development Act (1965), 116, 126
Appalachian Volunteers, 133, 134–35, 137
Area Redevelopment Act (1961), 119
Arrow, Kenneth, 37
Barlow Report (1940), 78
Beachman, Arthur, 98, 99
Beer, Samuel, 42, 43–44, 61, 71; liberalism of, 50–51
Bevan, Aneurin, 77
Bituminous Coal Operators Association (BCOA), 159, 168
Break-up of Britain, The (Nairn), 46–48, 61, 67, 72, 198, 225
British Steel Corporation, 161, 162
Brown, George, 80, 81, 82, 179, 190, 228
Burlage, Robb, 138

CAD. *See* Congress for Appalachian Development
CDCs. *See* Community Development Corporations
CSM. *See* Council of the Southern Mountains
Call to the Valleys, 101–2, 170, 172
Capacity, 202–3. *See also* Local capacity
Capitalism: and development of class consciousness, 47; and local capacity, 66–68; market, 62–65, 70; Marxist view, 51; technocratic, 62–66, 69, 71
Carrillo, Santiago, 48
Carter, Harold, 101
Castells, Manuel, 48
Caudill, Harry, 134–37, 144, 146
Centrality, 14–19; and changes, 61–62, 166–69, 173–74; definition, 14–15; high, 190–91; issues of, 18; and local capacity, 15–19, 52–59, 169, 171; relative, 15
Centralization, 42, 43, 83
Cirrillo, Marie, 134
Communist Manifesto, The, 51
Community, 10, 176; defense of, 13–14; notion of, changes in, 40, 221; organization, 22–23; territorial, 155–56
Community Development Corporations (CDCs), 134, 141, 235
Congress for Appalachian Development, 135–37, 144, 152
Conservative Party (Great Britain): government, 82, 91; modernization policy,

79; and planning, 20, 78, 91; and reform, 82
Council for Wales and Monmouthshire, 84, 89, 93, 94
Council of the Southern Mountains (CSM), 140, 142
Crowther, Lord, 109, 110, 184; Royal Commission on the Constitution, 82, 198, 226
Cymru Fydd (Young Wales), 74

DEA. *See* Department of Economic Affairs
Davidoff, Paul, 35–36, 37, 205, 206
Department of Economic Affairs (DEA), 80–81, 179, 184
Development districts, local. *See* Local development districts
Devolution, 86, 94, 95–96
Diffusion, process of, 41
Dyckman, John, 36–38

Ebersole, Gordon, 135–37, 144
Economic Development Administration (EDA), 119, 121
Economic growth, slow: political effects, 19–21; responses to, 21–23
Economic Plan for Wales, An, 152, 156, 173; clientele of, 184; difference from Welsh Office plan, 107, 108, 110, 112, 183; evaluation of, 27, 110, 113–15, 198; proposals in, 109–10
Ellis, Tom, 74, 75
Evans, Gwynfor, 105, 173

Federalist Papers, The (Madison), 42

Galbraith, John Kenneth, 206
Geddes, Patrick, 10, 11, 29, 205
George, Lloyd, 74, 75
Government: control of, 61–66, 70–71; response to territorial opposition, 160, 164–65, 171–72; structures in Great Britain, 6, 83, 161, 164; structures in U.S., 6, 41–43, 118, 161, 164
Gramsci, Antonio, 71
Great Britain: central institutions, 81–85; government of, 6, 83, 161, 164; growth of central control, 78–88; National Health Service, 77; national planning in, 31; regional planning, 80–81; regional policy, 6, 40, 73, 78–81; ruling class in, 47

Harris, Britton, 35
Heads of the Valleys Standing Conference, 112, 113, 154; establishment, 100; as opposition to Welsh Office, 102, 172; strategies, 170
Heath, Edward, 80
Hegemony, 16, 31, 33, 55, 59–60, 175; corporate, moves against, 23; definition, 153, 189; impact on planning, 189–93; planning under, 196, 198, 210; unstable, results of, 24, 56
Hierarchy: conditions of, 17; description, 17, 194; opposition planning and, 205; stable, 55, 56

Ideology, 200

Key, V. O., 40

LLDs. *See* Local development districts
Labour Party (Great Britain): modernization policy, 20, 79; planning programs, 77, 80–82; strategy for Wales, 95, 160, 161, 179, 187, 190; in Wales, 74–76, 89–90, 105–6, 114, 155
Lambert, John, 113–14
Land Authority for Wales, 97
Le Corbusier, 29
Lenin, 46
Lewis, Saunders, 75
Liberal Party (Great Britain), policy for Wales, 75, 95
Lipset, Seymour, 40
Litton report, 181, 187
Llantrisant (Wales), 93, 100, 188; inquiry, 100–101; opposition to development, 104, 206; proposal, 100–101, 108, 159, 181
Local capacity, 192; under capitalism, 66–67; and centrality, 15–19, 52–59, 171; and cultural differentiation, 67–68; growth of, 169–70, 172; low, 16, 17, 190
Local development districts (LDDs): establishment, 125, 127–29, 159; evolution, 129–32; professionalism in, 150–51; role of, 161, 164, 165, 167, 168, 169, 170, 172; strategy, 129, 148–50
Luxemburg, Rosa, 45–46

MCU. *See* Mountain Community Union
MWIDA. *See* Mid-Wales Industrial Development Corporation
Madison, James, 42
Markusen, Ann, 48
Marxist theories: vs. liberal, 50–51; on nationalism, 8, 45–46; problems of, 44–45; on regional development, 43–51
Merthyr Tydfil (South Wales), 76, 154, 155, 169
Meyerson, Martin, 30
Michels, Robert, 44
Mid-Wales Industrial Development Corporation (MWIDA), 98, 159, 188

Miller, Arnold, 141, 142
Miners for Democracy (MFD), 141, 142
Modern Capitalism (Shonfeld), 206
Modernization: alternative doctrine to, 201–3; in Appalachia, 165; British policy in Wales, 79–81, 172; liberal view of, 51; as planning doctrine, 190, 197
Morgan, Arthur, 10, 11
Morgan, Kenneth O., 75
Mountain Community Union (MCU), 140
Mountain Journal, 140
Mumford, Lewis, 10, 11

Nairn, Tom, 46–48, 61, 67, 72, 198, 225
National Health Service, 77
Nationalism, 13; and Marxist literature, 45–48; Welsh, 7, 13, 73–75, 86–87, 154, 155, 160, 198
Nationalist movements, 7, 12–13, 47, 74–75
New Deal, 11, 118, 216
New Industrial State, The (Galbraith), 206

O'Connor, James, 71; Marxist analysis of regionalism, 49, 50–51, 61
Odum, Howard, 10, 11, 35
Office of Economic Opportunity (OEO), 121, 133, 134–35
Opposition organizations in Appalachia. *See* Appalachian Alliance; Appalachian Volunteers; Congress for Appalachian Development; Peoples Appalachia Research Collective
Opposition organizations in Wales. *See* Call to the Valleys; Heads of the Valleys Standing Conference; Standing Conference on Regional Policy; Welsh Language Society
Opposition planning. *See* Planning, opposition

PARC. *See* Peoples Appalachia Research Collective
Patton, Janet, 123
Peattie, Lisa, 207–8
Penrose, Edith, model of, 52–54
Peoples Appalachia, 137–39, 140, 141, 152
Peoples Appalachia Research Collective (PARC), 135, 143, 144, 152; activities of, 137–40; analyses by, 199; establishment of, 137; impact of, 170
Plaid Cymru, 5; early history, 74, 105; economic policies, 106–12, 156, 172–73; goal of, 74–75; influence, 162; issues for, 13, 104–5, 106; and nationalism, 154, 155–56, 158; planning by, 27, 59, 112, 183–86, 187–88, 198; politics, 162, 168, 169, 170, 173, 175, 179; Research Group, 107, 156, 198, 200, 202; rise of, 87, 104–6, 230; strategy, 154–56, 162; and territorial organization, 155–58, 159, 172, 175, 193. See also *Economic Plan for Wales, An*
Planning: advocacy, 206–9; in Appalachia and Wales, contrasted, 178–83; clienteles for, 178–79, 182–83, 190; definition, 25; doctrine, examples, 25; future of, 210–12; goals, 178–79; indicative, 59–60, 197; for institutional change, failure of, 209; opposition to, 179; Penrose interaction model, 52–54; and politics, 177; roles of, 178, 196–97, 202; structural analysis for, 204–5; success of, 194; Young interaction model, 53–54, 58–61
Planning in West: evaluations of, 29–31; future of, 33–34, 38; history, 29–31, 37–38; new analytical, 34–37
Planning, official: in Appalachia, 25, 28, 30, 31, 59, 124–32; description, 184–85; local opposition to, 192–93; methods, 180–83, 192–93; and modernization, 192–93; role of, 200–201; in Wales, 26, 28, 30, 31, 59, 90–97
Planning, opposition, 24–25, 33; in Appalachia, 27, 28, 59, 132, 135–52; characteristics, 27; consequences, 178, 188, 189; methods, 184–86, 196–97; purpose of, 212; role of, 201; in Wales, 27–28, 59, 97–112, 183–86
Planning, regional: in Appalachia, 6, 123, 124–32; in Wales, 6, 73, 91–116
Politics, comparative, 40, 41
Politics, regional. *See* Regional politics
Politics, territorial. *See* Regional politics
Polyarchy, 18, 58, 59; documentation of, 193–95; limits of, 211–12; planning within, 196, 205, 209–11; stable, 54, 56
Public Utility District, 135–36

Rawkins, Phillip M., 105–7
Redcliffe-Maud, Lord, Royal Commission, 82
Rees, Gareth, 113–14
Regional development: changes in, 40–43; liberal analysis of, 41–43, 50; Marxist analysis of, 43–51
Regionalism: early, 10; kinds, 7–8; New Deal programs, 11; political doctrine, 10; Western, 48. *See also* Appalachia
Regional Planning Association of America (RPAA), 10, 11

Regional policy, liberal: failures of, 8–9; features of, 9, 10
Regional policy, socialist: attacks on, 10; lack of, 8; results, 9–10
Regional political mobilization, 7–8, 49, 69–72
Regional politics: Appalachian, 5–6, 172; characteristics, 12–14; definition, 12; liberal and socialist doctrine in, 7–8, 43; and regional development, 45; theories of, 51–60; Welsh, 5–6
Regional response to planning: lack of, in Appalachia, 120; movements, 20–23; problems, 23–25; radical element in, 23; in Wales, 97–104
Regional theory, 7–8, 12
Reiner, Thomas, 35–36, 37, 205
Roberts, Emrys, 105, 111–12
Roosevelt, Franklin Delano, 11, 70
Rosser, Sir Melwyn, 94, 97

Save Our Cumberland Mountains (SOCM), 141
Scotland, 7, 12–13, 47, 74, 80, 82, 86
Selznick, Philip, 42, 70, 119, 133
Separatism, 12–13, 18–19; planning under, 196–205; results of, 19; transition to, 24, 56, 170–174, 175, 189, 195; Welsh, 74–75, 87, 154, 155, 160, 173. *See also* Nationalist movements; Territorial opposition
Shonfeld, Andrew, 114; *Modern Capitalism*, 206
Simon, Herbert, 36–37
Solidarity, 54, 60; and centrality, 57–59, 224; definition, 57; increase of, 172–73; and opposition planning, 60
Southern Politics (Key), 40
South Wales, 74, 99–100; effects of industralization on, 76, 162; new town in, 100–101; regional organization in, 100–104, 164, 181; working class in, 76–77
Spence, Beth, 145
Standing Conference. *See* Heads of the Valleys Standing Conference
Standing Conference on Regional Policy (South Wales), 102, 114, 170; history, 103–4, 170
Sundquist, James, 40

TUC. *See* Trades Union Council
Tennessee Valley Authority (TVA): and doctrine, 25; goals, 119; as model, 121, 122, 123, 133; populism in, 70; regionalism in, 10, 11, 133; and regional policy, 118–19, 141; similar agencies, call for, 123, 135, 157, 171; study on, 42, 70, 133
Territorial opposition: in Appalachia, 156–58, 175, 179, 199; applications of, 205; government response to, 158–66; in Wales, 154–56, 179, 198–99
Territorial organization: in Appalachia, 154, 156–58, 162, 169, 170, 172; consequences, 175–76; and government reaction, 158–63; in Wales, 154, 155, 159, 162
Territorial politics. *See* Regional politics
Trades Union Council (TUC), 155, 159
Tug Valley Recovery Center, 143, 159

United Mine Workers: and local activism, 141, 142, 158, 159–60, 168; as national organization, 159–60; organization by, 133, 139; reform in, 138–39
United States: Department of Housing and Urban Development (HUD), 23, 121, 131, 149, 167; federal system, development of, 41–42, 61, 120–21; national planning, 20, 31; regional policy, 6, 40, 117–23. *See also* Appalachian Regional Commission; Government; Office of Economic Opportunity; Tennessee Valley Authority; VISTA

VISTA, 121, 133, 134

Wales: description, 4–5, 16, 213; economic performance of, 162; government planning, 91–97; government structure in, 82–85; incorporation into Great Britain, 73–78; industrialization, 75–77, 88, 100; institutions, 85; local government reform, 82–84, 96; new counties in, 165, 167, 169, 172; new towns in, 93, 99, 100–101, 104; opposition planning in, 97–112; regional planning, 6, 73, 91–97; regional politics, 5–6; selection of, for study, 4; separatist movement, 7, 12–13, 74–75, 87; variable centrality in, 168; working class in, 76–77, 155, 156. *See also* Devolution; Labour Party; Llantrisant; Merthyr Tydfil; Nationalism; Opposition organizations in Wales; Plaid Cymru; Separatism; South Wales
Wales: The Way Ahead, 107, 110, 115, 168, 177, 184, 187; criticism of, 91–92, 112, 164; flaws in, 92–95, 190–91; methods in, 184–85; problems surrounding, 104, 173, 179–83
Welsh Development Agency, 97, 163
Welsh Economic Council, 163, 168, 173;

Welsh Economic Council (*Continued*)
constitution of, 90–91; establishment of, 89; flaws in, 95; role in planning, 91–97, 161, 183, 184, 190–91
Welsh Grand Committee, 85
Welsh Language Society, 75, 159
Welsh Office, 167; creation of, 84, 88–90, 160, 168, 170–71, 173; functions, 5, 26–27; growth of, 97, 163, 166; local opposition to, 102, 103, 104, 192–93; power of, 198–99; response to opposition, 158, 160, 164; role in regional planning, 91–97, 100, 104, 107, 108, 112, 113, 114, 164, 177, 179–83, 191; Secretary of State for Wales, 89–90, 92, 164; weaknesses, 91–92, 158, 161
Whisnant, David, 137, 147–48
Whitehead, Donald, 147, 148
Wiley, George, 139, 140, 142
Williams, Phil, 13, 107–8, 109, 110, 155–56
Working class: and Marxist theory, 43–46; organization of, 44, 45, 47, 70; representation in government, 69–70, 72, 106–7, 111; support in regional politics, 14, 155–58
Wright, Frank Lloyd, 29

Young, Frank W., 52; interaction model, 53–54, 58, 59, 60, 61